*"I find Mr. Kyle's novelized account of the project to be most entertaining and - more important - informative. The style brings the reader willy-nilly on the quest for good project management, and we all become part of the project."*

**William Atherton, President, North American Life**

*"Thanks, Mackenzie! You've put a proven process for planning and managing projects into a great read. Now even I'm Making It Happen!"*

**Richard Pearson, Managing Director, Priority Management, Hong Kong**

*"Mackenzie's fable not only makes MAKING IT HAPPEN an easy read. laying out the fundamentals of organizing projects, but also brings to life the concepts..."*

**Gary Hamer, BC Gas**

*"...a novelty in helping non-project managers understand what a project is, and above all, to help them understand the art and science of project management. Easy to read and captures the approach I would recommend to anyone who feels that time and money in completing something is important today."*

**Calin Popescu, Phd. P.E., University of Texas at Austin**

# *MAKING IT HAPPEN*

*(A fable about project management)*

*Mackenzie Kyle*


*First Printing September, 1995*
*Second Printing October, 1996*
*Third Printing August, 1997*


*This book is intended to provide insights into and understanding of effective methods by which projects can be initiated and managed. It is designed to do this in an entertaining manner. Should the reader wish to obtain professional advice on legal, accounting or neurosurgical matters, certified practioners should be consulted.*

ISBN 0-9699703-0-7

# Contents

PREFACE

This book has two things to offer you as a reader.

The first is the unique and superior approach to the discipline of project management that it presents. Much is known about projects (and vastly more is written), but not much is widely understood. The methods presented here were refined over many years by individuals who have spent their careers in the field, making the concepts of the management sciences work. This useful approach was not developed without cost and frustration, and there is a great deal contained here that you will find nowhere else.

The second is the manner in which ideas are conveyed. Learning should always be an adventure, although sometimes it is not. If you've ever stumbled through a dry textbook struggling to make important information stick in your brain, you'll appreciate the alternative approach taken by this book. Without the excitement generated by discovery, it is very hard to retain, let alone implement, new ideas.

Making learning interesting has been one of the greatest challenges of my job. My colleagues and I have developed a number of techniques for doing this, and in the course of our work, experienced a great deal of success in improving how companies operate. In early 1993, I decided to take the approach that became the following story. This is not another attempt to make a simple subject complex, nor to make a complex subject *seem* simple. It is a demonstration of how simple it really is.

If you choose this book to assist you in your learning adventure, you will follow the 'real life' journey of discovery of a person not unlike yourself, and see the application of new and powerful ideas to the discipline of making things happen.

MK
Auckland, New Zealand
July, 1995

# GENESIS

# CHAPTER 1

"So you see, we'll need a work breakdown structure almost immediately," he said.

"I see," I said. I didn't.

"Ralph is also asking for earned value cost analysis, and he wants you to keep the scope flexible, understand?" he asked me.

"I understand," I said. I didn't.

"And he wants self-empowered work teams running the show on this one," he continued.

"Got it," I said, pretending to make notes on the pad in front of me. I didn't have a clue what he was talking about.

"And the whole thing has to be part of our new Total Quality Management Initiative," he said.

I groaned. For me, this was the last straw. Now was the time to get off this boat if I was ever going to.

"I'm not really sure you have the right person for the job, Stu."

I could tell by the way he looked at me that this was not what he wanted to hear. I prepared myself for his response, praying my lack of enthusiasm would get me bounced off the project team.

I didn't hold out much hope. "Stu" is Stu Barnes, the Vice-President of Operations at Hyler Recreation Systems Inc., and my boss. Me, I'm Will Campbell, and I'm in charge of Hyler's Information Systems group. Stu and I had worked together for almost three years by the time we had this conversation, and we knew each other pretty well. Although Stu looked and talked like a marine drill sergeant (which is exactly what he used to be), he is the best boss I have ever had. While this was a good thing most of the time, it also meant that Stu was very used to me whining and complaining about things I did not like.

"Look Will," he started in, "you know how I feel about all this stuff, but Ralph is the boss, and we all know that Ralph has his sights set on much bigger things than Hyler. If that means riding the crest of whatever wave comes rolling in from Head Office, that is exactly what he'll do. And that means that's exactly what we'll do."

"Ralph" is Ralph Borsellino, President of Hyler Recreation, and at 34, the youngest president ever. The top brass at Mantec, our parent company, was very impressed with Ralph, and word was that he was on his way up in the organization.

Inwardly, I groaned again. Stu was right. If Ralph wanted it, that is the way it would be.

The meeting had not started out badly. Twenty minutes ago I had been quite excited by what Stu had to say.

"So what we have here," Stu had been telling me, "is a major opportunity to complement our existing product line, and you know how they love that kind of thing back at Head Office in Denver. Not only will it create new customers, but if our experience is anything like what they've seen in Europe, it will lead to more sales of our existing products further down the line!"

This was exciting news. Although I had spent the last 18 months in the Information Systems area, Hyler was a small organization and everyone understood the ground rules. Our company was just a stopover for the up-and-coming movers and shakers at Mantec. Innovation leading to expanded sales was a sure ticket for promotion out of Hyler. But to put all of that in context, I suppose I should tell you a little bit about the organization.

Andrew Hyler started the company during the war ("WW ll, the big one," as Archie Bunker used to say) to make lifeboats and life rafts for the U.S. Navy. He located his operation in Enderby, Oregon, just outside of Portland. Like many wartime industrialists with a guaranteed demand and price, he was quite successful." After the war was over and new military contracts were not forthcoming, Andrew had the idea that he would go on making boats, but now they would be pleasure boats for fishing and hunting. Everyone called him crazy, especially since he lived way out in Oregon, where there were not a lot of people.

Old Andrew must have seen what was coming, because he did

very well for himself. After the war, just about all for
tion became popular, and boating was no exception. Since
was the only manufacturer on the West Coast, he had a significant competitive advantage. Not only could he build better quality boats than they made back east, he could sell them cheaper because his shipping cost was a fraction of the competition's. He had such a grip on the market that none of the eastern manufacturers even bothered to open up a West Coast plant. When aluminum boats became popular, Andrew was well positioned to scoop that market too.

By the time the sixties rolled around, Andrew Hyler was getting on and he decided that he no longer wanted the day-to-day hassles of running a business. In 1967 he sold the company to Mantec Corporation, a major conglomerate whose holdings included oil and gas fields, refineries, pulp mills, trucking companies, and vast amounts of real estate.

The purchase of a boat plant was the final step in an elaborate management development plan that the Mantec executives had worked out. Hyler was to be used as a training ground for developing managers. The idea was that the "trainees" could make their mistakes and learn at Hyler, where the stakes were small, before moving on to bigger and better things within the parent corporation. To this day, all of the top executives at Mantec, and the heads of most Mantec subsidiaries have spent time at Hyler.

Of course this means that managers who come through our company have some pretty high expectations placed on them, which is probably why Hyler has led the field in recreational boating and water sports on the West Coast for the last 25 years. The company now has sales approaching $40 million, and in addition to aluminum boats (which are a decreasing portion of our business), we make several models of windsurfers, fiberglass sailboats, boat trailers, fiberglass dinghies, and sails. Our last big product line expansion was into the area of personal flotation devices. That was the brainchild of the former Vice-President of Marketing, and it did so well that she is now president of one of Mantec's huge new box companies in Texas.

So what Stu was saying about this new product was bound to make a guy like Ralph Borsellino happy. Hyler would have more sales, and still be on the cutting edge of the industry.

Stu continued to give me details. "The really exciting thing about this new product is that it looks like it will overcome the windsurfing Resistance Factor."

The famed Resistance Factor. This was news indeed! The Resistance Factor, or the RF as we called it, was a term local to Hyler that described people's reluctance to take up windsurfing as a recreational hobby (or at least their resistance to get into it enough that they would actually purchase their own windsurfer, hopefully from us).

My first project as the new head of Information Systems had been to oversee a consumer survey about a variety of recreational activities, in the hopes of learning more about how people decide to purchase our products. The survey produced some interesting information about how people choose to recreate, and about windsurfing in particular.

Although everyone has seen the pros on TV skimming across the waves and doing spectacular acrobatics, the fact is that windsurfing is not a terribly easy sport for the average beginner. Anyone who has tried it knows that it can even be a little frustrating. Unfortunately, frustrated beginners rarely become windsurfer owners, hence the Resistance Factor. Ever since the survey, we've been looking for a way to overcome that problem.

In order to get comparative data, we surveyed several sports, not just windsurfing. Sports like downhill skiing scored very high for the beginner. Even the first time out, beginners can get their skis pointed downhill and can, in a manner of speaking, ski. With windsurfing, it is a different story. Many of the people surveyed reported that they couldn't even pull up the sail the first time they tried it. And somehow, windsurfing just isn't all that much fun without the sail.

Interested now, I said, "So don't keep me waiting Stu, tell me about it. "Have you got a new windsurfer design, or what?"

"In fact," Stu said, "the Europeans have a new design. WaterTrends out of Germany has a new product that they introduced to the market late this summer. I've seen it, and I think it can be very successful over here."

"So what does it look like?" I asked. "And how does it overcome the RF?"

Stu reached into his desk and pulled out a sketch. "It's essentially a cross between a small sailboat and a regular windsurfer," he said, as he put the drawing on the desk in front of me.

The sketch showed a board that looked like a regular windsurfer, but broader, with a seat with a back set into its surface. A woman was sitting in the seat, her legs extended in front of her, spread slightly, with her feet resting against a horizontal bar close to the front of the board. This bar was attached to a vertical shaft that disappeared straight down into the board. The mast sat forward of the bar/footrest, a foot or so from the tip of the board. It rose about four feet off the deck, and had a boom that extended horizontally back from the mast over the woman's legs, stopping a foot from her chest. There were two ropes attached to the boom, about three-quarters of the way back from the mast. These went out to each side, through pulleys attached to both edges of the board, and the woman held the ends of the ropes in her hands. The sail itself seemed a bit on the small side compared to the sail on a windsurfer or a small sailboat (though I was no expert).

"You see," Stu was saying, "the feet control the rudder with that horizontal bar there, and you have a sheet in each hand to control the sail." Being a non-sailor, I always have to remember that sheets are ropes used to control sails.

"I don't get it," I said. "How is this better than a windsurfer? It just looks like a screwed-up little sailboat."

"I was hoping you'd ask me that," Stu said gleefully. I could tell he was more than a little excited about the whole thing. "It combines the best features of both the sailboat and the windsurfer, and that is how it overcomes the RF."

I looked at him skeptically. I was not impressed. "It looks like a water slug to me."

Stu rolled his eyes to the ceiling. "Why am I cursed with these visionless peasants, God?" he asked, as if he was expecting an answer. Turning back to me he said, "Look, people like windsurfers for some very simple reasons. They're very portable, you can put them on your car top. They're very flexible in the water, you can go fast in very little wind, fall down, jump waves, and if you're very good, do really fancy things like complete loops. They also like them because they are a lot cheaper than sailboats. But beginners have a hard time with them. It takes a reasonable amount of skill and athletic ability to have any fun with them at all.

"On the other hand, a little sailboat is quite easy for a beginner to pilot. It doesn't go too fast, it's easy to figure out how to steer the thing, and there are no feats of strength required to get yourself going. However, a beginner doesn't want to rush out and spend four or five thousand bucks for a sailboat, and then have to tow it around on a trailer. Especially if they only use it a few times a year.

"Enter the WindSailor. It's lightweight and portable like the windsurfer, it costs the same or less, and yet it has all the user-friendly features of a small sailboat. There is no heavy sail to lift up, it doesn't go too fast, see how small that sail is, and it's almost impossible to tip over. It has a daggerboard that drops down between your legs for stability. And if you do tip it over, an eight-year-old could get it right side up again. It's got the best of both worlds. And guess what? After using the WindSailor for a year or two, the consumer wants to move up, either to a proper windsurfer or to a sailboat. And who do you think will be right there to supply them with that product?"

Stu sat back looking very pleased with himself.

"You'd almost think this whole thing was your idea," I said, suspecting it was.

"It was," he said, "at least the push to buy the manufacturing licence for North America. I saw this baby at a trade show in Europe four months ago."

"Why didn't we just steal the idea and design our own?"

"Will," he said with mock dismay, "I am shocked! How could you think of such a thing? Anyway, we don't have time. Our Marketing guys say that if we're not first on the market with this, we'll lose our edge, and it would be doubtful if we would ever recover the development cost. Besides, it could take more than a year to get it right. If we buy the rights on this one, we have a known quantity on our hands."

"Yeah," I said, "we know all about it, except whether or not it will sell." I paused. "This is a big risk for you to be taking personally. "What did Ralph have to say about it?"

Stu sighed. "Look kid, I've been at this plant for the last 15 years, and I've been stalled out in this job for the last seven. We all know that Ralph is going to be moving on soon. I want that top job. I'm sick of seeing hot shots come in here for a year or two and run this place like they want a promotion. I want control for a few years to make Hyler the kind of place where I want to work. This WindSailor is my ticket."

This was the first Stu had told me about his personal ambition. Not only was Stu the best boss I had ever had, a lot of others felt the same way. Although Hyler was certainly not in any trouble, it could have been a much better place to work. The constant shuffle at the top levels tended to make many of the longer-term employees unhappy. Stu had never been tapped for the top job, mostly, it seemed, because he was not on his way up within the bigger Mantec organization. He thought of himself as a mere manager, and he liked living in Oregon.

"Anyway," Stu continued, "you know Ralph. If it looks good, he's 100 percent behind you until it looks bad, at which point it was your idea. If this does go, he'll be promoted and I'll have a shot at his job. If it's a flop, well, I need a change anyway."

My predecessor was one of those people who Ralph had supported 100 percent until things started looking bad. She had developed a great idea about using the IS department as a clearing house for employee feedback about the company. Of course not all of it was positive feedback, and Ralph had started getting a little nervous about someone other than him knowing the dirty secrets about employee attitudes. She was fired for "poor performance," but everyone knew the real reason.

Stu sighed. "Besides, regardless of promotions or office politics, I happen to think this is a damn good idea, and it's what this company should be doing." He stuck out his chin heroically.

Whenever people start to get noble on me, I get nervous. Doing the "right" thing is nice until you haven't got a job anymore. I had to agree though. It sounded like a good idea.

"Well, you know me, Stu," I told him. "I'll support you however I can. I'd love to see you get into Ralph's job. What can I do?"

Stu looked at me, and suddenly I felt like a lamb being mentally barbecued by a wolf. He smiled. "Along with responsibility for this little project, Ralph agreed to let me choose who I wanted to work on it."

"Yes," I said, not getting it yet.

"Well, I've decided that I want you to be the project manager." Stu looked at me and smiled again.

I stared back at him. Project manager? A hundred different objections formed in my mind: I don't know anything about boat design! I know nothing about factory setup! I'm not an engineer! Who will take care of my job?

Instead of voicing these thoughts, I said, "Okay."

"Good!" he said, clapping his hands together and then rubbing his palms. My feeling of doom deepened.

"Now Ralph did, of course, impose a few conditions of his own on our little project."

Of course he did, I thought.

"Nothing too serious," Stu continued. "Nothing we can't work around." Just what I like: conditions set by the boss that don't help you. You have to work around them.

"For starters, I'll be the project sponsor, but you'll ultimately have to go to Ralph for spending approval."

"Right," I said, taking out a sheet of paper to write on. Oh good, I thought to myself. Up the bureaucratic ladder to the ultimate control freak before I can spend a dime. That will make life easy.

"Ralph wants Al Burton on the project team." Stu stopped and looked at me, anticipating some kind of response.

"What!!" I screamed, "that asshole? Look at the last project he was on. It was a total screw-up. What the hell do we need..."

"As you know," Stu interrupted, "the TQM project was a complete success."

"That project was a disaster!" I retorted.

A year ago, when Total Quality Management was picking up speed as the trendy management thing to be doing, Ralph had assigned Al Burton to implement TQM in our plant. I guess Al seemed like a logical choice because he was an engineer, head of Industrial and Production Engineering, and the only certified project manager at Hyler. Although it was supposed to have taken three months, according to Al, and cost $150,000, it was still going on, in a haphazard way. The bill was now at almost $800,000. Since no objective had yet been established, other than to "do things in a quality way," no results had yet been achieved. Morale in the plant had never been worse.

"Look," said Stu, "you and I both know it was and is a dismal failure. But Ralph needed it to be successful, and so it was successful. Putting Al on this team is Ralph's way of having an insider, a spy. Ralph can depend on Al, because Ralph had to make sure TQM and Al's project didn't fail." He sighed. "In this organization, politics are part of everything we do. You'd be stupid to ignore it. Just don't let it affect the success you want to achieve."

I knew it was good advice, but it got so frustrating having to work with those ground rules. I began to pray that Al would get hit by a bus.

"You know how Ralph likes jargon, and things that sound like Tom Peters said them," Stu continued. "Well, Ralph picked up a bunch of things from Al's last project that he wants to see on this one."

I readied my pencil and paper for more notes.

"Ralph wants you using some project management software to make reporting easier." Wonderful, I thought, more software to learn. Stu went on: "He wants you to produce a schedule of milestones for the project, using the software, by the end of this week. He specified that he wants to see it in a Gantt chart format. He's leaving the choice of the software up to you."

Stu began telling me that I had to provide work breakdown structures, earned value costing, and TQM integration, and this is where you came in.

I really didn't consider myself a project management "expert". I had survived many projects in the past, but the size of this one made me nervous, not to mention the employment implications. In fact I had a sign in my office that looked like this:

STEPS IN A PROJECT:

1) ENTHUSIASM
2) ACTION
3) CONSTERNATION
4) PANIC
5) OBFUSCATION
6) PUNISHMENT OF THE INNOCENT
7) PRAISE AND REWARDS TO THE NON-PARTICIPANTS

It was supposed to be humorous, but it rang just a little too true on the projects in which I'd been involved.

I had a vague idea about what a work breakdown structure was, what earned value costing was, and I had actually tried using things like Gantt charts for scheduling. I had done academic work in college with all of those tools in one of my courses, but none of them had helped me very much on real projects. I felt like I would need all the help I could get.

"Why me?" I asked Stu. "Why not Al? He's the certified project manager. He's supposed to know all of this stuff."

Stu sighed and stared off into the middle distance. "It's you because I want this thing to have a chance of succeeding." I guess his compliment must have shown on my face, because he immediately said, "Now don't get a swelled head over this. You could just as easily screw it up. The only thing is, I know that Al has the wrong approach. He's proved it on every project he's managed here at Hyler. And I don't have time to run the thing for him. I figure that you, on the other hand, have a fighting chance of trying something different, even if it's out of desperation, and we just might succeed."

As I sat there feeling somewhat deflated, he continued, "I know you, Will, and you don't put a lot of stock in what you read in textbooks if you see that it doesn't work in reality. Al believes that if the textbooks say it, it must be right, regardless of whether it actually works. It's obvious to me that his textbooks on projects don't seem to help him understand the damn things."

Feeling somewhat inflated again, I said, "So what you're saying, Stu, is that I've got a free rein on this one, to do whatever it takes to make it work?"

Stu hedged. "Within reason. You've still got to keep Ralph happy, and I don't know if there is a lot of leeway on the money side. But yes, I will try to run interference for you so that you can do whatever works."

That was the last good thing I heard all morning.

# CHAPTER 2

Before I left his office, Stu provided me with some more details about the WindSailor, and my new project.

The WindSailor board was made from a relatively new fiberglass resin compound, and because of this the board needed to be painted with a special sealant that required a longer than normal curing time. Since I don't know a great deal about the chemistry of reinforced plastics (or any chemistry, in fact), this didn't mean much until Stu told me that this would place constraints on our manufacturing facility. Specifically, we would have to provide extra warehouse space for the curing process. This space had to be part of, or connected to, the manufacturing space. The boards would not be able to be transported very far, and certainly not outside, after they had been sealed.

According to Leslie Frame in Marketing, who had been in Europe working with the WaterTrends people, we expected to sell about 2,600 WindSailors in the first year, at a price of about $1,600 each. Although that only represented an overall sales increase at Hyler of about 10 percent, Leslie was projecting sales of almost $10 million by the third year. That represented a significant chunk of money for the company.

The Europeans had introduced the WindSailor in only a few geographic areas in late July, having missed their beginning of the season target date by a wide margin (my ears pricked up when I heard that), so they did not have much marketing data to go on. The response in those selected areas, however, had been impressive. Their initial run of 2,500 boards sold out within four weeks, and they had back orders for next year equal to three-quarters of their production capacity. They were increasing their capacity to meet what they hoped would be an even greater demand next season.

By purchasing the North American manufacturing and distribution rights to the WindSailor, Leslie estimated that Stu had given Hyler a least a full year's head start on any North American competition, and on other European manufacturers who might try to export to our market. Since this was a brand new product, Leslie figured that this head start would give us market dominance over any competing boards for as long as three years, longer if our marketing and promotion efforts were done well.

There was, of course, a catch that Stu seemed almost happy to relate. Leslie and the WaterTrends folks in Germany figured that it would take the competition about 16 to 18 months to design, test and produce a board that would get around the WindSailor patent protection, and compete head-to-head with our product.

"So you see," said Stu, "we have to get our WindSailor into the marketplace before the end of next summer." It was now August. "That leaves you almost 10 months to get this project done. No problem!" He actually reached across the desk and slapped me on the shoulder in a macho-friendly sort of way.

Great, I thought to myself. No problem. Design the new facility, build it, buy all the equipment and get it running properly in less then 10 months. As I thought about this, I became even more appreciative of the fact that we were located near Portland, where it does not snow, and you can do construction work all year.

Our distribution system always pushes our production dates back earlier than you would expect. Hyler only owns one retail outlet, which is located at our plant, so the rest of our product is sold through a variety of privately owned sporting goods stores. This means we have to have our products ready for sale well before the final customer wants to buy them. Distribution time is a reality that has to be factored into all of our production schedules. If we wanted to get the WindSailor out to the public for the last part of next summer, the month of August, for example, we would have to have it ready for sale by June. This would allow time to get it out to retailers.

Stu interrupted my little reverie. "As you might expect," he said, "the Hyler Board of Directors, in all of its wisdom, has already decided how much this project will cost." I always hated these pronouncements. We only had a rough idea of what work was going to be involved, and the board was already telling us what we would be spending, regardless of anything we might discover to the contrary. Based on my past experience, I expected that we *would* discover to the contrary, with respect to both cost and schedule. Then there would be hell to pay, even though the board must have pulled the cost estimate out of thin air.

"...have $1 million to spend on this one. The new equipment costs are not included in that figure." My attention returned to Stu as I heard the budget I was to have. "Think you can do it for that?"

"Stu," I began, "just how am I supposed to answer that question? You know as well as I do that I don't know what this thing is going to cost. I just found out about it 20 minutes ago."

"Good," said Stu, apparently turning a deaf ear to my complaints. "I'll tell Ralph that you can. I wouldn't want to disappoint him."

"Hold on a minute, Stu," I said, getting my courage up. "I am going to play this one straight. One million may be the board's budget figure, but I refuse to be caught out on this project like every other one. As soon as I know differently, Ralph is going to have to approve a new budget for this thing."

Stu looked at me with his "long-suffering" look, as if there was a whole world of pain out there that I just didn't understand. "Sure, sure," he said. "Whatever it takes. Just make sure you pass it through me before you go off talking to Ralph." He sighed. "You may want to keep yourself pure and clean and out of the office politics, but one of us has to keep an eye on it. In fact, I think you had better look at me as your political advisor on this one, as well as your sponsor."

That seemed fair enough, since his neck was out on this project even further than mine was.

"Well," I said, standing up, "I better get going on this thing." I had a last-minute thought. "Who will I be coordinating with on the Human Resources end of things?"

Stu just looked at me and didn't say anything.

I prompted him, "You know, with all the new machines, we'll have to hire and train a bunch of people." Stu still didn't say anything, and kept on looking at me. I started to get it. "Aw, Stu. " I sounded like a little kid whose bedtime had come halfway into his favourite TV show. "There's a hell of a lot of work there. I don't even know what I'm doing on the manufacturing side!"

Stu finally spoke. "This one is important, Will. We have to do it right, and I'm not going to break it into a million little pieces in hopes that everything will get done. The whole thing is part of the same big project, and I want it run that way." I must have looked depressed, because he added, "You won't have to do this thing all on your own, you know. With my help you can pull team members from every department, and they'll be doing most of the work in their areas. But I want you coordinating the whole thing."

Resigned, I said, "I suppose I'll be responsible for the new systems as well?"

"The whole thing," Stu said, "except for the marketing campaign and the actual rollout, which Marketing will handle. I want you to coordinate it all."

With those words ringing in my ears, I headed back to my office. The more I thought about the whole thing, the more unhappy I was. Not only was this project important for the company, it looked like Stu's hopes of promotion were riding on it too. It wasn't so much that I minded pressure, it was just that projects always seemed to turn out poorly, or with mixed results at best. Hard as I had tried, I had never figured out a way to improve the result.

If my budget was $1 million, Marketing would probably have nearly that amount too. Recreational products are very marketing intensive. Two million dollars was a lot of money for Hyler to invest, and that didn't take into account the increase in operating expenses that would result from this product. Head Office would never let Hyler get into serious trouble, but it would let people's careers get into serious trouble. If things didn't go well, not only would Stu not be getting his promotion, but I would probably want to dust off my résumé too. All of this, hanging on a project. I felt something funny happening in my stomach.

My loyal department staff were not much help for my stomach or for my lack of knowledge about projects.

"Better dust off the old résumé," said Amanda Payton after I told her about my meeting with Stu. Amanda is my second in command in Information Systems, and one of my favorite people at Hyler. "It sounds like one of those projects that can really go down in flames!" She smiled encouragingly.

In an effort to reduce her smugness to a more bearable level, I said, "Yes, no question it will be a challenge." I tried to look forlorn, then continued, "But thank God I have you around to help! The project is going to take up a lot of my time over the next 10 months, so I will need you to take over my responsibilities on a regular basis. Of course, we won't be getting any extra people to help us here in IS, so you will still have your own stuff to look after." I paused, and then because it didn't sound like enough, I added, "And I think I will be needing your expertise on the project team as well. Looks like we will be spending a few late nights together." I gave her my best "team" smile.

Her smugness transformed into minor depression, and I felt a little better. Then I told her about Al Burton being assigned to the team by Ralph. Amanda was not impressed. "Al is going to be a major burden to the whole thing. You know him, he does everything by the book. And half the time he has the wrong book!"

I wished that everyone else's opinion of Al was not quite as dismal as mine. After all, I was going to have to work with the guy.

"When are you getting started?" Amanda asked.

I looked at my watch. "I've scheduled the first team meeting for tomorrow morning at 10:00 a.m. Want to come along?"

"I wouldn't miss it," she said, although I got the feeling she was only interested in the entertainment the meeting would surely provide. I would definitely have to find a lot of work for her to do.

"Why that's wonderful, Will!" Jenny said. She obviously wasn't getting the message.

I tried telling her again. "But dear, my future is riding on this project! And so is Stu's. Remember him? He's my boss. You like him!"

Jenny is my wife. She's a great person, and I value her opinion above just about anyone else's. The only thing I don't like about her is that she is not terribly sympathetic. She has crazy ideas about dealing with problems in a rational way, and sometimes I just find that hard to take. Tonight for example. The whole drive home (which, admittedly is only about 10 minutes, since we live on the outskirts of Darfield, the next town over from Enderby) I had been looking forward to complaining about my troubles, and then listening to her appropriately sympathetic noises. As usual, she was not playing her part.

"Look hon," she continued, "from everything you've told me, it seems like Stu made a great decision buying the rights to this product. If Hyler can get it to the market before the end of next summer, it will be a great success!"

I guess my wife's positive attitude is something I have always admired. She needs it in her job. Jenny is a writer; a freelance journalist. When we had Sarah, our first child, six years ago, Jenny and I decided to move out of the big city (then Baltimore) and live the small-town life. We thought it would be better for the kids, and for us. By the time we had our son Jake three years later, I had managed to find the job with Hyler.

Moving to the country sounds like a really trendy, yuppie thing to do, but we have never regretted it. Unfortunately, Jenny's career was harder hit than mine. Before the kids and the move, she had had stories published in *Newsweek* and *Time*. Now she writes mostly for local papers and magazines. As she always says, when the kids are older, she will be able to get back into traveling more, and write higher-profile stories again.

Anyway, as a writer Jenny has seen a lot of rejections, often for arbitrary reasons. She has this disgusting habit of shrugging them off and trying again. For some reason, she has always encouraged me to do this.

I tried once more to convince her that it was hopeless. "But Jen, I am supposed to modernize the plant. That's my project! I don't know anything about construction or installing machinery or anything. And worst of all, I don't know anything about projects!" I could feel my lower lip trembling, as if it wanted to stick out in a pout.

It was clear that my behavior was not eliciting the least bit of sympathy. "Will, it seems to me that if you are going to be managing this project, you will be able to get people on your team who have expertise in specific areas. Is that right?"

"I suppose," I admitted grudgingly.

"So your only problem is that you don't know anything about projects. Is that right?"

I hated it when Jenny reduced my nice, big, insurmountable difficulties to simple, solvable problems. Fortunately, not knowing about projects was not a simple problem.

"It's not that I don't know anything about projects, Jen," I began. "I've worked on plenty of them. It's just that they always seem to be too big and complicated to handle. It's almost as if the outcome is randomly determined by the Project God, and He is a close relative of Thor."

Jenny looked at me and thought for a moment. "Do you honestly believe that a project can't go well?" she asked me.

"I suppose not," I said. "I just haven't run into anyone who seems to know how to do it." I paused. "There are lots of people who claim to know. God knows I've been to enough seminars. But most of their ideas don't make sense, and don't hold up when I try to apply them."

I stopped. Now I was really feeling depressed. When I had come home, I had just wanted someone to feel sorry for me. Now I was starting to understand the magnitude of my problem.

At least half a dozen books about projects had made their way across my bedside reading table in the last few years. I had been to three seminars on the topic. All in vain. Sure, I got ideas, but it was as if the approaches I had seen lacked some kind of internal consistency. They seemed to depend on the goodwill of your boss, and everyone on the team, in order to work. They did not take into account individuals who were disorganized, who did not want to spend a long time doing mathematical analysis of plans, or project managers who did not want to trust their team. Plus, they were always very construction oriented. There was nothing wrong with that, but most projects I had ever worked on had a big administrative component that directly affected everything else.

While I was able to criticize other people's approaches, I had never figured out an alternative of my own. Who had the time? In the past, whenever I had finished a project, it was time to get on with some other work or a new project. There was never any time to sit down to try and learn something from what we had just done. So of course we always did the next one the same way.

"...should go and see Martha." Jenny interrupted my thoughts.

"Sorry hon, what was that?"

"I said, if you want to figure out how to do projects better, you should go and see Martha."

I looked at my wife for signs of mental distress. "Martha?" I asked.

"That's what I said," Jenny replied.

I considered this suggestion. "You mean, Martha, your grandmother?" "Yes, Martha, my grandmother," Jenny said.

They say that if you want to know what someone will be like in 30 years, just look at his or her parents. I have often wondered if looking at the person's grandparents gives you a picture of what they will be like in 60 years. This always gives me a fright when I think about Jenny's grandmother.

To be fair, the old woman was not that bad. It's just that Martha (as everyone, including her own daughter, calls her) was perhaps the weirdest senior citizen I had ever met. She was somewhere in her eighties, and she lived with her daughter (Jenny's mother) in Darfield. She seemed to spend the whole day sitting on the porch in her rocking chair, smoking her pipe (yes, a pipe), thinking, and being crusty to people like me. Admittedly, she did have a mind like a steel trap, but she made people uncomfortable (at least people like me) every time she opened her mouth. It seems she could not speak without pointing out how someone was doing something wrong, or how they could do it better.

The most annoying thing about Martha was that she was almost always right. If she told you there was a better way of doing it, there was. Unfortunately, Martha would tell you in such an unpleasant way that something inside of you did not want to give her the satisfaction of showing her she was right. Anyway, you always felt that if you had all day to sit around in the rocking chair thinking about things, you would have lots of better ways of doing things too.

I looked at Jenny. "What does Martha know about projects?" I paused. "Come to think of it, what does Martha know about anything except rocking and pipe smoking?"

"What do you know about Martha?" Jenny asked me.

"Other than the fact that she's your grandmother, and that I often hope your mother was adopted, not much. Why?"

Jenny gave me an exasperated look. "If you don't know anything about her, how can you be sure she can't help you?" There was that logic again.

"I don't go up to drunks on the street asking for help on projects do I?" I asked rhetorically. "And I don't know anything about them either. C'mon Jenny, you have to give me a reason to subject myself to her." I liked the way that sounded. You didn't visit Martha; you subjected yourself to her.

"To be honest Will, I don't know that much about her background. I do know that when I was a little kid and Martha was living with us, she used to travel all around the country, and even overseas. When I used to ask her what she did she would always tell me she was 'helping set people's thinking straight', as she put it.

"My mother told me that Martha was a consultant. I've asked Martha about it directly, but she doesn't say much other than what she used to tell me as a kid.

"According to Mom, Martha and my grandfather started a manufacturing business together before the Second World War. They did very well with it, even better after Pearl Harbor. When my grandfather was killed in London in 1942, Martha ran the whole thing herself. I guess she sold out sometime before I was born, and came to live with my mom."

I was kind of interested in all of this. In a way, it made sense. Martha looked like someone who was used to ordering people around.

"That's fascinating family history and all, but what makes you think she can help me with launching the WindSailor?" I asked.

"Look, Will," Jenny began, "you know how Martha likes to think about things and improve on how others do them. With her experience in business, don't you think she might have run across a project or two? Maybe she has some ideas that will help you."

I sighed. I guessed it wouldn't hurt to go and talk to her. Anyway, it probably wouldn't take long. I had one last line of defence.

"Jen, she calls me Willie, and you know how I hate that!" Jenny just looked at me. "Okay, I'll go over and see her tonight." Anyway, I reflected, when Martha is not able to help me, maybe my wife will give me the sympathy I deserve.

# CHAPTER 3

One thing that I have always liked about Darfield, from the first time I saw the place, is the town's "oldness." I don't mean ancient, stone-age oldness, I mean the way the whole little village looks like it came from about 1920 (which, I suppose, most of it probably did). The streets are wide and lined with big old elm and oak trees, and behind the trees sit the houses. Big two- and three-storey places, with porches that run all the way around the front; houses that really do have the character that real estate listings always claim. Every time I drive through the place, I feel nostalgic for the smalltown America that was gone before I was born.

Fortunately, my nostalgia is tempered with practicality. Jenny and I were not crazy enough to buy one of those old places. 'Way too much upkeep! When I get home from work I do not want to spend my evenings installing new plumbing, replastering walls and fixing rotting floorboards. We bought a much newer place on the outskirts of the village so we would not have to deal with all of that.

Jenny's mother, however, loves old houses. She and Jenny's father bought one of the places on Elm Street in the sixties, and have been fixing it up ever since. Personally, I am glad. I can live out my big-old-house dreams whenever I go to visit, knowing I will soon be returning to a place that doesn't require nearly so much work.

Because of this, the prospect of visiting Martha was not all bad.

It was still light out as I cruised slowly down Elm, admiring the scene, thinking about what it must have been like 60 years ago. I pulled into my in-laws' driveway and sat in the car for a moment, drinking in the atmosphere. On this late-August evening the trees were still in full leaf, the air was warm, and you could almost hear kids playing baseball in the vacant lot behind the house.

"Looks like Willie's coming for a visit!" Unfortunately you could also hear Martha making comments from the front porch. I sighed and got out of the car.

"Hi Martha," I said politely. She was in her usual place on the porch by the corner of the house, sitting in her rocking chair, pipe clenched between her teeth. Sometimes when I looked at her she made me think of a cross-dressing Popeye, but maybe that was being unkind.

Jenny's mother Natalie came out through the screen door at the front. "Oh hi Will. Jenny called and said you would be coming over."

"Hi Natalie," I said. "I just thought I would drop by to visit for a few minutes." I did not feel like admitting the true reason for my visit just yet.

"Would you like some lemonade?" Natalie asked.

Lemonade on the front porch on a summer evening. It sure helped my little fantasy along. I walked up the steps and tried to look casual as I sat in one of the porch chairs close to Martha. "And how are you tonight?" I asked.

"Not too bad, Willie," Martha answered, and then went back to smoking her pipe. I sat there for a few minutes feeling uncomfortable until Natalie brought out my lemonade.

"Here you are, Will," she said, putting it on the small table beside me. "Now, Jenny told me you wanted to talk business with Martha, so I'll just leave you two alone out here." Natalie turned and went back inside.

We sat in silence for a few moments while Martha smoked. I have to admit, I love the smell of pipe smoke, regardless of who is producing it.

"Well Willie," Martha finally said, "You're making me nervous just sitting there. What did you want to talk about?"

I started hesitantly, "Jenny was telling me that you used to be a consultant."

Martha looked at me. "After I quit doing real work I spent some time trying to help other people get their thinking straight. Yes, that's true," she said.

"Well...," I continued haltingly, "when you were helping people straighten out their thinking, did you ever do any work with projects?"

Martha laughed. Actually, it was really more of a guffaw. "Yes indeed Willie. I've spent some time working on projects. Why do you want to know?"

I still had no indication that Martha knew anything, but I figured what the hell, I'm here. I might as well tell her the story. I gave her a brief overview of my project at Hyler.

"But you see Martha, my real problem isn't really this specific project. It is projects in general. This one is important, but it just points out that I don't know what I'm doing with any project." I felt a little naked admitting that to Martha. I was worried she would come back with some scathing reply about my lack of intelligence.

To my surprise, that was not what happened at all. "You've made a big step Willie," Martha said slowly. "I never was able to help straighten out anyone's thinking who didn't understand they had a problem. That's good." She paused.

I felt absurdly pleased at that comment. I guess her opinion meant more to me than I wanted to admit. "So can you give me some suggestions that will help?"

Martha looked thoughtful as she took a long draw on her pipe. She leaned forward and said, "You know Willie, there isn't a lot that I can tell you."

Oh well, I thought, just as I expected. It is always nice driving down here anyway. Time to go home for some real sympathy from my wife.

"But what I can do is help you figure out how to do them better." She sat back in her chair looking rather pleased with herself.

I paused and sipped my lemonade. "Help me figure it out? I don't mean to be rude, Martha, but if I knew what to do, don't you think I would have done it already? I need to know more about projects. I don't have time to figure anything out."

Martha took her pipe stem from her teeth and said, "Willie," – I am sure she kept calling me that because she knew it bugged me – "Willie, I bet you already have just about all the knowledge you need to have to do projects well."

I reflected on my formal and informal education in project management. I had taken a course in Operations Research when I was at university. We had done a lot of mathematical analysis of PERT charts and arrow diagrams, both project management tools.

But the guy teaching the course had a PhD in Project Management for God's sake! It seemed to me there must be a lot of knowledge that I did not yet have.

I told this to Martha. She just smiled. "I suspect that you don't have time to go back and get a PhD before you complete the WindSailor project. And anyway, you probably wouldn't learn much to help you." I had to agree with that one. So far, academic knowledge had been of no help to me in my projects. Martha continued, "If you want to improve the way you do something, like projects, do you always need to increase the quantity of your knowledge?"

"Yes," I said, without hesitation. As soon as the word slipped out, Martha's expression told me that I should have thought about it for a little longer. I tried to defend my answer. "Look at all the technological advances we humans have made in the last few years. All the latest discoveries like the silicon chip and fiber optics. They all came from research that increased our knowledge."

"Fiber-optic technology has been around since World War II," Martha told me. Like I said, she loves to correct people. "So it hardly qualifies as new technology. However, you are right to a certain extent. New discoveries and solutions do require knowledge, and that knowledge may not yet have been discovered. But I'll ask you again. Is gaining more knowledge always the way to improve things?" She sat back in her chair and tried to take another draw on her pipe. It had gone out by this time, so she busied herself cleaning it out in preparation for relighting.

While she was occupied, I thought a little more carefully about the question. Intuitively it made sense that the more you knew, the better you would be able to do things. But I was acquainted with a number of people who seemed to have a large quantity of knowledge yet were not very good at what they did (my project management professor being one of them). I tried to emulate my wife and apply a little logic instead of getting exasperated with Martha's questions.

If knowledge had to do with the quantity of information you had, what more would you need except more information to help you improve how you did things? I was at a dead end. I also began to feel impatient. I wanted to spend some time tonight preparing for my 10:00 a.m. meeting.

I told Martha that I was stumped.

"Tell me, Willie," she said, "you're an educated boy. Have you ever heard of Emmanuel Kant?"

The line "Emmanuel Kant was a real pissant..." from Monty Python's "The Philosophers' Song" came back to me, but otherwise I drew a blank. I did not want to admit this to Martha though, so I thought hard. I took a wild stab. "He was a philosopher, wasn't he?" I asked as nonchalantly as I could manage. It is amazing what you can learn from television.

"Very good," Martha said, "there is hope for you yet." She continued: "Kant is going to help you solve your problem." When she said this, I started to get very impatient, but being a polite kind of guy, I let her finish. "Kant wrote about some very interesting things, and one of them relates to our conversation. Kant had an interest in knowledge and human thinking, and he made a very important observation about how we humans make new discoveries." She stopped rocking and leaned forward in her chair, as if she were getting interested in the conversation.

"Kant proposed that the way we choose to look at what we already know is the source of the 'new' discoveries we make. In other words, it is not the acquisition of new information, so much as how we look at what we already have, that is important in learning new things."

Martha's pipe had gone out again during her little speech, so she paused to light it. What she was saying appeared to make sense, but I am the kind of person who relates better to examples. "Can you give me an illustration of how this has worked in the past?" I asked.

"I'm getting to it," she said, "just let me get my pipe lit." She kept on puffing. One thing I cannot understand about pipe smokers is why it doesn't drive them crazy that their pipe goes out all the time. Come to think of it, maybe they are all crazy.

Finally she continued. "The example Kant used is probably one of the best. Did you know that people used to believe that the sun moved around the earth?"

This was deteriorating. I looked at my watch and said, "Yes, and people also used to think the world was flat. Where is this going?"

Martha looked a little annoyed. At least I think she did. It was hard to tell her annoyed looks from her regular ones. "How do you suppose we figured out that the sun didn't go around the earth?" she asked.

"I don't know. I guess somebody made some measurements of the stars or something, and worked it out."

"Not at all," Martha said smugly. "Copernicus was the person who figured it out, but he had exactly the same information that everyone else had at the time. He did have something that no one else had though. What do you think it was?"

"I have no idea," I said.

"You don't, but he did," Martha told me. "Copernicus had an idea. That was all. No new knowledge, just an idea. His idea was that maybe the earth revolved around the sun, not the other way around. All the existing knowledge actually supported that idea, just like it fit into the perspective of the sun going around the earth. But no one had ever thought of it before." Martha sat back in her chair and puffed her pipe. "Kant pointed out that Copernicus had proposed a new mental framework."

I looked at her. I figured she expected me to sum things up like a schoolboy at the end of the lesson. I summed things up. "So what you are saying, Martha, is that in order to improve things, or make discoveries about how things are, we might not need new information, just a new perspective on what we already know." The lesson seemed to be ending, and I figured I could be out of there in five minutes.

"That is exactly it Willie, exactly." She looked as if she had solved all of my problems. Needless to say she had not, especially the one that would occur if Jenny turned into a Martha in the next 60 years.

"So what is your point?" I asked, figuring she did not have one.

"My point, Willie, is that you don't need to learn a whole lot more about projects, you need to get a new perspective on them."

I stared at her. "Don't keep me in suspense. What is the new perspective?"

She looked at me. "I already told you, I can't tell you what it is. I can only help you discover it for yourself."

This was getting just a little too mystical for me. I stood up.

"Well, thanks for your help Martha," I said, "but I've got to be getting home. I have a big day tomorrow." I started to walk off the porch.

Martha stared over the edge of the railing. She said, "You haven't got it yet, Will." My ears pricked up when she called me that. "But you might. One way or the other, it won't affect me."

I stopped on the porch stairs, waiting for her to finish. "I want you to do one thing. Tomorrow, at your team meeting, ask everyone what they mean by the word 'project'."

I shook my head and glanced at the sun sinking into the western horizon. "Goodnight Martha," I said as I walked to my car. I figured that Martha must be just a little too theoretical, what could defining projects have to do with anything? The woman was crazy or something, but at least I had visited her, like Jenny had asked.

# CHAPTER 4

At 9:55 the next morning, I entered the Hyler conference room. As usual, there was no one there yet. That is to say, no one I was expecting for my 10:00 a.m. meeting. In fact, there was another meeting still going on. I checked the room schedule beside the door, and discovered that this meeting was supposed to have ended at 9:00 a.m. It was a status meeting about a marketing project, and like all project meetings, seemed to be running long. I sighed as I imagined all of the long meetings I had in store for me.

I thought about last night. When I had told Jenny about my conversation with Martha, all she had said was, "Are you going to ask them?"

"Ask who, what?" I answered.

"Ask your project team what a project is?"

"Hon," I began, "what does that have to do with anything? Everybody knows what a project is! And anyway, I need some serious help. I don't need to spend my time defining things that everyone already knows."

Jenny did not want to hear about my troubles after that. All she said was, "Don't write Martha off. She knows what she's doing."

I tried to explain to her that she thought that solely because Martha was a relation, there was some kind of trust there because of a complicated Freudian grandmother-granddaughter relationship, but she would have none of it.

I did spend some time preparing for the meeting, and the most important conclusion I came to was that I would need a lot of help from my team members, because this was one project where I did not have the expertise to do it all myself.

At 10:05 a.m. the Marketing meeting was still going on, and none of my team had shown up.

By 10:10 a.m. people started to arrive, and I gave the marketing folks the boot.

By 10:15 a.m. everyone was there, seated around the conference table. I, of course, occupied the head chair. Interesting, I reflected, how often in the meetings I had attended in the past I had thought that the person sitting in the head chair did not know what he/she was doing. Now I was sitting in the chair, and I knew I had been right.

Gathered around the table were Amanda Payton from Information Systems, the infamous Al Burton from the Production/Industrial Engineering group, his engineering assistant Sheila Chan, Alice Sorensen from Accounting, Mark Goldman from Human Resources, Leslie Frame from Marketing, and Luigi Delgarno, who was kind of the plant general foreman.

Except for Al, I was pretty happy with the group. As head of Information Systems, I had worked with all of them on various projects, and I had a good relationship with each, including Sheila, Al's assistant. Personally I thought she was a much better engineer than Al, but that could have been due to that fact that she seemed to get along with most people.

I looked around at them, took a deep breath, and started into my pitch. "As you have all probably heard by now, Hyler is taking on a new product. It's something that we're tentatively calling a WindSailor, and it fits nicely into our existing product line." I continued to give them some general information about the product.

"As to why we are all here, " I went on, "in order to manufacture the WindSailor we are going to have to make significant changes to our existing plant. This will likely include building new space, and buying new equipment. We are also going to have to hire and train more people. And we will have to develop some new information systems to support all of this expansion." I paused and took a sip of water. "Our friend Stu Barnes, the vice-president, is sponsoring this project, and for some reason he has chosen me to manage the whole thing. The only part we will not be responsible for is the marketing campaign. Our Sales and Marketing people will handle that."

I stopped for a minute and tried to gauge everyone's reaction to all of this. It appeared that more coffee would be needed before I could hope for much response.

I continued. "Stu has given me a pretty free rein to run this thing whichever way works, and we are going to need it. We have to finish everything in time for the production people to make 2,600 boards by July." I was happy to see that this got some reaction from the group. Most of it was resentful looks and under-the-breath mutterings, but at least I was sure they were alive.

"I am a firm believer in figuring out where we're going before we start spending any money," I said, although I was not sure how we were going to do this. "So I want to invest enough up-front planning time on this project to ensure that there are no surprises. To facilitate this, I want to run this team in a very informal way. I want everyone involved. If you have ideas, we all want to know about them. If you have criticisms, we all want to know about those too." I took a deep breath and prepared to be honest. "I am not what I would consider a project management expert. I've worked on a lot of them, but I hardly ever feel I have the control I think I need to do them well. This project is important, expensive and on a very tight deadline. I want to make every effort to make sure that it doesn't get away from us."

I stopped and looked around at all of them. I was hoping that this little speech would start pulling us together as a team.

Unfortunately Al spoke first. "I'm not sure what Stu was thinking about, making you project manager. You don't know anything about construction, and that is clearly the most important part of this project." That was Al: the picture of a supportive team player. "It would probably be simpler if you just assigned all of the construction work to me."

Before I could say anything, Luigi, the general foreman, spoke up. "Al, anytime you do anything around the plant, it screws up operations. When we're not making boats and boards, we're not making money. You just don't seem to understand that. Personally I'm glad you're not in charge of this one. We would be bankrupt in a week." Al and Luigi exchanged dirty looks.

Alice from Accounting piped in: "And I am sick of running around after you, Al, trying to keep track of your costs, and paying your bills. Every time you get involved in something, it creates a big problem for us in Accounting."

They were sounding like a well-functioning team to me. Us against Al. I figured that it might be time to say something before things got out of hand. "Regardless of what we all think, Stu has already decided. Believe me, I tried to convince him he was making a mistake, but he wouldn't buy it. Given that we don't have a lot of choice, I want to make the best of it." Al stared down at the floor, looking sulky. I thought everyone else seemed to look pleased, but that was probably my imagination.

"As I said before, I am no expert on projects. Right now I would like to figure out where we are going, and roughly who is going to do what. Where do you guys want to start?"

"As project manager," Al said, "you should start by establishing the project goals with the team." One thing you had to admire about Al: personal animosity from everyone he worked with would not stop him from speaking what he thought was the truth.

"Okay Al," I said, "let's begin with project goals." I got up and walked to the flip chart. "I'll write them up here as we go."

Leslie volunteered the first one. "I think the main goal of your project, as well as of the Marketing project, is to make the WindSailor a big success for Hyler."

That sounded good to me, and everyone nodded agreement. On the flip chart I wrote:

***Project goal: Make the WindSailor a success***

Sheila, Al's assistant, had some concerns with that. "That sounds pretty fuzzy. If we are going to make that the goal, shouldn't we have some kind of measurement of success?"

"That's fine," said Leslie. "How about meeting the projected sales of 2600 units in the first year? Let's use that for a measure of success."

Under the first line on the flip chart, I wrote:

***by meeting the first-season sales target of 2,600 units.***

"Everyone happy with that?" I asked the group.

Luigi spoke up again. "How about putting something in there about minimizing the disruption to our current production operation, which, I will remind you all, is what gives us grocery money every week."

I hesitated. "I'm not quite sure how that would be classified. It's not really a goal...."

Al spoke up again. "In project management terms, that would be a sub-goal. See, it supports the main goal, but it's secondary."

I still hesitated. I was starting to wonder exactly how goals and sub-goals and maybe even sub-sub-goals were going to help us.

Al looked a little peeved that I had not acted on his suggestion and written something. "For God's sake, Will, I'm a certified project manager. I know about goals and sub-goals. It's the accepted way to do it."

Certified people always made me nervous, but I wrote on the flip chart:

***Project sub-goal 1:To conduct the project in such a way as to minimize the negative impact on our existing production operation.***

Alice said, "If we are going to include this kind of stuff, I want something in there about doing this project so it doesn't cause me and my staff another million and one accounting headaches."

"Fair enough," I said. On the flip chart I wrote:

***Project sub-goal 2:To conduct the project in such a way as to minimize conflict with the accounting function.***

I turned to Alice for approval. "How's that?"

"Fine," she said. "If you can get anyone to pay attention to it."

Al chimed in with his comments on accounting. A real team builder was Al. "Look Alice, the reason I don't bother getting anything to you on time is that your costing system doesn't work for projects." Nobody said anything for a moment, and although I hated to admit it, I agreed with Al on that one. Fortunately Sheila spoke up and saved me the trouble of doing so publicly.

"He's right, you know, Alice," Sheila said. "Any reports you provide us about projects are always so far out of date by the time we get them that they are useless."

Alice looked a little flustered. "Look," she said defensively, "my main responsibility is to keep track of financial information for the company. All this project stuff is just a sideline for me, and I don't have the resources to be able to jump every time you people want something!"

I sensed more of a problem, so I stepped in again. "Obviously getting enough resources will be important to getting this project done properly. Everyone, including Alice, will have to let me know about their requirements well in advance. With Stu's help we should be able to hire extra staff, or whatever it takes, to get this work done." Personally, I hoped that we could figure out very soon what kind of resources we would need.

"Let's get back on track. Any other goals or sub-goals we need to add to this?" I asked the group.

"What about your budget?" Leslie asked. "Shouldn't there be something about budget in your goals?"

"Good point," I said. "Our budget on this one, as officially approved by the Hyler board, is $1 million."

"That's a nice round number," Amanda said. "From outer space," she added under her breath, loudly enough for everyone to hear.

Al must have agreed with her. "Take some advice from me, Will. I've worked on a lot of projects, and it really doesn't help to put the budget or the schedule in the statement of project goals. It will just get you into trouble. The cost and schedule just change all the time anyway, and it upsets the sponsor. Once he sees them written down, he gets very excited when you change it."

"Are you nuts?" asked Mark Goldman, the human resources guy. "Not put anything down about schedule or cost? Since his neck is on the line, don't you think Stu is going to want to know that we are at least aware of when this is supposed to finish and how much it will cost?"

Al leaned back in his chair and assumed his most annoying I-know-what-I'm-talking-about-and-you-know-nothing look. "Stuff changes all the way through a project. If someone has decided he wants something done, he's got to be prepared for the changes. We don't want to get hung out to dry when we can't meet some unrealistic budget and schedule put together by some turkey who doesn't know anything about the project." He paused. "What I suggest is this: Let's put in a project sub-goal that says something about doing all of this work on time and on budget, but let's just not write down what the time and budget are. If we can get away with it, it will save us a lot of headaches in the long run."

I wasn't sure what to do with this one. Here was something else that I felt I had to agree with Al about. Most of the projects I had worked on had a time frame and costs that were pulled out of thin air. Invariably, by the time the thing was done, one or both were significantly different from when I had started. Maybe it would be better not to mention cost and schedule.

"Al, what does the sponsor say to you when you leave those two things out of project goals?"

Al looked a bit sheepish. "To be honest, I have never been able to get a sponsor to go for that." Everyone in the room, including me, let out an exasperated sigh. "But it's a good idea!" Al said quickly, "if you can get it by the sponsor."

I did not like the idea of trying to "get anything by" the sponsor, for God's sake, we were supposed to be working together!, but past experience had me in agreement with Al. On the flip chart I wrote:

***Project sub-goal 3: To conduct the project in such a way as to complete it on time and within the specified budget.***

As I finished writing, Mark said, "I'll tell you right now, that looks stupid. I for one vote to put the schedule and budget constraints up there before we go any further."

I turned to the group. "What do the rest of you think?" There were various murmurings for and against the idea of including the cost. The only thing I could determine was that there was no agreement.

I decided to move on. "Look, we will come back to this later. Maybe we can agree after thinking about it for a while." I turned back to the flip chart. "Anybody have anything they would like to add?"

No one did. "Right," I said. "Moving along. We've identified the project goals. What about responsibilities?"

As usual, Al had some suggestions to offer. "Let's just divide things up functionally. I'll handle all the construction and equipment stuff, Mark will handle human resources, Alice, accounting, and so on."

"So what do I do?" I asked. This did not sound like teamwork.

"You coordinate," Al said.

Before I could respond, Amanda spoke up. "Al, you know that isn't going to work. There is too much interaction among all of the areas. You said yourself that Accounting doesn't supply you with the information you need. How is that going to change if everyone is operating independently?"

"Look," Al said, "if each person looks out for themself, we'll be able to work quite efficiently. When I need something from one of you, I'll let you know. If you can't supply it, I'll take care of it myself. If you want to look at your Accounting example, I don't even bother with them anymore. We track our own costs."

Alice's face turned very red. "When you do that, you make my job even more difficult! You don't tell me what you are spending where, and then I have to deal with suppliers who want to know why I haven't paid them!" Alice sat back and crossed her arms. "If I had a choice, I wouldn't even be here."

Then Mark added fuel to the fire by saying, "You have to admit, Alice, that things do run on a different schedule in Accounting. It takes weeks to get things paid, like moving expenses for new employees."

Alice blew up again. "That's because no one ever tells us anything! We only find out what's going on when you guys start to complain!"

I suppose that I should have been happy. My team was starting to spread the blame already, a skill we would likely need in the coming months.

I decided to move on again. "Perhaps we will leave responsibilities until we have a little better picture of the work we have to do."

Al said, "If we would just divide up the responsibilities, each of us could figure out the work to be done on our own, and we wouldn't have to waste any more time in this meeting."

As was the case before, this did not sit well with Luigi. "If I don't have any say in your activities, Al, you won't do things in the most efficient way from a production point of view. And," he said smugly, "that conflicts with our first sub-goal."

"I don't need you telling me how to do my job!" Al said, his voice rising.

"You don't even know what your job is!" Luigi said, his voice louder than Al's.

"I agree with Al," Leslie said. "We're all wasting our time in this meeting. Let's just figure out what we each need to do, and get on with it."

Amanda jumped in. "I already explained to you, Leslie, everything we do is going to have some impact on everyone else...."

I sat back down at the table, and my mind drifted out of the conversation as everyone seemed to start talking at once. I thought to myself, at least this meeting is not like any other project team meeting I have been involved in: it's worse. I tried to be positive and think about what we had achieved so far: we had a very fuzzy project goal, a couple of fuzzy sub-goals that would apply to any project being done at Hyler (or anywhere else), and a lot of disagreement about how to do things.

I tried to get a little perspective on why things were going as poorly as they were. Granted, we did have people from several of the different functional areas. They were bound to have their own ideas about projects and what was important. But a project in Accounting would be essentially the same as a project in Marketing or construction. It would follow the same basic process, although the end product would be different.

Or would they really be the same?

More importantly, what if everyone thought they were different? Perception is reality, as they say. If a bunch of people were trying to deal with a particular situation, and they all had a different understanding about that situation, might it not be hard to get consensus on how to proceed? And suppose that not only did everyone have a different understanding of the situation, but that everyone's understanding was wrong. Not completely wrong, but maybe off just a bit. Might that not cause some difficulty?

I stood up again and went to the flip chart. I turned over a fresh page. "What is a project?" I asked the group.

No one responded for a second because they were all too busy arguing. They started to quiet down when they saw me standing there.

"What was your question Will?" Amanda asked.

"What is a project?" I repeated. "What is the definition of a project?"

"No offence, Will, but what does this have to do with anything?" Mark asked.

"Look," I said, "I think this will help. What is a project?"

"It's some work that has a goal," Amanda volunteered. I nodded and wrote that on the flip chart.

"That's not exactly it," said Mark. "It also has a beginning and an end and a life cycle." I added that to the chart.

"It has a budget and a schedule," said Alice.

"It has resources assigned," added Leslie.

"It's a one-time activity," Luigi said. "You never do it again. It's unique."

"It's a bunch of tasks that achieve a goal," Mark said.

I frantically scribbled all of this on the flip chart.

Then Al said, "A project is any undertaking that has defined start and end points, and sets specific objectives to be accomplished. Projects are unique, time-limited, goal-oriented, major undertakings, and they require a commitment of varied skills and resources."

Without even pausing for breath he continued, "Project management is the discipline that has developed a set of tools, methodologies and a process to manage projects. Specifically, project management is the art of directing and coordinating human and material resources throughout the life of a project, by using modern management techniques to achieve predetermined objectives of scope, quality, time, cost and participant satisfaction."

It sounded like something he had memorized out of a textbook.

I tried to jot down a few of the highlights. "Anyone have anything else?"

"That's a nice definition and all," Amanda said to Al, "but if that is a project, what isn't?" She was right. It seemed that Al's definition could be applied to just about anything.

Al apparently agreed. "If you choose," he said, "you can manage anything as a project."

I felt confused. Everything could be managed as a project?

It was time to move on. "Anyone have anything else to add?" No one did.

I stepped back and looked at what I had written on the flip chart. No two people agreed on what a project was, except that Al's definition seemed to encompass them all. Everyone seemed to be describing the same thing, but they all had their own ideas.

"Anybody notice anything about all of these definitions?" I asked.

"Yeah," said Luigi, "you killed a lot of trees to write them all down. Where is this going?" I remembered asking Martha the same question last night. No one else said anything.

The problem was, I didn't know where this was going. I just knew that there was something important here that I didn't want to miss.

"Nowhere," I answered. "It's almost half past ten. I would like each of you to make a list of the things that need to be done in your area, or with your area and one of the others. Have that done by tomorrow, and we will meet at 1:00 p.m. Then we'll try to put the lists together and come up with some kind of integrated plan."

Grumbling, everyone got up and left the conference room. I did not blame them for feeling a little dissatisfied; I felt that way myself. I went to the flip chart and tore off the pages we had used. When I turned around, Al was the only person still in the room. He got up slowly from his seat, obviously wanting to talk to me.

"Will," he began, "you know I'm not happy about you getting this project. Quite frankly, I don't think you have the knowledge or the experience to do a good job on it. Ralph Borsellino thinks along the same lines as I do. He wants me to make sure that you stick to the rules on this one, so it doesn't get away from you." He paused and looked at his notes. "So think of me as the policeman on the team. I'll be looking for things you are doing wrong, and I will be letting Ralph know. But I will also be telling you what I tell Ralph, so don't think I will be trying to stab you in the back." I didn't feel comforted.

But at least he was honest. No dancing around the issue for Al. He wanted to let me know just where he stood, and I respected him for that.

"I'm just hoping you will screw up early enough that I can save the project when they turn it over to me."

On second thought, there was such a thing as too much honesty.

"Now," he said, "as I understand it, Ralph wants a work breakdown structure for this project. You haven't mentioned that to the team yet. He also wants to see earned value costing reports. You haven't told Alice about that yet." He studied his notes. "And," he continued, "you haven't told them about integrating this with the TQM project."

He stopped, and I was thankful. Another two items, and physical violence would have been unavoidable. "Listen Al," I said with controlled rage, "I gave you every opportunity to participate, so I expect you to bring these things up with the entire group. I don't need you giving me a private report card when everyone has left the room." I paused. "And anyway, what does Ralph want that stuff for? He probably doesn't even know what a work breakdown structure is."

"He wants that stuff, as you call it, because I told him he wants it! He doesn't have to understand why." Al glared at me as he put his notes away. "It's not easy being the project manager. Just remember, I'll be watching." He picked up his briefcase and walked out of the room.

I slumped down into one of the chairs and stared at the ceiling. I was doubly disadvantaged. Not only was I not a project expert, but I hated office politics, and it seemed that Al was intent on playing them to make me look bad. Neither he nor Ralph seemed to realize that making me look bad could have serious consequences for this project, and for Hyler.

I picked up my stuff and the flip charts, and headed back to my office.

# CHAPTER 5

Back at my office, I sat down and put my feet up on my desk. Although people have told me that this particular position looks arrogant, disrespectful, lazy and just plain impolite, I find it extremely comfortable. Whenever I need to think, I always sit like this and stare at the ceiling, sort of my own version of Rodin's sculpture.

I spent a moment examining my motives. I had worked on many projects before this one without spending so much time wondering if there was a better way. Why now? Was it the size? The fact that there were many aspects of the project with which I was not familiar? Maybe because my career with this company was riding on it. Anyway, it didn't seem to matter why I was suddenly concerned, I couldn't shake the feeling, so I would just have to continue trying to figure out a better way.

That decided, I got up and stuck the flip charts from the meeting around the walls of my office. I looked first at the project goals flip chart.

| | |
|---|---|
| ***Project goal:*** | ***Make the WindSailor a success by meeting the first-season sales target of 2,600 units.*** |
| ***Project sub-goal 1:*** | ***To conduct the project in such a way as to minimize the negative impact on our existing production operation.*** |
| ***Project sub-goal 2:*** | ***To conduct the project in such a way as to minimize conflict with the accounting function.*** |
| ***Project sub-goal 3:*** | ***To conduct the project in such a way as to complete it on time and within the specified budget.*** |

I felt uneasy with those. It wasn't that I disagreed with any of them; it was just that they didn't seem to provide me with anything that would help me do the project better. Maybe they were not specific enough.

I gave up on them and looked at the definitions of the word "project." Like I thought before, they were all a little different, and all a little vague. Take the one that went: "Something with a beginning and an end and a life cycle". Intuitively I felt that this was a characteristic of a project, but a phrase like that could be talking about a giraffe, and I was not prepared to admit that giraffes were projects.

So what was the definition of the word "project"? Suddenly I had an idea. Where do you go when you want to know the definition of a word? Of course! The dictionary.

I went down the hall to where the three administrative people sat. Hyler's (and Ralph's) commitment to the self-empowered manager and the flattened, federated organization meant that I did not rate my own secretary. This was fine with me, because the age of the computer meant I did most of my own typing and correspondence anyway.

They all looked busy, so I helped myself to the big, fat Oxford Concise Dictionary from their bookshelf, and returned to my office.

Feet up on the desk I again, I began flipping through the pages looking for the word "project." I always have a little trouble finding words in dictionaries, maybe I didn't learn my alphabet properly as a kid. In fact, my wife always teases me about it. As a result, I always open the book up well ahead of the word I am looking for, just so I don't miss it. As I turned pages toward the p's, a few words caught my eye: fetal (the position I felt like curling up in right about then), hateful (which described my feelings towards Al), Pizarro (Spanish conqueror of Peru, you never know when this might come up in Trivial Pursuit). Finally I found the word "project":

***project (noun): plan, scheme, planned undertaking***

I got up and copied this definition onto a blank space on one of the flip charts. Then I sat down again at my desk, put my feet up, and stared at the words.

A project is a plan? That is it? The word "plan" did not seem to be mentioned in any of the definitions I had gotten from my project team. Even Al's long, rambling one did not say anything about a plan.

I tried to consider things logically. What did a plan have to do with a project? Intuitively, one would think it obvious that a plan is required for a project. So how come no one mentioned it when they defined the word? I knew from past experience that most projects do not have anything that one might call a plan. Actually, that was not quite true. Someone always claimed to have a plan inside their head, but I could never be sure, because I could not see in there.

This line of thought brought me to the question of what a plan is good for in the first place. Why make a plan? We make a plan, I decided, to help us organize all of our jumbled ideas about how we want things to go in the future, and what we are going to do to make things turn out that way. If we figure out how we want the future to be, we can figure out the things we have to make happen in order to get the future we want.

I got up and went to the flip chart again. Underneath the dictionary definition of the word "project" I wrote:

***A plan helps us structure our thoughts about:***
- ***how we want the future to be***
- ***what we have to do to make that future happen***

I felt that I was onto something. Just then the phone rang. It was Stu.

"So how did the first meeting go?"

"Not too badly," I lied. "There seems to be a little disagreement about how to proceed, but we will get around it."

"That's good," said Stu, "because there is going to be a meeting of the Hyler Board of Directors tomorrow evening at the Four Seasons Hotel in Portland."

I was a little surprised. "You mean a face-to-face meeting?" I asked. Hyler's board included several key executives from Mantec, our parent company. They were busy people, and most Hyler board meetings were held via conference call.

"Yeah," Stu confirmed. "It seems they want to come out and visit with Ralph, see how he's doing, and make sure that this WindSailor project is going to go okay."

"So I guess you'll have to give them a little presentation on the project?" I asked, thinking of all the information he was probably going to want before tomorrow night.

"Actually," said Stu, "you are going to do a little presentation on the project."

"Me?!? Why me? It was your idea!"

Stu chuckled. "Both Ralph and I thought that the board might be interested in hearing from you directly, instead of those of us who are a little removed from the whole thing."

My heart sank. "What are they going to want to see?"

"That's up to you, Will," Stu said. "I just want to show them something that gives them confidence that we are in control of this thing."

"It hasn't even started yet!" I moaned. "I haven't had time to do much of anything with it."

"Just show them you have it under control," Stu said. "Talk to me tomorrow afternoon so you can give me a run-through of what you are going to tell them." He hung up.

I slumped back in my chair. My first impulse was to start throwing task lists, charts, graphs, cost estimates and coffee beans together for the presentation the next day. Fortunately, my innate sense of sloth prevailed. That seemed like an awful lot of work unless it was going to take me in the right direction, and I was not convinced that it was the right direction.

I decided to spend at least a little more time on what I had been thinking about before Stu called.

Where had I been? Ah, yes. I looked at what I had just written on the flip chart about why we plan. Good thing I wrote it down, I thought. Otherwise, with the distraction of Stu's phone call, I would have completely forgotten where I was.

Just then a light came on inside my head. Of course! A plan does serve to structure our thinking about where we want to go and how we will get there, but just as importantly, it serves as a communication device! And not only is a plan a communication device for others, it also serves to remind you of what your intentions were. No wonder I used to question people who said they had the plan all thought out inside their heads. There was no way they could communicate it! For practical purposes, just thinking about something does not mean you have planned it. You still need to be able to communicate it.

Before I could forget, I jumped up and wrote on the flip chart:

***A plan:***

***1) Helps structure your thinking***
***2) Communicates your intentions***

A project is a plan. The purpose of doing a plan is to structure your thinking, and to provide a way to communicate your intentions. I did not know why, but I believed that this was important.

I call-forwarded my phone, grabbed my jacket, and headed out the door. It was only 11:30 a.m., but I had more important places to be. It was time to visit Martha again.

# CHAPTER 6

I did not take the time to notice the big houses and the tree-lined streets on this drive through Darfield. I was too busy thinking about projects, plans, and presentations to the Hyler board. Wherever I was going with all of this, I hoped that I could get there in a big hurry.

As I swung into my in-laws' driveway I could see Martha sitting on the porch in her rocking chair, smoking her pipe, just as I had left her the night before. She was reading something, and looked up as I got out of the car. "Aren't you supposed to be at work, Willie?"

Before she could say anything else, I said, "A project is a plan!" I rushed up on to the porch and sat down in a chair beside her.

She smiled a little and took the pipe out of her mouth. "I'm kind of surprised to see you back here today, Willie," she said. "Seems to me I wasn't giving you too much help last night." She took another draw on her pipe and I felt a bit sheepish.

"I got to thinking about what you told me last night, and the question you asked when I was leaving," I admitted. "Anyway, I pretty much forgot about it until things started to fall apart, as usual, at the first project meeting today. I was desperate, so I asked the group your question. Everyone gave me a different answer, and I started thinking about how this might cause problems. Anyway, I looked up the word "project" in the dictionary and, well, things started to make more sense. And since it was your idea, I decided I needed to talk to you again."

Just then the front door opened, and my father-in-law Fred Sparks walked out. Fred works the afternoon shift at the local sawmill, so he is usually home until about three. "Oh hello Will, " he said. "Aren't you supposed to be at work?" It seemed like a popular question. I started to feel like I was 17 and cutting school.

"I had to talk over some things with Martha," I explained. "I won't be long."

"Nat!" Fred turned and yelled back into the house, "Will is here, and he'll be staying for lunch!" I started to refuse, but Fred would have none of it.

"So," Martha said as Fred went out to the garage, "you've figured out that a project has something to do with a plan. Did you think about what a plan is good for?"

Feeling absurdly pleased, I said, "A plan has two purposes: it helps structure your thinking, and it allows you to communicate your intentions."

"Very good," Martha sounded surprised. "Understanding what a plan does is very important if you want to make one. So what did you come out here to ask me?" Her pipe was out, so she pulled her tobacco pouch out of her dress, and started stuffing tobacco into it (the pipe, not her dress).

That one stumped me for a second. Why had I come rushing out here? Just because I had figured out a few vague things about plans and projects? "To be honest Martha, I am not really sure. You got me thinking about what a project really is, and about what a plan is good for. Now that I have thought about it, it seems to me that this is really important stuff. How can we do a project if we don't even agree on what it is? And if a plan is for communicating, that will mean certain things about how we record the decisions and logic that make up a plan." I paused for a moment. "The only thing is, I have to make a presentation to the Hyler Board of Directors tomorrow about this project, and I don't think they are going to be all that impressed with what I've got so far. I need you to help me figure out quickly what all of this means, and take me to the next step."

By now, Martha had her pipe going again, and she eyed me speculatively. "You didn't seem all that keen last night." She sort of sighed this out and then stared out into the distance, playing the injured party.

I figured a full apology was in order. "Martha, I really want to know what you have to say. I'm sorry I doubted your approach, but I'm ready to listen now."

She turned and looked at me. "Like I said before, I can help you figure things out. If I tell you things, you won't understand the why, and you won't be able to use the ideas properly. Then you will blame me when things go wrong." At this point I did not think that was terribly likely, but I kept quiet.

Martha leaned forward in her chair. " 'Ignorance ain't so much not knowin', as knowin' a lot of stuff that ain't so'. You ever hear that, Will?" I shook my head. "Will Rogers said that a long time ago, and it is still true today. And it doesn't just apply to projects!" She was really getting going now.

"You see, people always want things to be better, but they never want to change how they do things." She stopped and looked at me. "If you want to do projects better, you're going to have to change how you do them."

"That sounds fine to me," I said. "I know it's not working. The only question is, what do I do differently?"

"Remember what we talked about last night? About mental frameworks? That is what you are going to have to change if you want to improve projects."

I was game to try. "Okay. Where do we start?"

Martha had been leaning forward in her rocker as she was speaking, but now she took a draw on her pipe and leaned back. "You tell me," she said.

I was ready for this one. "Well, I understand the purpose of a plan, and I understand that we need a plan to have a project, but it seems to me that there are all sorts of things in a project that just aren't covered by that simple definition of 'project'."

"A good place to start," Martha said. "Fetch me a piece of paper." I went back down to my car and got a pad of paper from the passenger seat. I always like to have something to write on, wherever I am. I took it back to Martha, and gave her a pencil from my shirt pocket.

Martha took the pad, and right in the middle wrote the word "project". She asked me, "What was the definition of this word again?"

I told her, "Plan, or planned undertaking." She wrote this down beside the word. "So which is it?" she asked.

"Which is what?"

"Which is the definition of 'project'? We need to clarify what we mean by the word 'project' if we are going to be able to think about it in a useful way." She looked at me.

I felt a little puzzled. I thought I had solved all of my definitional problems by going to the dictionary in the first place, and now Martha was trying to confuse me further. I looked at the definition again, and it hit me. Was a project a plan, or was it the undertaking, the one the plan was for? It was like saying: is a project the cake or the recipe for the cake? "I'm not sure," I said with finality.

Martha gave a little disgusted sigh. "You can't depend on the dictionary to solve all of your problems; you still have to think. Is it more useful to think of a project as a plan, or a thing that the plan is about?" I thought about kids I had known when I was growing up who had lived in the "projects." Were they projects, or were they high-rise apartment buildings? "A project is a plan," I said finally. "It makes more sense to think about the finished product as whatever it is, and reserve the word 'project' for how you are going to get the finished product."

Martha seemed pleased by this. "Good idea. But if a project is a plan, are all plans necessarily projects?" This women was driving me nuts with her questions. I thought about the classic false syllogism: All dogs have feet. All rats have feet. Therefore, all rats are dogs. Didn't it go something like that?

I considered plans. There were strategic plans, project plans, house plans, game plans, and God knew what other types of plans. So the question was: is a strategic plan the same as a project plan? I did not think so.

"I guess all plans are not necessarily projects."

"Which means," continued Martha, "that a project is a special type of plan. In fact, a project is a special type of plan called an Execution Plan."

On the pad she wrote:

***project = execution plan***

"It sounds to me like the execution plan just describes the actual work to produce the final product," I said.

"Exactly," said Martha.

"So, for example," I continued, "if you were building a house, the Execution Plan would just be the plan for pouring the foundations, putting up the walls, painting and all of that. Is that right?"

"Exactly," she repeated.

I had a problem with this. "There has to be more to it than that! What about project initiation, and the design? What about where you figure out if you want a three-bedroom house or a one-bedroom? That doesn't fit anywhere in this definition!"

Martha stopped rocking and leaned forward. "That is exactly right," she said as she stared at me without blinking. I got the feeling that there was an important message here.

Martha leaned back and started sucking on her pipe again. It was out, which was how it seemed to spend most of its existence, so I had a chance to ponder while she refilled.

If the definition of a project did not include all of that other stuff, it did not mean it was not done. "Martha, you are telling me that project initiation and design, and even the actual execution, are not part of the project."

She nodded in agreement. "I didn't say they weren't part of the project manager's job, I just said they weren't part of the project." Her pipe was going again and she took a few puffs. "Think about a golf game, Willie." This was easy for me, I often think about golf games. The only problem is, I do not get to play them very often. Martha continued, "It really helps your game if you use the right club. Now what helps you determine which club to use?"

The answer was obvious. "Where the ball lies," I said.

"That's right. If you are driving off the tee, you might select your 3-wood or your driver. If you are in a sand trap, you might choose a wedge, and if you are on the green, you would likely select a putter." Briefly I wondered how she knew anything about golf. If she could help me with projects, maybe she could help my golf game.

She went on. "Now suppose for a minute that you are a really great putter." That was a hard supposition for me to make, but I let her proceed. "You can sink anything within 25 feet of the hole in one stroke, just about every time. Let's also suppose that your driving isn't all that great. You have a bad slice, and most of the time when you hit off the tee, you end up in the next fairway or in the bushes. But once you get on the green, you are very accurate. Would you consider using your putter to hit off the tee, since you have so much success with that one particular club?"

"Of course not."

"And why not?" she countered. "You can use your putter well, and your driver isn't working. Why not use the putter?"

"Well...because it is the wrong club. It would take a lot of putts to get you anywhere near the green. Your best bet would be to try to improve your drives, not putt your way off the tee."

Martha puffed out a thick cloud of smoke. "You know Willie, as a rule, I hate analogies. They are just too full of holes. Why use one instead of talking about the real thing? But because I am partial to the game of golf, I want to point out a couple of things to you." She raised her index finger. "First, things we would not think of doing in a golf game, we do all the time in real life. You have some skill with your putter, does this mean you would drive with it? Of course not. Yet in life, when we find something that is successful for us, we tend to apply it over and over again, even though the situation has changed. How much sense does that make?

"Second," here she raised her middle finger, "to know what tool, or club, you should apply to help you out, you need to lift your head up and look around! You can't make a good decision about any club until you know where you are on the course.

"So with projects, the first thing we need to understand is what the course looks like, and where we are. We need to know that so we can figure out what club or tool to use to get us closer to the hole. We don't want to use the driver in the sand trap; we want to use the wedge. While picking the right club, or tool, doesn't guarantee success, it certainly increases our chances."

Martha stared hard at her pipe, trying to determine why no smoke was coming out of it. Apparently it had gone out yet again during this little speech, and she started the relighting process once more. All that would drive me crazy if I were a pipe smoker.

Although Martha was not in love with analogies, I liked this one. I certainly felt that I had been using my putter to drive on most of the projects I had worked on, and that I had never thought very much about what the course looked like.

"So, Martha, not only do you have to help me see what the course looks like and where I am, you will also have to help me get some more clubs. I think I am a little short in the club department." If I even have any clubs, I said to myself. Maybe what I had right now was a baseball bat.

"It isn't the only place, Willie," Martha said brightly, "but don't worry. That is another way projects are like golf. You can certainly acquire a huge bag of clubs, but there are really only a few basic ones that are essential to playing the game." She was right, at least about golf. With maybe a 3-wood, a 5-iron, an 8-iron and a putter you could hit out of pretty much any situation. Specialized clubs like sand wedges and drivers could be useful, but they were really refinements of the basic tools. That made me feel better. It also made me wonder why I bothered lugging all those clubs around with me on the golf course.

I was anxious to get my head up and have a look around the "course" for a project, but just then my mother-in-law stuck her head out the screen door. "You folks ready for some lunch?" Natalie asked. I was not ready to stop just yet.

"Sure am!" Martha answered before I could say anything. "Willie here is tiring me out. Don't worry," she said to me when she saw the look on my face, "we'll talk more after we eat."

It was a summer-style lunch of cucumber-and-tomato sandwiches, and it was actually quite refreshing to stop thinking hard for a few moments, and talk about the weather and other important things with my in-laws. By the time everyone had finished eating, I was ready to get back to work.

"I know you two have a lot to talk about," Natalie said as she got up from the table. "You go on back outside, and I'll clean up." Normally I am quite diligent about not leaving someone else to do all the cleanup work, especially when they have just made me lunch. Today, however, I was happy to oblige. Martha got up slowly from her chair and ambled back out to her rocking chair. She started working on lighting her pipe once again.

That pipe seemed to play a major part in her life, so I asked her about it.

"This old thing? Why Donald used to smoke a pipe, and I always loved the smell. After he died, I just couldn't bear to live without it, so I took it up myself. It always reminds me of him." She stared into the middle distance, thinking, I assumed, of Donald.

"Who was Donald?" I asked.

"You don't know much about this family, do you?" Martha scowled at me. I had to admit I did not. "He was my husband."

We sat in silence for a few minutes as I waited for Martha to begin again. Finally, I looked at my watch and decided to take the initiative.

"So Martha, can you help me see the layout of the course?" I figured that staying with her analogy might be a good idea.

Martha was ready to continue. "As you know Willie, every golf course is different, just like every project, and the things that surround it are different. But just as there are elements common to every golf course, there are some underlying, fundamental principles that describe what goes on around a project. In order to be successful, we must understand these."

That made sense. Every hole on a golf course is going to have a tee, some fairway, some rough, a hazard or two like sand or water, and a green. "Martha," I said, "can we get away from the analogy and on to actual projects? I am starting to lose track of reality." Besides, I was starting to wonder if I could still get a three o'clock tee time, and I was far too busy for that.

Martha took the pad and pencil from where she had put them beside her rocker, and wrote:

**Genesis**
**Design**
**Execution Plan (Project)**
**Execution**
**Reviews (3)**

I looked at it for a moment. It was not talking, so I looked at Martha. "And?" I prompted.

"All projects fit into the same structure, Willie, and these words describe that structure. Once you understand the structure, you can apply the right tools, and get the job done." She looked kind of proud of herself, as if these words represented a lot of work for her.

"So what do I do now?" I asked.

"I am going to help you understand each phase in this process, help you figure out the tools you need, and you will take it from there."

I looked again at the paper. Intuitively, it seemed to represent most of what I would have said a project was. I noticed though, that the word "project" actually showed up halfway down, beside "Execution Plan."

"Martha, why add to the confusion? Why don't you just call this whole thing a project?"

Martha lowered her eyebrows as a dark cloud seemed to pass over her face. In fact, until she lowered them, I never realized how dark her eyebrows really were. "Did you forget what we talked about before lunch? You told me what a project was, a plan."

"Well," I said defensively, "isn't this whole thing on your paper a plan?" I could tell from Martha's expression that she did not think so.

"This," said Martha, "is a framework that describes what happens around projects. Clearly, we need to have more discussion around planning in general."

I felt desperate. There was only so much understanding I could deal with in a single day. "Martha, I am afraid I just don't have time for that. I will take your word for it. This is a framework, not a project. Let's just go from there."

I could tell that she didn't really want to, but in the end my pleading look won out. "Okay," she said, "but it is a discussion we must have later. In order to be clear, you must accept that a project is a special type of plan called an Execution Plan."

"Fine," I said, relieved that we were moving on. "But what do I call all this stuff that includes a project?"

Martha drew on her pipe before she answered. "There is no really good name for it. I like to think of the whole thing as an assignment." She circled all the words and wrote "assignment" underneath them. "Trouble is, lots of folks call the whole thing a project, never create an execution plan, and try to manage something that doesn't exist."

"Okay," I said, "at this point, what I've got is an assignment." After all, Stu had assigned this thing to me. He hadn't projected it on me. "Now explain Genesis to me. What is supposed to be going on during that phase?"

"Willie, I think it will be more useful for you to think about each one of these phases in terms of what should result from its completion. Knowing what must come out of it will determine what should be going on during the particular phase." When I thought about it, that made a lot of sense. Let the end determine the means.

"Fine," I said. "So what is the result of Genesis?"

Martha did not say anything, she just looked at me and smoked her pipe. Then I remembered: she was going to help me figure it out, she was not going to just tell me. I sighed and sat back in my chair. How did most projects, excuse me, assignments, begin?

Usually some higher-up in the organization decided that he or she wanted to make an impact, so they would set something in motion, hopefully for the better.

"Genesis is when someone in a company decides to change things," I said.

Martha was not displeased with that answer. "That is part of what is going on, but what is the result?"

The result? The result was usually some executive's rough ideas about what should be done. Half of the problem with projects, I mean assignments, seemed to come from the fact that the executive in question was not really sure what he or she wanted.

"The result of Genesis would be some kind of fuzzy statement about what was supposed to be accomplished."

"Even with your editorial slant, you are pretty much correct." She wrote on the pad of paper:

***Genesis (Results):*** ***An idea about how to improve the existing situation.***

It sounded kind of airy-fairy at first, but the more I thought about it, the more I realized that that was exactly how projects started. They did not always improve things, but that was their intention. Something seemed to be missing, though. "Shouldn't there be something in there about the project sponsor or the project champion? You know, the person whose idea it was. There should be something about responsibility."

"You are partly right, Willie," Martha told me. "Although you have made an assumption that is not always true. Do the ideas for assignments always originate high in the organization, with people who are likely to be sponsors or champions?" I was feeling a little confused, mostly by what Martha meant by sponsors or champions. In our company, lower-level people were often assigned to be project champions or sponsors, but the ideas for the projects were always approved by people higher up.

Then I realized what I was assuming. The ideas could come from anywhere, but they needed to be approved by someone who had authority, someone higher up.

"So not only does there need to be the idea," I said, "there also needs to be some kind of authority behind it."

On the paper, Martha added:

***Genesis (Results):*** ***An idea about how to improve the existing situation.***
***An assignment of the authority to act***

"What else?" I asked, eager to hear more.

"What else what?" Martha replied.

"What else is supposed to come out of Genesis? There must be more. People need more than this when they do multi-million dollar projects! There must be more to it. What about project goals and sub-goals and work breakdown structures and all of that?" I guess I sounded a bit hysterical. I was imagining my presentation to the Hyler Board of Directors the next day, and so far I did not have much to present.

Martha looked unconcerned. "Willie my boy, the beauty of letting the results you require determine your actions is that you waste little effort on superfluous things." She looked at the floor and said in a distracted way, "Assuming of course you pick the right results." She looked back at me again. "Cocker spaniels and strategic planning once were useful, but popularity messed them both up. But never mind about that. You didn't pick this assignment, you just have to carry it out. Now, don't you agree that a clear definition of your assignment up front is important to success?" Of course I said yes.

"Well," she continued, "getting that clear definition is the first phase in an assignment. Once we have completed that, we have the results we need to go on to Design. That is the beauty of this framework. Each successive phase depends on the previous one. You know you did the last one right if you can do the next one."

"If that is true," I asked, "how come I've never seen this framework, but I see people doing projects all the time?" Martha just looked at me and did not say anything for a moment.

"Seems to me," she said, "that I've heard of more than a few 'projects' not going too well." That was certainly true, and not just on the level that I dealt with. You could not open up a newspaper without reading about some mega-project that was four years late and $300 million over budget. "And besides," Martha said, "people do follow this to some extent, because this framework deals with how projects actually happen. Most people working on projects have their heads down, and they can't see it. And anyway, if one or more of the phases is not completed properly, it leads to all of the troubles you observe with 'projects'. You'll see what I mean as we go, Willie." Her nickname for me was really starting to grate.

"Okay Martha, I know what the result of Genesis should be. Any suggestions on how to get that clear description of the idea to improve the situation?"

"As a matter of fact, I have." Martha wrote eight questions on the paper:

1) ***What is wrong with the existing situation?***
2) ***How will things be better when we are done?***
3) ***What are the design criteria? (How does this thing have to perform when it is completed?)***
4) ***What is the scope of the assignment? (What is in, and what is out?)***
5) ***What are the other constraints (cost, time, quality)?***
6) ***Who is the sponsor?***
7) ***Who is the project manager?***
8) ***What authority is being given?***

"I call the answers to these questions the objective statement," she told me, handing me the paper. "And I think we are just about finished for the day."

"Finished? But I haven't got enough to go on yet! I haven't even answered these questions." I felt panicked. Just when I thought I was understanding things, she was going to send me off.

"Willie, I can't answer the questions. You and the project team have to do that. I just need to tell you three more things, and then you can go away and stop pestering me. I need to have a rest." She did not look very tired to me.

"First, you need to be able to identify the sponsor and the project manager. We'll talk more about the others next time you visit." I waited for her to tell me who they were. As usual, she told me by asking a question. "Tell me, what is the one characteristic that tells you who the sponsor is?"

I thought about it for a second. "Authority," I said. "The sponsor usually has some authority over the project."

"Close," said Martha. "What is it that gives the sponsor that authority?"

I thought again for a second. Then I had it. "Money! The sponsor controls the cash."

"Correct," Martha said. "The sponsor controls the money. You have to know who is making the money decisions, because that person has ultimate control over the entire assignment. He or she is the person you must go to when changes happen, because the sponsor is your client and he or she is paying the bills."

"Second," Martha continued, "you must get the objective statement signed. By whom and why?"

I felt like I should be on Jeopardy, saying "Projects for $600, Alex." Instead, I said, "The sponsor should sign-off the objective statement. As to the why, I suppose because that way I, as the project manager, can cover my butt if the sponsor starts to change his mind." I had a feeling the whole signing thing would not go over too well at Hyler. Sponsors usually like to protect themselves a little better than that.

Martha sighed. "The signature is a cultural ritual. It indicates that the sponsor has read, understood and agreed to the objective statement. It is not supposed to be for assigning blame. It shows the project manager that the person who will be paying the bills is clear on what he or she wants. If the custom was to cut off the heads of chickens and wave them in the air while dancing naked around a bonfire, then I would tell you to do that. The signature is a mechanism that gets the sponsor on board. Without it, you are at the mercy of the whimsical sponsor.

"Third, the objective statement will change." Great, I thought. We will put all of this work into something just so we can change it. I imagined I would probably spend the whole project writing and rewriting objective statements. Martha went on, "In the beginning of an assignment, we really know very little about the assignment, it is just someone's idea about how to make the world a better place. As we get further and further into it, we will learn more and more, and that may change our original assumptions about how the assignment was going to be. Whenever that happens, you must update the objective statement!" She punctuated each syllable in the last few words by tapping the pencil on the armrest of her rocker.

"And you must get the sponsor to sign each new objective statement. Otherwise, the sponsor will be out of date, and probably not very happy when he or she finally learns about the changes."

I was frantically making notes as she told me all of this. When she stopped and I finished writing, I said, "It seems like a lot of work."

Martha lowered her eyebrows again. "Shouldn't you be meeting with your project team right now?"

I took the hint and left.

# CHAPTER 7

As I drove back to the office, the excitement of Martha's revelations started to fade. What had seemed like critical knowledge was starting to pale in the cold, harsh light of reality. It was now 2:30 p.m. and I had a major presentation to prepare by tomorrow night. While I could appreciate what I had learned, I still was not convinced that it was taking me anywhere that was going to make Stu or Ralph very happy. Nevertheless, I was determined to change things, so I resolved to stick with Martha's ideas.

When I got in, there was a stack of pink message slips on my desk, and my in-basket was full of memos, notes, letters and other urgent things relating to my real job. Fortunately, I am the type of person who can ignore the urgent in favor of the really, really urgent. I started calling my project team.

Twenty minutes later we were sitting around a big table in the Dunkin Donuts shop across the street from the plant. The conference room had been booked, and no one had an office big enough for the eight of us.

The team's faces were not looking too pleased, despite the fact that I had sprung for a 24-pack of donut holes. It sat untouched in the center of the tables we had pushed together. Mark spoke for the group when he said: "What is this all about, Will? We all have a lot of work to do, and I for one haven't had a chance to put anything together on this project yet."

I wasted no time. "Like I told all of you this morning, I want to do whatever it takes to get control of this project. I wasn't all that happy with what we achieved at our meeting, so I contacted an outside consultant for some assistance." I had decided to exaggerate a little about Martha. I figured that if I didn't, none of these new ideas would have credibility with my team.

No one except Al seemed very interested in the news. He looked a little ticked off that I would go outside instead of coming to him.

I continued, "The consultant introduced me to a framework that describes what happens during a project..."

For the next 15 minutes, I gave them a condensed version of my discovery in the dictionary, the purpose of a plan, and my conversation with Martha, concluding with the fact that we were at the Genesis stage in this particular assignment.

"So you are saying we don't even use the word 'project', right?" Alice asked when I was done.

"It's not really about right and wrong," I told her. "The point is that if we agree on what we mean by the words, we have a solid foundation on which to build. If we don't agree, we'll be flailing around in the dark."

Heads around the table were starting to nod and Luigi said, "So far, this makes a lot of sense. Even if it does seem obvious, it would be nice if we were all thinking about things the same way for once."

Apparently Al was not in agreement. "This is an absolute waste of time!" he said as Luigi finished talking. "I've already told you what a project is, and this doesn't have anything to do with it." He stood up. "I have more important things to do. I'll have a work breakdown structure for my tasks by tomorrow." He turned and looked at me and said, "I'll be talking to Ralph." With that, Al pushed his chair back into the table and left.

Everybody was silent for a few minutes, a little taken aback by the outburst. Finally Leslie said, "If Al doesn't like these ideas, well, that says something for them." This made everyone smile.

Sheila, Al's assistant, asked if I thought this consultant knew what he was talking about.

"Absolutely." I tried to sound confident. I hoped that "he" did.

"So what does this guy say is the next step?" asked Mark.

I pulled out the sheet with Martha's questions written on it. "We need to clearly define what the assignment is," I said, "and to do that, we need to produce an objective statement."

"That should be easy," said Amanda, "since we've already got our project goals."

Pointing to the questions, I told them that I thought the project goals would probably help us, but we needed to answer each question pretty specifically.

"So, what are the questions?" Amanda asked.

I read the first one aloud. "What is wrong with the existing situation?"

Everyone looked at each other. "Nothing," said Leslie. "Everything is fine."

We all thought about that for a second, and then Amanda said, "But the result of Genesis is supposed to be an idea about how to improve the situation."

"That doesn't mean there is anything wrong," retorted Leslie. "It just means there is an idea about how to make things even better."

"But if there isn't anything wrong," said Sheila, "then how can we make things 'even better' as you say?"

"The question is just so negative. Why does it have to be so negative?" Leslie liked to think of herself as a very positive person. Her reasoning was a little weak, but I was not sure that there was anything wrong with the existing situation either. Hyler seemed to be doing just fine without the WindSailor. My life had certainly been much better before.

Fortunately, Sheila came to our rescue. "Look you guys, you are getting emotional about the words instead of thinking about what they really mean. It's obvious what is wrong with the existing situation. There is an opportunity to exploit the new product, and Hyler doesn't have the facilities to take advantage of it. There is nothing negative about it."

As I looked around the table, people's heads started nodding again, and I felt my own going up and down. "When you put it that way, Sheila, it seems pretty obvious," Mark said. "What is wrong is we can't take advantage of the opportunity. I like it."

"Let's not get too happy about everything yet," I interrupted. "Who volunteers to write all of this stuff down? Amanda, you look like you want something to do." She gave me a dirty look, but she took my pad of paper and pencil, and at the top of a clean page wrote:

***Objective Statement***
***Hyler Recreation Systems***
***The WindSailor***

"Okay," she said to the group, "how do we want to word this?"

Mark said, "Just like Sheila put it a minute ago. We have this opportunity with the WindSailor, but we can't take advantage of it because..." Here he trailed off. "Why can't we take advantage of it? It seems like we are going to. Isn't that what this whole project is…"

Alice interrupted him and said, "Assignment."

"Excuse me, assignment, is about?"

Sheila was way ahead of him. "We can't take advantage because we don't have the physical facilities, people and systems to make the thing, and we don't have a marketing plan."

"Remember," I interjected, "the marketing plan isn't part of our assignment. That's Leslie's job."

"Hang on a minute," Amanda said, "and let me get this down." We all waited as she scribbled furiously. When she was done, she read it back to us. ***"What is wrong with the existing situation? Hyler does not have the plant capacity, people or systems to support its intention to take advantage of the opportunity created by the introduction of the WindSailor product."***

We all thought for a minute. "It sounds kind of limited," Mark said, "but when you think about it, from our perspective on this particular project, I mean assignment, that is exactly what is wrong right now."

"Everyone okay with that?" I asked, as everyone nodded. I helped myself to a donut hole. "Okay, the next question is: 'How will things be better when we are done?' "

The answer to that one seemed pretty obvious, and everyone said so. "What is the point of this one?" Amanda asked. "The answer is just the opposite of the answer to the last one."

"I'm not sure," I said, "but let's stick with the questions. Our consultant had something in mind when he gave us these. Let's not break the pattern until we really understand it."

Everyone agreed, and Amanda wrote for a few moments before reading back to us: ***"How will things be better when we are done? The manufacturing capacity, trained workers, and administrative support systems will be in place, and Hyler will be able to start producing the WindSailor, along with all of its other products."***

When I heard Amanda say the answer out loud, I started to have some ideas about why the question was there. I decided to wait until we were finished the objective statement before bringing it up.

Everyone agreed that Amanda's summary sounded pretty good, so I went on to the next question. "What are the performance criteria?" I looked up at the group. "The consultant said that the answer here should describe how the end product has to perform when the assignment is done."

We all looked at each other. I found this question a tough one to answer, because our final product was somewhat intangible. I had another donut hole to hide my ignorance. "Anybody got any ideas?" I asked the group.

This time it was Alice who put it into perspective for us. "If our final product is to be an expanded manufacturing facility with a trained workforce and all the systems to support it, the performance criterion is simple: the new facility, people and systems must be capable of producing 'X' WindSailors of appropriate quality."

Everyone nodded. "Will," Mark asked me, "how many of these things do they want us to make?"

I flipped through the notes I had made at my meeting with Stu. "Looks like 2,600 in the first year, and then 6,000 per year after that."

Amanda wrote as I was reading the numbers out, and read back to us: ***"What are the performance criteria? Hyler must be capable of producing 2,600 WindSailors in the first year of production, and 6,000 in the second year."***

I thought that sounded fine, and everybody else seemed to agree, except Luigi. "I think we need some performance criteria in there about the workers," he said.

"What did you have in mind?"

"Something that talks about their ability to work with this manufacturing process. Don't forget, this is new to all of us. If it's coming from Germany, we can't afford to be flying technicians over here every time something breaks down. I think we need to mention that."

We all looked at Amanda. "Summarize that in 10 words or less," I told her. Her result was more than 10 words, but we all liked it anyway. She read: ***"The workers must be fully conversant with the manufacturing process for the WindSailor, so that we do***

***not require outside technical support after the WindSailor has gone into production."***

Luigi was satisfied, and nobody had anything else to add to the performance criteria, so I went on to the next question: "What is the scope of this assignment?"

Leslie answered without hesitation, "Our scope is to make the WindSailor successful. That is what we are all here for."

Sheila did not agree. "Our hope might be that the WindSailor is successful, Leslie," she said, "but really, our scope is all the work that gets the company ready to manufacture the WindSailors."

Luigi nodded in agreement. "There's a whole bunch of other work that goes into making this thing a success, like your marketing project." Here he looked over at me and said, "Excuse me, your marketing 'assignment'. Anyway, we don't want to lose focus on our work. Let's keep our scope to the work that needs to be done to get this thing ready for manufacturing."

Everyone except Leslie seemed to be happy with this. "I still don't think that's right, but it's your project. I'm just here as a liaison."

"How detailed should we get, Will?" Mark asked me, as if I knew. I answered anyway.

"I think that right now we want to keep it to some broad statements about the work. We will figure out the details later."

"For starters," Mark began, "there is hiring and training of all personnel,"

"Purchase of new equipment," added Luigi.

"Design and construction of new buildings," said Sheila.

"Upgrading of old information systems, or design of new ones," said Amanda as she wrote down the other points. We waited for a few moments while Amanda finished writing. No one volunteered any more scope items.

That seemed like everything to me, so I said, "I think that about covers it. Anything else and we will be starting to get into too much detail."

"Let's just add one more statement to kind of tie things up," Alice said. "Let's say something like: 'And all other activities related to preparing the WindSailor for handover to production'. That kind of spells out even more clearly where the end of the assignment is, for us at least." Amanda dutifully wrote it down.

"What about marketing?" Sheila asked.

"Our group is taking care of all of that," Leslie told her.

"I know that, Leslie, it's just that I almost think we should mention that fact in our scope. Something to the effect that marketing is NOT part of this particular assignment."

"What is the point of that?" Mark asked. "Everybody knows that the marketing project is separate. If we try to list everything that isn't in this assignment, we'll be here for weeks!"

I agreed with Mark, but Sheila seemed to have a good handle on what we were doing so far, so I asked her to explain.

"In projects I've worked on in the past, there has often been a key activity or bit of information that had to come from somewhere else, and that we needed to continue with the project. Since it, whatever the thing was, was outside of our scope, we didn't worry about it until it came time for the other person or project team to deliver. If they weren't ready, then we started to worry, because if they were late, or didn't do their job right, it delayed our project. Then the sponsor wanted to know why we were behind. It doesn't seem fair, but that's what happened.

"Anyway, it just seemed to me that if we let Stu know for certain what is not part of our assignment, he can make sure those things are ready for us."

Theoretically, it sounded like a good idea. There was only one problem that I could see. "Sheila, what do we have to do with marketing? Other than getting the WindSailor ready for production in time for them to roll it out, I don't see us having anything to do with them."

Sheila looked blank. "I'm not sure."

"The name," Leslie said.

"Exactly!" replied Sheila.

"What?" I asked.

"Of course!" chimed in Luigi. "Good thing to think about now."

I felt left out. "Would someone please explain this to me?"

Luigi did the honors. "Part of what Leslie will be doing is coming up with a suitable name for the Hyler version of a WindSailor. That name, and all of the appropriate artwork and color scheme that go with it, are produced by Marketing."

"So?" I said.

"So, in case you forgot, we have to get the plant ready to produce these things. And part of that manufacturing process will include painting, decorating and displaying the product name prominently on each board. And before we can buy the paints, order the molds and templates, and train the painters, we need to know what this thing is going to be called, and what the graphic layout looks like."

I was beginning to see.

Sheila said, "Thanks Leslie. That is exactly the kind of thing I was thinking about when I brought this up. Coming up with the name and color scheme and the rest of it is all your responsibility, but at some point we are going to need that information, or else we won't be able to continue."

Amanda, who had been busy writing, waved her pad of paper and said, "How's this?: ***'The scope of this assignment specifically excludes all marketing-related activities, including the development of the product name and decoration'.***"

We all liked that, and I could tell that things were flowing smoothly because we were out of donut holes. Mark got up to get some more, and I read the next question. " 'What are the other constraints?' These are things like time, cost and quality. I'll start, because I have been told by Stu that the total cost of the project will not exceed $1 million."

"Where did he get that number?" Sheila asked a little skeptically.

"Beats me. Thin air, probably. Or maybe it came out of Ralph's head." I was tempted to say it was the same thing, but I kept my mouth shut.

"I kind of like Al's idea about costs," Sheila said. "Especially if the top brass are just making up these numbers."

"I really doubt that they are making them up," Alice jumped in. "I think it probably makes sense to put down what the constraints are. Then, when we have a better idea about how much this will cost, we'll know where we started from." This sounded like Accounting reasoning to me, although I agreed for a different reason.

"We are going to record all of the constraints that we know

about, even if we don't think they are reasonable. If the top management group wants to impose constraints on us, so be it, but I don't intend to withhold any information to keep their egos intact. If their estimates are off the wall, I want them to know about it. Put down the cost constraint." I gestured to Amanda.

"The schedule we also know," said Luigi. "We have to be ready to produce these things by the middle of June." The way he said it, it seemed like he didn't think we would be ready in time.

"I've got one that I bet no one has thought about," Amanda volunteered. "I'll bet that we have to maintain access to Hyler Lake during the whole assignment."

She was right. I certainly had not thought about that, and judging by the looks from the others around the table, none of them had either.

The Hyler plant is situated at the corner of Ascot Street and Thurlow Avenue just outside of Enderby, and has been ever since the beginning. However, the town fathers had been farsighted back when Andrew Hyler wanted to put the original factory out here. Located just behind the proposed plant site was a beautiful, 130-acre freshwater lake. The Enderby town fathers agreed to let Hyler have the site, but required him to build and maintain a public access to the lake. This proved to be a well-liked move (at least by the townspeople), and in the forties Hyler Lake was a popular place for people to take picnic lunches and go swimming, sailing or fishing.

Today the lake is just as popular, and it fits well with our business. Situated as it is in a valley, the winds blow moderately and consistently all year round. We hold windsurfing races and sailboat regattas most weekends in the summer, and we use the lake to test all of our new products. The lake is the main reason we have a successful retail outlet at the plant site.

Having said all of that, the lake is also a bit of an inconvenience. Our manufacturing facility is spread out among several buildings, and public access to the lake is right through the plant site. This means that we have to maintain a security guard 24 hours a day, seven days a week to make sure that the public doesn't get a little too friendly with our stuff. And we have to put up with the "civilian" traffic around the factory.

When the original plant was built, it was significantly smaller than today's version, and all in one building. At that time it seemed simpler to Andrew Hyler to extend the road that went to the parking lot at the plant site, until it reached the edge of the lake. Hyler did not want to pay to put in a new access off Ascot Street, because this would have meant crossing a small creek and spending more money.

That setup had worked all right until the plant had started to expand. The town fathers were adamant about keeping their new found lake/park open, and they did not want to pay for another access. Hyler had agreed when he built the plant that it was his responsibility to provide a road, and the town was not about to let him back out of that promise.

Out of stubbornness, or just plain cheapness, Hyler decided not to build a new road. He simply expanded around the access road until we had to live with the situation Amanda brought up.

"Put it down," I told Amanda. "Although that is going to give us a whole new set of headaches."

"No kidding," Luigi said. "I've lived in Enderby for 25 years, and anything that the town council even looks at takes a long time." I was not particularly grateful for that news.

Amanda read out: ***"Public access to Hyler Lake must be maintained during the assignment."*** We all nodded that it sounded okay.

"Cheer up," Mark told me. "Maybe this project will be the excuse the company needs to lay down the cash and put in a separate public access." I could imagine a hundred other things that might get tacked onto this project.

"Are we done yet, Will?" Leslie asked me. "It's past 3:30, and I have some phone calls to make before the end of the day." Everyone seemed to be getting a little anxious to get back to the office to do some 'real' work.

"Just three more questions, and then we're done," I told her. "The first is: 'Who is the sponsor?' "

Sheila seemed to have a much better knack for all of this than I did, because she asked, "How are you defining 'sponsor', exactly? It seems to me that word gets abused as much as the word 'project'."

"Good question, Sheila. The consultant said that the true sponsor of a proj- I mean assignment, is the person who is paying the bills, the person supplying the funding." I looked around the table for suggestions.

"I can see why you would want to have that person as sponsor," Mark said, "but that is not how it works at Hyler. The sponsor usually doesn't have any spending authority, but they deal with the person who does."

"You mean, that's how it doesn't work," Sheila retorted. I could see that she felt strongly about this one. "Half the reason that projects are finished late around here is that project sponsors don't have any real decision-making power. Whenever something comes up, we have to wait while the sponsor goes to ask the person who can actually decide. And then, since the real decision makers haven't been close to the project, they usually decide the wrong thing. And, guess what?, it always turns out to be the project manager's fault when that bad decision screws up the schedule or the cost." She turned to me. "I think it makes a lot of sense to put the real sponsor's name down on paper. Let's put the responsibility where it belongs."

I could relate to Sheila's experience with sponsors. The only problem was, I had already been told who the sponsor of this project was: Stu Barnes. Amanda was quick to point this out.

"Does Stu have spending authority on this assignment?" she asked me.

"No, he doesn't. In fact, he specifically told me that I would have to go to Ralph for approval of all funding." I didn't like the way this was going.

Sheila did though. "That's it, then. Ralph Borsellino is your sponsor." She turned to Amanda. "Put it down."

I wasn't so sure. "Hold on a minute, Amanda. What do the rest of you think?" I looked around the table.

"If we're going to use your consultant's framework for projects, I think we have to follow his rules all the way through." This was Luigi talking. "If we start breaking his rules, how can we expect his ideas to work? I'd say Ralph's name should go on this thing."

"I agree," Mark said. "It looks like Ralph fits the definition of the sponsor."

"But guys," I said, "do you have any idea what it will be like having to deal with Ralph?"

Sheila was not sympathetic. "Ralph is the ultimate decision maker, regardless of whether we call him the sponsor or not. However, if we are clear about his role up front, maybe we can avoid a lot of the difficulties we have run into before when the real sponsor is removed from the assignment." I couldn't disagree with the logic, but I really would have preferred to have Stu deal with Ralph.

"Okay, Amanda," I gave in. "Put it down." I paused and then said, "Last questions: 'Who is the project manager?' and 'What authority is being given?' "

"That is an easy one," said Alice. "You are the project manager. And if Ralph is going to be the sponsor, you won't have any authority." Alice smirked, but I knew she was only half kidding.

"I don't know about what authority is being given, so let's just put down something that seems reasonable," I told them.

Once again, Sheila jumped in. "Why not put down that the sponsor must approve the completion of each phase and the plans for next one? That way, we'll keep the sponsor up to date on exactly what's happening, and if he has a problem, he can let us know before the assignment progresses any further." Sheila seemed to be really getting into this whole process. So much so that I started wondering whether I could get her to take over project management responsibilities. I didn't think it was likely, so I said only, "Let's put something in there about getting the sponsor's approval for expenditures over $50,000. Ralph will like that."

Amanda wrote for a while, and then read: ***"The sponsor of this assignment is Ralph Borsellino, President of Hyler Recreation Systems. The project manager is Will Campbell. He will report on the progress of the assignment in a biweekly meeting, and will get the sponsor's written approval to proceed at the completion of each phase of the assignment. The project manager must also get approval for all expenditures over $50,000, while approval of ongoing costs will be provided at the biweekly progress meetings."*** She stopped reading and looked around at us. "I put in the part about the progress meeting on my own, but I think that would be a good idea." We all nodded our approval.

Amanda ripped the top two pages off her pad and handed them to me. "There you go. Now what happens?"

"Now," I said, "I have to present this to the Hyler Board of Directors, and I have to get Ralph's signature at the bottom, giving the approval to proceed." Everyone looked at me sympathetically for a moment. Then they all got up to leave.

"Good luck!" said Luigi. "You're going to need it."

# CHAPTER 8

I stayed behind in the donut shop after everyone else had gone back to the office. I got myself another coffee and a chocolate-chip cookie, and thought about how different our objective statement was from the project goals we had developed that morning. Those goals had been broad and vague and, as it turned out, not even all that accurate. Our assignment was not to make the WindSailor successful; it was just to build the facilities. And what we had originally put down as sub-goals showed up as constraints in the objective statement.

Something else I had learned: there seemed to be a big difference between the objective of an assignment, in our case, building the facilities, and the expected outcome or benefits of doing the assignment, success of the WindSailor. It appeared to be very important not to confuse one with the other, because you really only had control over achieving your objective. The expected benefit would only happen as a result of achieving the objective. Even then, your expectations might not be met if your objective was wrong in the first place!

Fortunately, I was not responsible for the WindSailor being a good idea. That was a strategic planning concern. I just had to get Hyler ready to make it.

On the whole, the objective statement approach had provided me and the project team with a much more concise definition of our assignment, and a much better starting point. I was finally starting to feel comfortable with Martha's ideas.

A little more than 24 hours later, I was not feeling quite so comfortable. I was in the Ambassador Room at the Four Seasons Hotel in Portland, standing in front of the Hyler Board of Directors.

"And so you can see," I told them as I concluded my presentation, "the assignment has been clearly specified, the constraints noted, and the people playing the essential roles of project manager and sponsor identified. All we need at this point is approval from the sponsor to proceed with the design." I stopped, looked around the room, and then sat back down in my chair. Nobody said anything for a few minutes. Finally Ralph spoke up.

"I'm not sure I'm comfortable with that objective, Will. I don't see anything in there about the WindSailor being a success."

I was ready for that question, and I tried not to sound too confrontational when I answered.

"That's a good point, Ralph," I told him. "The thing is, I don't think this assignment has the success of the WindSailor as it's objective." That raised a few eyebrows around the table, so I hurried on to explain. "We're just preparing the facilities and the people to manufacture it, that's all."

"I find that a little hard to believe." This comment came from Leon Goldberg, another board member and a vice-president at Mantec. "Surely everyone involved with this project," I was starting to wince every time someone used that word, "has responsibility for the success of the WindSailor." A quick survey of faces seemed to indicate that there was general agreement about this. I also thought Ralph was looking a little smug, but maybe I was being unkind.

"Don't misunderstand me, Mr. Goldberg," I assured him. "I'm not telling you that I don't feel that I have some responsibility for the success of the WindSailor. It's just that Hyler will have a better chance of achieving that objective if my project team identifies exactly what our piece of the puzzle is." No one said anything, so I continued. "Someone has already decided that the WindSailor has potential, and they have identified what needs to be done to exploit that potential. My assignment is only a piece of all of that. The product needs to be marketed, contracts need to be negotiated with the Europeans, all kinds of things need to be done in addition to upgrading our facilities. Our piece alone is not enough to achieve the overall objective. Consequently, we don't want to assume responsibility for that overall objective, because we can't achieve it by ourselves. It makes more sense for us to focus on our piece."

I could tell that Ralph was not happy with this response, but the other board members, and especially Henry Stanton, the President of Mantec, were nodding their heads in agreement. Mentally I scored one for the good guys.

Ralph wasn't ready to quit yet. "I noticed that you identified me as the sponsor of this project. I specifically named Stu Barnes," gesturing at Stu, who was sitting beside him, "to play that role. I did that because I felt I wouldn't have enough time to devote to this project. Why did you change this?"

It seemed to me that Ralph was out to embarrass himself. I had no intention of doing the same to myself, so I told him. "Ralph, you also specified that all spending decisions would have to be approved by you."

Ralph interrupted before I could continue. "That's exactly right." He looked around the table at the other board members. "I am responsible for this division, so I approve whatever gets spent." He seemed to be assuring everyone that he was in control.

I didn't get a chance to continue, because Carrie Starblanket spoke up. She was a board member and the Vice-President of Marketing at Hyler. "Ralph, If you want to have approval over all the money decisions on this project, what is it that you want Stuart to do?"

Good question! I thought to myself. Ralph hesitated a bit before answering. "He will help the project manager get necessary resources..." he paused, "and act as my liaison with the project team," he finished quickly.

James Graubard, president of a local public relations firm, and the only board member from outside of Mantec, asked another question: "Having Stuart around seems like an unnecessary layer in the management of this project. Why do you need it?"

Ralph was looking peeved. "I told you, I don't have time to sponsor this project. Besides, Stu is much more familiar with the whole thing than I am."

Mr. Graubard continued, "But it seems to me that before you can approve any spending, you will have to have a detailed understanding of what you're deciding on, won't you?"

Ralph obviously did not see where this was going. "Not really," he answered. "I run a pretty self-empowered management team. I trust Stu, and I would normally go with what he recommends." As soon as he said it, he realized his mistake. Mr. Graubard asked him anyway.

"So why don't you just remove that extra step, and give Stuart spending authority?"

Ralph squirmed a bit in his chair. "This is an important project. I think I need to keep my finger on it."

Lou Teves, another board member and a vice-president at Mantec, chimed in, "But you just told us that you will probably take Stuart's recommendations regarding spending decisions anyway. Why do you need to be involved?"

Henry Stanton finally spoke up. "Ralph, you appear to have two choices. Delegate spending authority to Stu and make him a true sponsor, or make the time to be a proper sponsor yourself."

Beautiful! I couldn't believe it had worked out so well. Best of all, I hadn't had to say anything to get them all to the conclusion I wanted, so Ralph couldn't blame me for what happened. Or so I thought.

Ralph was flipping madly through his diary, checking, I assumed, to see if he could take time to be part of this assignment. Finally, he said, "I guess I'll make time to sponsor it." He didn't look too happy.

Henry Stanton looked pleased. "I think that is the right choice, Ralph. This is the most important new product that Hyler has taken on in some time. I think it requires your involvement." Ralph looked somewhat mollified at this. "But that leaves a question," Mr. Stanton continued. "Where does Stuart fit into this assignment? It was his idea to take on this product." Everyone looked around the table at each other until all their eyes ended up on me.

An important lesson I have learned in life is that if you are asked a question in a roomful of people, and you don't know the answer, never confess ignorance. Instead, look thoughtful and stall, because someone else will almost always volunteer something you can use. I followed my own advice, and I was not disappointed.

"I'll act as a kind of business analyst for the project team," Stu volunteered. "I did the original feasibility analysis and laid out the general parameters of both this project and the marketing one. I'll be on hand to advise Ralph about the impact of his decisions on the success of the product."

Everyone seemed to think that this was a good idea, including me. I was glad that Stu would be involved somehow.

Ralph had one more question for me. "Have you got a work schedule yet? Or a work breakdown structure to show us?"

Honesty seemed to be working well for me today, so I told him, "Actually Ralph, I don't have those yet."

This was not strictly true. In fact, at 9:00 a.m. that morning Al Burton had presented me with a list of what he thought of as his tasks, a work breakdown structure chart, and a schedule for his work. After looking it over, I asked him why he was planning to build an entirely new building south of our existing plant. I had been under the impression that expanding our current facilities would be cheaper.

"It's what Ralph wants," Al told me, a little peevishly. "He doesn't want to add on to this dilapidated factory, he wants a whole new facility for the WindSailor."

I was instantly full of questions. "Can we afford a new building? And have you consulted with Luigi over in Production on this new site? What about the Inventory people?" I guess I sounded a little concerned, and Al must have thought I was not confident in his work.

"We'll go over all of that stuff later," he told me. "If people want to change it, we'll change it. Meanwhile, here is a schedule that you're going to need for your presentation for this afternoon. We'll worry about the details afterward."

I had a problem with Al's logic in that regard. "Al, don't you think that our schedule is going to be just a little bit different, depending on whether we actually build a new building or add on to one of the existing ones? I don't feel comfortable committing to a schedule when we haven't decided yet what we are going to build!"

This seemed to fluster Al. "It has to be done by June next year, right?" he asked me.

"That's the deadline we have been given," I confirmed.

"Well, this schedule fits in that time frame, and that is all that matters!"

As Al got more upset, so did I. "Don't you think it might make just a bit more sense to figure out how long it will actually take, and then look at our time constraints? I don't want to commit to anything that can't be done. Look what happened in Europe! They missed their window by months!"

Al stood up and leaned over my desk so he was looking down on me. "You just don't know much about projects, do you?" It was more of a statement than a question, and anyway, he didn't wait for an answer. He turned and left my office.

I nudged myself out of my mental reverie about Al, and concentrated on Ralph's question. "Ralph, we don't have a schedule yet because we don't know exactly what we are doing yet."

It was perhaps not the best choice of words. More raised eyebrows around the table, and once again I hurried to explain. "You see, we know how the final 'product' of this assignment has to perform. We have to be able to produce WindSailors. But we still need to determine the best way to do that. For example, we need to examine whether to expand our current plant facilities or build an entirely new, separate building."

Here, I was interrupted by board member Jeannie Granato. "You have to go to production by June, and you don't know how you are going to do it yet?" She sounded incredulous, and I had to fight not to lose my temper.

As calmly as I could, I said, "The time constraints will certainly influence how we decide to expand our manufacturing facility. Once I get approval to proceed, that will be my next step." I hoped that I was understanding what Martha meant by the Design phase. "To get the best final product, we need to take the assignment one step at a time, starting with the objective statement. Once we have that, we can figure out the best way to do it."

Ms. Granato did not look convinced. Ralph didn't help things when he said, "Can you give us an estimate on how long the design will take?"

I honestly did not know, so I told them. "I spoke with one of the designers this morning, and he told me that it will depend on which option we go with. It might take three weeks or it might take two months."

Everyone was looking uncomfortable with my reluctance to put a time frame on getting the design done. Fortunately, one of the board members came to my rescue.

"Mr. Campbell is perfectly correct in not giving you a firm date for completing the design." My savior was Mr. Graubard. "I've worked in public relations and advertising for 30 years now, and that business is almost all design. Any time someone puts a firm time frame on how long it will take, I get worried." He paused and looked around at the other board members. "Design is a creative process. I've never been very successful in keeping it to a firm schedule. How long does it take to come up with a good idea?"

This did not satisfy Ms. Granato. "But this whole project has to be completed by June! How can we be sure it's going to get done?"

"How long will the actual construction and the hiring and training of personnel take?" Ralph asked me. I couldn't believe it! He seemed to be missing the whole point here.

"I can't tell you that until we know what we're building, Ralph," I said. "Constructing a new building will take longer than just expanding our current facilities. When we've finished the design, then we'll have a better idea." After I said it, I realized that I had never thought about it like that before. I had often told people how long it would take to do something before I knew exactly what it was. For some reason, I was hardly ever right.

Mr. Graubard backed me up again. "Our marketing experts have provided us with their best guess about when this product has to be ready for the market. We have to realize that just because we want that to happen doesn't mean that it will. Things take as long as they take." He turned to me and said, "I'm glad you are not giving us a firm deadline for completing everything."

Henry Stanton stepped in to close the discussion on this point. "Will, keep your sponsor informed of the progress, and as soon as you have completed the design and can estimate a completion date for the whole thing, get the sponsor's approval."

Ms. Granato spoke up one last time. "What if his estimate is later than our June deadline?"

Mr. Stanton responded. "There is always a trade-off between time and money, Jeannie. I'm sure that our project manager and sponsor will figure out a way to bring this thing in on time. They just may have to spend more money to do it." I didn't take much notice of it then, but later I was very glad about that comment, and the fact that Mr. Stanton had made it rather than someone else.

There was more discussion about some of the points on the

objective statement, and I had to give the group an explanation about why we would have to maintain pubic access to Lake Hyler. In the end, Ralph signed the objective statement right there in front of everyone. He also made me sign it, but that didn't make me uncomfortable at all.

After that, the board was ready to move on to the next item: a presentation by Leslie Frame and Carrie Starblanket on the marketing of the WindSailor. I wished Leslie good luck as I passed her on the way out, and headed for the parking lot.

# The Project Team

# CHAPTER 9

"I thought you said Design was the next step," I said to Martha. She glared at me in a way that made me wish I hadn't opened my mouth. It was the evening following the board meeting, and I was back in what was quickly becoming my accustomed spot on the front porch of my in-laws' house, trying to learn more from the old woman.

"How do you expect to play a round of golf if you don't know what clubs you've got?" Martha snapped. She seemed to be in a bad mood today. "You can't go on to the next step until you know who is supposed to do what on your team!"

"Wait a minute, Martha. I thought you told me that the golf clubs were like the planning tools that I was going to use during the project," Martha gave me a warning look and I quickly corrected myself, "I mean, during the assignment."

She didn't seem too pleased with my comment. "I also told you I don't like analogies! Forget about the golf clubs, then. But you can't go on to the next step until you know who does what!" She tapped her pencil on the notepad in front of her. She had written:

SPONSOR
FEASIBILITY ANALYST

PROJECT MANAGER
DESIGNER
IMPLEMENTOR } THE TEAM
USERS' REPRESENTATIVE
ADMINISTRATOR

REVIEWERS

"That doesn't seem like a lot of people, Martha," I said. "I think there will be a lot more than that on this assignment."

"If you would just let me explain, Willie! Boy," she muttered under her breath loud enough for me to hear, "he learns one thing, and now he thinks he knows it all." In her normal voice she continued: "There are certain responsibilities that need to be fulfilled during every assignment, big or small. These responsibilities are easier to think about when we group similar ones together and give each group a name. That name happens to sound like a name that might go to a member of the project team. On a small assignment, the same person might play more than one role. And on a big assignment..."

"...you might have many people in one particular area of responsibility," I finished for her. "That makes more sense."

Martha continued as if I hadn't interrupted. "On a bigger assignment, with many people in a single role, it is important to have one person in charge of each role." That sounded logical. Just like you want only one project manager, you would probably want one person in charge of the design process, even if a lot of people were working on it. The whole thing would be much easier to coordinate that way. Martha stared at me over the top of her glasses. "Please note Will, this is not a committee!"

I decided not to question that remark, and continued on. "So I guess we need to define these roles like detailed job descriptions..." I trailed off as Martha sneered at me.

"That is exactly what we don't want to do," she told me. "We could never cover everything. It is far more useful to define these roles in terms of what they must contribute to the assignment. That way, we don't restrict what they do." I wasn't sure I understood that, but Martha looked too cranky for me to ask for an explanation.

She pointed first to the sponsor. "We already talked about this one. What does he or she contribute?"

How could I forget. "In my case it's a he, and he is supposed to contribute the money."

"And all the responsibility that goes with it," Martha finished for me. "Since he is paying, the sponsor can decide everything. Of course a good sponsor doesn't want to do that, which is why he hires a project manager. However, the basic framework of an assignment provides the sponsor with neat, controlled times to provide his approval. At the very minimum, you should get the sponsor's signed approval of the just-completed phase, and the agreement to continue on."

I was thinking of Ralph, and I wasn't so sure. "Why does the sponsor want to be bothered that much? Why not just talk to them when something bad happens?"

Martha just sat and stared at me, and I knew there would be no answer unless I provided it. I considered the situation. If the sponsor was able to sign-off on each phase, that would mean that he would be very aware of what had happened so far, and how this would affect the future of the assignment. It was obvious: if he understood the current state of the assignment, he would be in a much better position to make decisions about the future of it.

I told Martha this. "Correct," she said. "You learn more and more about how your assignment will turn out as you get farther and farther along. By the end, you know everything there is to know, except it's a little too late to help you. So as you go, you want the sponsor to be continually aware of what the situation is. The end of each phase happens to provide an ideal point for review. For example, what will you have a better idea about once you finish all the design work for your assignment?"

I had thought a lot about this after the presentation to the board. "How much it will cost, and how long it will take."

Martha wasn't quite satisfied with that. "You will have a better idea about those things, Willie," she said. "You won't know them in detail until after the Execution Plan phase. But yes, once the design is complete, we will have a better idea about cost and schedule. Now what do you suppose your sponsor would do if you estimated that instead of $1 million, your assignment would cost $5 million to complete?"

Knowing Ralph, I didn't have to think about that one for very long. "He would probably stop the project."

"He might," Martha allowed. "What he should do is go back to his feasibility analyst to see if the assignment is still justified at that cost. If it isn't, he should stop the project." She took a pull on her pipe and blew a smoke ring out over the porch railing. It was a still evening, so the ring hung together for a long time as it floated out over the lawn.

"The point is, when you finish each phase, you have more information. The sponsor needs to be aware of the information, because he needs to decide whether to proceed. Far too many assignments build up their own momentum and continue well after they no longer make sense." The way she puffed her pipe and stared out across the lawn into the middle distance made me think she had seen a few of those assignments.

"What about the feasibility analyst?" I asked Martha. "My boss was the person who started this whole WindSailor thing, and that is the role he volunteered to play. Although he used a slightly different name, I'm sure it's the same thing."

"Well, what do you think your boss will be doing on this assignment?" Martha asked. I thought back to what Stu had told the board yesterday.

"He'll be advising the sponsor on the viability of the assignment as we go along," I told her.

"That is what a feasibility analyst does. They provide the sponsor with an objective assessment of the idea, usually from a financial perspective."

"Why not have the project manager do this?" I asked. "They're right in on the action."

"How objective do you think the project manager is likely to be after the assignment begins?" Martha asked.

Good point, I thought to myself. In my experience, once someone had asked me to do something, my focus tended to narrow. The questions I asked myself did not have to do with whether this thing was a good idea, only with how to accomplish it.

Martha must have been able to read what I was thinking, because she didn't wait for me to answer. "As I said before, on a smaller assignment, this might not be a separate person. But on something the size of your assignment, an outside, objective person doing the feasibility analysis is an asset."

Martha picked up her pencil and tapped the next name on the list. "What about the project manager? What are you supposed to contribute?"

That was easy. "The finished product, as it was spelled out in the objective statement. I'm responsible for creating the project, or Execution Plan, then seeing that the actual work gets done."

Martha nodded her head in agreement. "That is essentially it. Of course, good communication with your sponsor, and good planning techniques, as well as lots of performance management tricks will help you to deliver the finished product, but you will find out more about those later." It sounded like a lot of work to me, but I didn't say anything.

We continued on, and one by one I figured out, with a little help from Martha, what each of the players on the team was responsible for. The designer was to coordinate the production of the design. The implementor was the person 'on the ground' who actually built the finished product. The users' representative was supposed to canvass the people who had to live with the finished product, and convey their interests to the project team, especially to the designer.

"A very misunderstood role!" Martha told me about the users' representative. "It requires a lot of work, because there are often many users, with a wide variety of requirements, for every assignment. Frequently this is ignored, and no one is happy with the final product. No matter how good your idea is, if you don't accommodate the actual users, it can still be unworkable in reality!"

The project administrator, according to Martha, was also an unsung hero of the team. "It takes a special kind of concentration to re-project schedules, keep everyone informed of progress, produce reports, keep track of costs, and do all of those important things that so often get neglected. No wonder so many projects go over budget and take too long. Everyone is too busy doing things to keep track of where they are!"

Martha suggested that we leave the role of the reviewer to discuss later, and then she started coughing. Martha gets these funny spells where she coughs and coughs and coughs, to the point where you get alarmed by the color of her face. Her doctor says it's because of her pipe smoking, but Martha has no intention of giving that up.

I called Natalie, and she came out on the porch. Between us we carried Martha inside to her bedroom. Fortunately her room is on the ground floor, because Martha was not the lightest person I had ever tried to carry off to bed. I stood around in her room while Natalie gave Martha her medicine, until Martha finally waved me away. I went out to the kitchen to get a glass of water, and when I came back to the living room I could still hear her hacking.

Finally it stopped, and a few minutes later Natalie came out of Martha's room and shut the door. "She's dropped off to sleep," she told me, looking very concerned. I asked if she seemed okay, which was really kind of a dumb question. Fortunately Natalie had not inherited her mother's caustic wit.

"She always seems so weak after all of that coughing. I wish she would stop smoking that pipe!" I tried to reassure her, saying that the pipe hadn't killed her yet. Personally, I thought Natalie's concern might be justified. Martha was looking a little worse for wear. Of course she was almost 90.

As I walked out to my car, I had a very selfish thought: I hoped she wouldn't die before she finished telling me about projects!

"Why don't you get the first round, Will? You can just bill it to the project." Al gave me a weak smile to go with his weak joke, and gestured toward the bar. I sighed, got up from our table and began pushing my way through the crowd to buy the drinks. It serves you right for being so keen, I thought to myself.

As soon as I had arrived home from visiting Martha, I began calling my team to set up an early-morning meeting for the next day. I wanted to waste no time identifying who would be assigned which roles. I had left Al until the end, because I was a little nervous talking to him about the WindSailor. Instead of simply agreeing to be there the next day, he insisted that we get together that same night. There were 'important issues' that we needed to discuss.

It was now 10:00 p.m., it had been a very long day, and I was standing at the bar of an English-style pub called the Gasping Goose or the Twisted Chicken or some such name that I was now too tired to remember. Al had suggested it. I finally flagged down the bartender and ordered a couple of mugs of some strange English-style brew. As I walked back across the room, I spilled beer on three different people. Nobody seemed to mind.

"Here you go Al," I said, sliding him a mug of something called

Ruddles Bitter, "it's on the project." We sat silently looking at our beer for a few minutes until I could stand it no longer. "So what was it you wanted to talk about?"

"Do you know," he asked me, still looking at his beer, "what my first job out of college was?" I shook my head, but I don't think he was waiting for me to answer. "I was the assistant supervisor of a drilling crew on an oil rig."

"Mmm," I said.

Al took a sip of his beer and continued. "Armadillo Oil was the company. Down in Texas. I was fresh out of college with my shiny new Engineering degree, and they put me in charge of a bunch of roughnecks. Know what happened?"

I tried my beer. It had a thick, bitter taste, and it didn't seem to be carbonated. It was also warm. "No," I told him.

Al laughed. "They just about tore me apart. Literally. Ever work around an oil rig, Will? No? Well, let me tell you, rigs are a very dangerous place to be, especially if you're an uppity young college graduate who is supposed to be the boss. There's a hundred ways to lose a hand, an arm or your life." Al took another drink of his beer and laughed again. "Yessir, those guys pulled every trick in the book on me. Had me believing and doing all kinds of dumb things. It took a while for me to figure out that they knew what they were doing, and that I should learn from them, not tell them how to do it. Things went much better after I got that through my head.

"I spent 10 years working in the oil industry, all over the world. Spent some time up in the North Sea, which is where I got to know this beer. But I never forgot the lesson I learned back in Texas."

I took another sip of the beer and began wondering if those Texan roughnecks had removed Al's tastebuds during one of their little pranks. "What exactly was it that you learned in Texas?"

Al looked up at me for the first time since I brought over the beer. "The same lesson you need to learn right now Will. You don't know it all. Others have gone before you and picked up a trick or two, and if you try to figure out everything for yourself, you'll end up looking silly in the best case, and in a downright bad situation in the worst case!"

We had obviously moved a long way from armadillos and cute

pranks involving hand loss, but my mind had not made the jump. "I'm not sure I understand what you mean, Al."

He gave me an exasperated look. When he spoke his voice was high and tense. "Do you know how long I've been managing projects? Over 20 years! And I've been a certified professional project manager for the past seven. So don't you think that just maybe, between me and all of my colleagues, we might have some good ideas about how to make a project run smoothly?"

"Of course Al," I said, hoping to placate him somewhat.

"Then why don't you listen to anything I tell you? It's bad enough having Stuart Barnes insist that someone as inexperienced as you take on the WindSailor, but you continually question everything I tell you. Why is it so hard for you to accept that I might be right?"

I tried to sound calm and non-threatening. "You are misinterpreting my actions, Al. It's not that I don't trust you, it's just that I want to try to find an even better way of doing things. And besides," I added, perhaps foolishly, "I don't think that your ideas work in every situation."

Al did not agree. "You don't think that work breakdown structures are useful? You don't think that earned value costing, which is endorsed by the United States Government, is useful?"

I decided to try a different tack. "That's not what I'm saying at all, Al. I just want to think things out from the beginning. I want to work out each move logically before we do anything."

"How can you possibly hope to apply logic? You haven't got any experience to go with it. Certainly not as much as I have."

I tried to be conciliatory. "Don't forget, I'm also relying on my consultant's experience...."

Al cut me off before I had a chance to finish. "That's the thing that bugs me the most, Will! There isn't any consultant. I checked with Ralph, and he hasn't authorized any money for a consultant. So that's how I know you're doing it all yourself. You just think your ideas will have more impact with the project team if you tell them that a consultant came up with these weird notions."

I tried to change the subject. "I think parts of your approach work, Al, but I need to think out my understanding of projects from the basics, from first principles..."

Al leaned back in his chair and took a long drink from his beer. When he spoke his tone was much calmer. "Look Will, the WindSailor is a big deal for Hyler. We can't afford to screw it up. That means that we can't afford to have you trying out your pet theories about project management on something so vital to the company. Why not practice on something smaller? Go with the conventional wisdom on this one."

I leaned forward and tried to keep my tone as calm and reasonable as Al's. "Let me ask you a hypothetical question. Let's suppose you were in a situation where you had to do a very important job. Let's also suppose that a standard, prescribed method for doing the job existed, but that method was not a very good one. It wasn't completely wrong, but it wasn't a very good way of doing the job, despite the fact that many people and many books supported that method.

"Now pretend that you had worked out a new way of doing the job. You figured this new method would produce much better results than the old way. You had never actually tried the new way, but you had thought about it very carefully, and you were as certain as you could be that it would work better than the old way. Which way would you do the job?"

Al looked at me with narrowed eyes. "The new method is totally untried?" he asked.

"Totally," I told him. "You just thought it up yourself."

"As a responsible manager, I would have to do it the accepted way."

"But Al!" I exploded, all semblance of reason gone from my voice, "the old way isn't any good! How could you still use it?"

Al took another sip of his beer. "You missed the whole point of the oil rig story didn't you, Will? I told you, other people have been there before you. They've probably already tried all of your harebrained ideas, but they're not using them because they don't work."

"But if the old ideas don't make sense..." I began.

"You might not be able to see their logic, Will. Your whole perspective is different from mine. You probably couldn't figure out why I do things the way I do them."

Biting back a nasty reply, I said, "If we can't use logic to come to agreement on things, how are we going to get along?"

"I already told you Will, experience is the best teacher." He paused and drank the last of his beer. "Now look, Will, it's getting late. Are you going to agree to stick to accepted project management principles on this or not?"

I shook my head. "Al, I have to keep questioning things I don't agree with. I'll try to do it in a way that is less offensive to you, but I have to keep doing it. Think of it this way: if the things I question actually do make sense, you'll have no trouble explaining them to me."

Al gave me a cold look, then glanced at his watch. "I don't have any more time for this. I'm going home." He pushed back his chair, grabbed his coat, and started to stalk off toward the door.

"See you in the morning?" I called after his departing back. He didn't turn around, and if he said anything, I didn't catch it.

Many sleepy eyes greeted me at the donut shop across from the plant at 7:00 a.m. the next morning.

"Couldn't this have waited for a more reasonable hour?" moaned Mark Goldman. He was the kind of guy who had a hard time being at his desk before nine, but everyone else seemed to agree. Except for Al, he hadn't shown up yet.

"Afraid not, folks," I told them. "But look at the bounty that nature provides when you rise early!" I pointed to the tray of Danishes and the large pot of coffee in the center of the table. "Eat, drink, and think along with me now, as we try to figure out the next move. By the way, does anybody know what happened to Al? I talked to him last night and he didn't say anything about skipping out." No one knew. I decided that we would have to start without him.

I began by telling the group about the presentation to the Hyler Board of Directors, and how our objective statement had been signed-off by Ralph. Everyone was pleased about that, so I went on to talk about roles and responsibilities on the project team.

I had been in even earlier in the day, and written on a piece of flip-chart paper all of the roles that Martha and I had discussed. I spread that out on the table in front of everyone and gave them a brief synopsis of what my "consultant" had been telling me.

"How can you have just one users' rep?" Alice asked. "There are a lot of people, especially on this job, who need to be involved. Maybe we should have a committee of users."

For some reason, the word "committee" always makes me nervous. I was not alone. "Have you ever tried to work with a committee?" Sheila asked. "If we have to deal with a whole committee, it will be a nightmare!"

"I realize that," said Alice, "but how else are you going to hear all of the users' concerns?"

I stepped in with my interpretation. "I believe the consultant was getting at the idea that we need to have one person on the project team in charge of each role. For example, whoever is the users' rep might organize a committee of users. It would probably be an effective way to get all of their concerns on the table. But the users' rep, not the committee, then comes back and works with the team." I paused. "It's like the team member is the funnel through which everything pours. But we only deal with the team member, not the 150 people they talk to in order to get their information."

"That setup works well," Leslie told us. "When we contract for assistance in advertising campaigns, a lot of people in the contractor's company work on our stuff, but we only deal with one key contact. In fact, the contractors insist on it. They find that it's the only way they can stay clear on exactly what we want."

Everyone seemed able to relate to that example. "Any other questions about the general responsibilities of the team players?" I asked the group.

"I've got one," Luigi said. "I'm not really clear on this implementor person. Aren't we going to be doing most of the actual work?"

"If we are, then I guess we will be filling the role of implementor," I said. "But there may also be others from outside the project team who do the actual work. Let me give you an example. We are going to have to hire a bunch of people to build the WindSailor. We might use a headhunter or employment agency to do that. In that case, we would be turning over a bunch of work to them to take care of."

"I've got a better example," Sheila told us. "When we do the actual construction work to expand the plant, we will hire a construction contractor. The contractor will supply a person to look at our design and then direct the people and equipment to construct the plant to our design. That person would be an implementor." Luigi nodded.

It was 7:30 a.m., and time to move on. "Now all we have to do is decide who gets to play which role."

The discussion became quite involved at this point, and it took us another 30 minutes to finally divvy up the roles. In the end, the team looked like this:

| | |
|---|---|
| **Sponsor** | **Ralph Borsellino** |
| **Feasibility analyst** | **Stu Barnes** |
| **Project manager** | **Will Campbell** |
| **Designer** | **Al Burton** |
| **Implementor** | **Unsure, everyone?** |
| **Project administrator** | **Sheila Chan** |
| **Users' rep** | **Amanda Payton** |

"I guess that means I'm the implementor by default," I remarked, "unless we assign someone else later.

"You have to recognize that some of us will be involved in other areas," Sheila said to me when we had written down the assignments. "I will undoubtedly be doing a lot of work with Al on design, and several of us will work on the implementation."

"And what about me and Leslie and Mark?" Luigi asked. "What are we supposed to be doing?"

"First of all, I don't think that helping out with some one else's responsibility is a problem, as long as you keep in mind what your primary role is. We have limited resources, so I'm sure we will all have to provide support to other people.

"Secondly," I turned to Luigi, "I expect that you will be one of the implementors, you are one of the users, and you will be helping out on the design. Don't worry," I assured him, "there will be plenty for you to do. Same with you, Leslie." I thought for a moment. "And besides, you two won't have to come to every one of these meetings anymore." They were happy about that, so I decided to wrap things up.

"Okay everyone, the next phase is Design. My consultant is out of town for a few days", I was thinking about Martha's coughing spell, "so we are going to start tackling this one on our own. Amanda, you get together a list of the users, so we know who we need to run the design by, and I'll get going with Al on the design itself."

"What about our list of tasks and work breakdown structures?" Sheila asked. "The things we decided to do after the very first meeting?"

"Let's forget about those for now," I told her. "I want to stick with the consultant's process. Anyone who has done that work already, save it. We may be able to use it later."

As we got up to leave I asked Sheila if she could let Al know that I wanted to meet with him.

"Look at that, people," I said, pointing at the clock over the donut counter. "Only 8:00 a.m. You've still got the whole day ahead of you! We'll have to do this more often."

Everyone rolled their eyes at me as they walked out and headed back to the plant.

# CHAPTER 10

My feeling that things were finally under control should have been my signal that something bad was about to happen. I was not watching for omens though, so I was totally unprepared for what was waiting for me back at the office. Or who.

"Good morning, Mr. Early Bird." Stu was sitting at my desk, feet up, looking, I supposed, the way I did when I sat there. I could see why people didn't like it. It's different when you are on the other side. "And how is my project manager this morning?" I could tell by the way he said it that he was not in a good mood.

"I'm going to save you a little time this morning, Will. When you check your voice-mail today, you will find a personal request from Ralph Borsellino himself to be in his office as soon as you get in today. I recommend that you pay attention to it, because The Great One has requested my presence as well." He took his feet off the desk, stood up and walked around it, planting himself right in front of me. Stu is about six inches taller than me, and when he gets close, it seems like a big six inches. In his best drill sergeant tone he said: "What the hell are you doing with this project, Will?"

It didn't seem like he really wanted me to answer, and I wasn't sure whether a salute would have been appropriate either, so I said nothing. Leaving me facing the desk, Stu started to walk around behind me like he was talking to a marine recruit who was about to do an extra 200 pushups. "Remember Al?" he asked me.

This time I guessed he wanted an answer, so I said, "Yes." I stifled the urge to add 'sir'. Then I added, "You're the one who put him on my team."

That was not strictly true, and I guess that was not what Stu wanted to hear, because, still sounding like a movie drill sergeant, he said, "And you managed to get him off your project team!"

I listened as Stu gave me the facts in his rapid-fire manner. Apparently Al had complained to Ralph two days ago about how I was handling the WindSailor project. Last night, after our meeting at the Throttled Duck, he had called Ralph at home and demanded to see him face to face, saying that it couldn't wait until morning. I guess Ralph was not at all happy about being disturbed outside of work, and he was even less happy when he heard what Al had to tell him.

California Water Sports Inc., one of our competitors based in San Francisco, had been talking to Al for some time about him going to work for them. Al had repeatedly declined, he told Ralph, for a number of reasons, including, he claimed, his loyalty to Hyler. Lately though, Al hadn't been feeling like he was appreciated as much as he should be around the company, and not being made project manager for the WindSailor was the last straw. The fact that an incompetent like me would be put in charge indicated to Al that there was no longer any place for him at Hyler. He had accepted a job with the San Francisco company, and Hyler wouldn't have old Al to kick around anymore.

To be honest, I saw this news as a cause for celebration more than the dressing down I was now getting from Stu. In fact, I figured that I should be rewarded. I had managed to make Al leave of his own free will. Not only would this help the WindSailor project, but all future work at Hyler. Maybe this project management stuff wasn't so bad after all!

My face must have given away what I was thinking, because Stu said "Get that smart-ass grin off your face! You know damn well I don't like Al any more than you do. If he had been under my authority, I would have fired him long ago! But he wasn't. The point is, Ralph specifically chose him to be part of this project. It was one of the conditions I had to agree to in order to get Ralph to go along with the WindSailor in the first place. And now you go and make him quit!"

Happy as I might have been, I really had nothing to do with it. I had to defend myself. "I had nothing to do with it!" I told Stu. "I was busting my butt to work with him, and he was doing nothing but trying to bring the whole WindSailor assignment down. He was the one trying to make me quit. He even told me so!" I was starting to sound very defensive, even though everything I said was true.

Stu didn't care. "It doesn't matter! You just don't understand the politics of the whole thing. Al was Ralph's representative on the project team. When Al quits and says it is because you are cutting him out of the project, who do you think Ralph will believe?"

"Are you saying the truth doesn't matter?" I asked him hotly. I have some strong opinions about organizational politics.

Stu took a deep breath and sat down in one of the visitor's chairs in front of my desk. He motioned for me to sit in my own chair. When we were both comfortable, he started to talk in a much calmer voice. "Look Will, I'm sorry for getting upset with you. I know you didn't try to make this happen. It's just that I get a little frustrated sometimes because you like to try to ignore the realities of the situation." Personally, I thought the reality of the situation was that we were all better off without Al, but I didn't voice my opinion. Stu continued: "I think that the WindSailor will be good for Hyler, so I want to do whatever it takes to make it happen. That means keeping Ralph happy, while still getting the job done. And your part in that little drama was supposed to have been to keep Al happy. Or at least to keep him from quitting, and claiming that you are incompetent. Can you see how a little thing like that might have an impact on Ralph and his opinion of the whole project?"

When he put it that way, I allowed as how I might be able to understand it. "But honestly, Stu, I was trying hard to work with Al. I guess I didn't try hard enough."

Stu sighed. "Well, now that you know what has happened, I want to tell you what will probably happen next. With Al gone, our illustrious president is going to be very concerned about his ability to keep his paws on this project. Negotiations with the WaterTrends people in Germany are at the point where we can't really back out of the deal. Luckily Ralph signed that objective form thing of yours in front of all the board members two days ago, so as much as he may not like to, Ralph will have to go ahead with the WindSailor. However, he will threaten to cancel the project and fire you or me or both of us before he lets us know that it will continue. Your job in this meeting will be to act humble and wrong and very willing to do better in the future. I really don't give a shit who is right. I want this project to go ahead." His face took on that army look again.

He stared me in the eye and barked, "Do you understand?" This time I couldn't resist. "Yes, sir!"

"I should fire you on the spot! Al was here for five years before you showed up, and after only two days in charge of this project, you manage to get him to quit!" I was amazed. The scene was playing out exactly as Stu had predicted. I tried to look humble. "I'm sorry it happened, Ralph." And then because I really wasn't all that humble, I told him that I was just trying to get the project done.

Ralph was not impressed. "Well you're going to have to try harder to get along with people!" Yeah, I thought, there was one of Al's really strong suits. He turned and walked over to his office window overlooking the plant site. "I consider losing Al a great detriment to our ability to complete this project, and I have thought seriously about canceling the whole thing." I glanced at Stu with admiration. The man was a genius. He could obviously read company politics like a road map.

Ralph sighed and assumed an expression that he thought made him look like a man of wisdom. "In the end, I concluded that this project is too important to the company." He turned back to both of us. "I want to continue on with it. But you," here he looked at me, "are going to have to work on your people skills. Stu, make sure that he gets some communication skills training as soon as possible. I consider it important to our success."

Stu glanced at me but said nothing. "By the way," Ralph continued, "I have to admit that I like some of the things you are doing, Will. The more I think about that objective statement I signed, the better I like it. But don't forget, you're supposed to meet with me every week to bring me up to date." He went to his desk and flipped open his calendar. "Let's set a date right now. How's Tuesday?" This was Thursday, the last day in August, and I wasn't sure that I would have much to report by Tuesday, but I agreed. It seemed like the wisest move.

On that note, we were dismissed. As we walked down the hallway toward Stu's office, I had to express my reverence for Stu.

"You called it exactly! Everything went just like you predicted." I slapped him on the back. "Man, am I impressed!"

Stu was not in the mood to celebrate. "You just don't understand the situation, Will. You seem to think that we are the good guys, and Ralph is out to get us. That's just not true. Ralph is not such a bad guy. He really does want to do what's best for the company. It's just that he has to play the game like the rest of us." He stopped walking and turned to face me. "If you try to understand Ralph a little better, and then give him what he needs, he won't cause us so much trouble. If you expect him to simply know the right thing to do, you will be allowing him to fail. This is not about being right or wrong or scoring points, Will. This is about making the WindSailor work. I want you to think about that." Stu turned and went into his office, closing the door behind him.

# Design

# CHAPTER 11

"Quit?" Jenny said. "Just because of you?" Sometimes my wife has a way of making me feel inconsequential.

"Well, at least partly because of me," I told her, trying to preserve my place among the causes for Al Burton's resignation.

"He must have been thinking about it for a long time," Jenny continued, as if she hadn't heard me. "You've been telling me ever since you started working there about how Al doesn't get along with anyone. It's funny that anyone else would hire him." I had to agree with her on that one. Maybe he seemed okay if you only had to deal with him in short bursts. "Is anybody worried that he might help your competitor scoop you on the WindSailor?" My wife, always the cheerful one.

"No one seems too concerned," I told her. "I talked to Stu about it and he assures me that WaterTrends has enough patent protection to keep our 18-month head start intact, no matter what. Meanwhile, my biggest concern is Martha's health." Her coughing fit yesterday had led to a visit to the hospital today. The doctors said she just needed to get some rest and quit smoking her pipe. According to Natalie, this diagnosis only confirmed Martha's already-low opinion of the medical establishment.

"I've always told you that you would get to like Martha if you just gave her a chance," Jenny said, mistaking the cause of my concern. I didn't bother to correct her about my true motive. "Mom told me to say that Martha would like to see you tomorrow sometime if you're not too busy. She seems to be getting fond of you, too!" All of this fondness was making Jenny very happy.

Just then our daughter came downstairs, and saw that I was home. "Daddy, Daddy, look at my ribbon. I won today!" she said, waving her prize in my face.

"Quiet, Sarah," my wife said. "Your brother is having a nap. You'll wake him up."

Sarah toned her voice down about five percent and continued. "I won the chess tournament. I beat all of the older kids! I won, I won!" This was definitely good news, and I picked her up and gave her a big hug.

Sarah and chess have always been a source of amazement to me. Normal in every other way, she became fascinated by chess when she was four. At first, I thought she would just want to put the pieces in her mouth, but right from the beginning she wanted to learn how to play, just like a grownup. After two years, she didn't play just like a grownup, she played better than most. Her skill level had reached the point where I would soon have to stop playing her, or face defeat at the hands of a six-year-old.

"Everyone thought Alistair was going to win 'cause he's in Grade 6," she said, "but I just concentrated like you told me, and I beat him easy!"

" 'Easily', honey," my wife corrected. Chess genius or not, Jenny is determined that our daughter will learn to speak correctly. "Why don't you go wash up for dinner?"

"Daddy, will you play me after dinner?" Sarah asked me. "I need to practice." I told her I would play a game with her as soon as we cleaned up the dishes, and I prepared my ego for a beating.

As I helped Jenny set the table and finish the last-minute preparations, I was deep in thought about the design process. I was comfortable with the idea that we couldn't do an Execution Plan and schedule until after we knew exactly what we were going to build. That now seemed obvious. My question, at this point, was one that I thought Martha would ask me: What is the result of the Design phase? What do you have when you are completely finished? Ideas popped into my head: blueprints, drawings, diagrams, pictures, these were the things you might have after you did a design.

Soon after I took over as the head of Information Systems at Hyler, I re-organized the department. It took me quite a while to figure out how I wanted my little organization to look, and at the time I thought I was doing 'organizational design'. If that was true, what did I have when I was done? In fact, I had drawn up an organization chart showing the new positions and how they related to each other. It was different from a blueprint for a house, but it showed the same thing: a picture of what the final product was going to look like. There was a lot more detail of course, enough to fill an operations manual.

I went around the table, putting knives and forks on the placemats. I can never remember which side the fork goes on, and this distracted me. I guessed the right-hand side, and went back to my thoughts.

For the WindSailor assignment, we would need both new organization charts and blueprints. We would also need flowcharts and other plans for the new software that would have to be produced, and written specifications for any new hardware. Not to mention a scheduling system, a staffing document, standard method instructions, and other items too numerous to remember. There would be lots of ways to communicate the design on this assignment.

If the Design phase produces plans or drawings or flowcharts, what is it that they do? They are, after all, only ways of conveying what the design is. If I could answer this question, I would have the result of the Design phase.

The one thing they all had in common was that they described something, the final product. Each one of those tools was giving a clear picture of exactly what the final product would look like, whether that product was a building, a department, or a software program.

Aha! I thought, as I put the water glasses at each place setting. The process of design has to do with describing the final product in detail. Therefore, the result of the design is a description of the final product, an exact description of the final product! Or at least detailed enough so that you could build the thing, whatever it was.

Martha would have been proud of me. It seemed so obvious now that I had worked it out, but I still felt like patting myself on the back. **The design process describes the final product in enough detail so that you can produce it.**

This led me to my next problem with design. Mr. Graubard had said at the board meeting that design is hard to schedule. He said something about the process being creative and difficult to predict. Why would that be? Surely a good architect can tell you how long it takes to design a building. Why would it be uncertain?

"...the left side," my wife interrupted my thoughts.

"Sorry hon, what was that?"

"I said the forks go on the left side, not the right. What kind of example is this setting for our children?" She gave me a look of mock horror and helped me switch them back.

Dinnertime conversation was about chess tournaments and Jake spilling his carrots all over the floor. Fortunately Max, our dog, has learned to lie underneath Jake's chair. He ate most of them before he realized that dogs aren't supposed to like vegetables. I cleaned up the rest.

By the time the dishes were cleared up and everything was back to its pre-dinner state of disorder, I was anxious to head into the study (as we call the spare bedroom that we have turned into an office) to think more about design. Then Sarah reminded me of my promise.

"Time to play, Daddy. You promised."

"Don't worry, honey," I said. "I'll play. But I can't play for very long. I have some work to do tonight."

"Okay," she said excitedly, "just until my bedtime." That was two hours away.

"Forty-five minutes," I told her firmly, thinking to myself that at about 20 minutes each, this would allow time for two games. With a little luck I could then get back to thinking about design, my ego still intact, at least until our next match.

Sarah held out her two fists to me. I tapped the right one, and she turned over her hand and opened it. There was a black pawn. "I get to play white." Sarah considered this a significant advantage. We sat down in the living room at the chessboard that was set up on the coffee table. I sat down on the couch, and she sat cross-legged on the floor opposite me. Suddenly my rambunctious little girl was gone, and in her place sat a serious-looking chess master. She picked up the pawn in front of her king and moved it two spaces ahead. I did the same with my king's pawn.

I should have started concentrating on the game in front of me. Instead, my mind started to wander back to design. Sarah moved her king's bishop diagonally across the black squares until it sat three spaces in front of her other bishop.

Why should scheduling design be so tough? I asked myself. I thought back to my own experience with software design. I had often run into trouble, but it was mostly because the users kept changing their requirements. Every time we would complete something, they would add a requirement, and it caused endless delays. I moved my queen's knight to bishop three.

I concluded that I would make sure we had the requirements clearly stated before we did any design work. That way, we wouldn't have to put up with ongoing additions, so we would have a much better chance of sticking to our schedule. And I would make sure that Ralph signed-off on the design when it was complete, to try to minimize changes to the design during execution. Of course that was built into Martha's process. Slick! Sarah moved her queen to bishop three.

If I could get a clear set of requirements for the design, which I had already started to do with the objective statement, and Ralph signed-off the completed design, where was the problem? Why had Mr. Graubard made his comments about the difficulty of scheduling design work? I moved my pawn to queen four and looked at my watch. Only three minutes gone. Sarah and I almost always took 20 minutes to play a game, and I was beginning to feel impatient. Maybe I should have agreed to only one game.

"Checkmate Daddy!" Sarah said delightedly as she moved her queen in to take the pawn in front of my king's bishop. She jumped up, the serious chess master gone. "I won! I won! I beat Daddy!" she went streaking into the other room to tell her mother. It appeared that some lessons in good sportsmanship were in order.

I have to admit, it didn't feel that bad. True, I had been beaten by a six-year-old, and as I stared at the board I could see that I must have been half asleep to let it happen, but she was my six-year-old, and I was pretty proud of her. I could hear her giving a play-by-play account of her victory. She told her mother that she had used a variation on the Lopez Opening, whatever that was.

Boy, I thought to myself, I can't even predict how long a chess game with my daughter is going to take. No wonder people are thinking that I will have trouble scheduling design. Then I stared at the board again and thought about it in a slightly differently way.

"Sarah," I called to the next room, "come here honey. I need to ask you a question."

Sarah came bouncing back into the room. "You're not mad are

you, Daddy? I mean, 'cause I beat you?" I tried not to smile too much.

"Of course not, honey. I'm very proud of you." And I'll pay more attention next time, I thought to myself. "But I need your help, Sarah. It has to do with something I'm doing at work." Sarah became serious again when I said this, concentrating like a chess master.

"Sarah, how long does it take to play a game of chess?" I asked her. She looked puzzled.

"I don't understand what you mean, Daddy. What does this have to do with work?"

"It's not a trick question, honey, I just want to know. You play a lot of chess games. How long does it take to play a game?"

"It's different every time, Daddy," she told me. "Sometimes it takes a long time if I'm playing someone good, and sometimes it only takes a little while if I'm playing someone who isn't that good." Since she was only six, I ignored the back-handed insult.

"So why can't you tell how long a game will take?" I asked her.

She thought about it for a minute before answering. "Every game is different, Daddy. And so they all take a different amount of time."

"Do you have a plan in your head when you start a game?" I asked her.

"Sure. I didn't used to when I was little. I just moved the pieces. But now I always have a plan on how I am going to win."

"What do you do if your opponent doesn't do what you expect?" Sarah looked at me like she wasn't sure what I meant, so I explained a little further. "What if I hadn't opened by moving my pawn; what if I had moved my knight here instead?" I asked, indicating the spot in front of my bishop's pawn.

"I would have tried a different plan," she told me, as if this were obvious. It was, of course, but I was sure there was a reason behind my questions. I didn't normally humiliate myself in front of six-year-olds.

"Want to play again?" I asked.

I caught myself feeling just a little too much satisfaction when I emerged victorious 25 minutes later.

# Chapter 12

"What is there to design? What happened to the idea of building a new building for manufacturing the WindSailor?" Ralph asked me, and mentally I sighed to myself. It was going to be a long meeting.

This was our first official sponsor/project manager get-together, not including the one that happened after Al quit, and I was prepared for a hard time. I had planned to educate Ralph about what would take place during the Design phase. Before I answered him, I thought back on my own education over the past four days.

On the day that Al quit, I had quickly informed everyone on the team, and arranged to meet Sheila and Amanda in my office first thing the next morning.

When they arrived, we talked a little about Al's sudden departure. "I assume he's gone to that California company?" Sheila asked me. I nodded. "He's been talking about it for some time," she continued. "I guess seeing you in charge of this project got to him more that I thought it would."

Amanda still couldn't believe it. "Sure, nobody liked him, and we all thought he was an idiot, but was that any reason to quit?" Sheila and I looked at her. Amanda is a very team-oriented person, and sometimes this gives her an unusual viewpoint.

"Since that is the situation," I told them, "and since the WindSailor waits for no man, I've made a couple of adjustments to our team." I turned to Sheila. "You are the new designer. Congratulations. And you," I said to Amanda, "are taking over the duties of project administrator, as well as being the users' representative."

Sheila looked happy about her new role, but Amanda didn't seem too thrilled. "I thought you said the users' representative role was a lot of work. How am I supposed to do both?" She was starting to sound like me.

"Don't worry," I told her. "I'll help you out. Anyway, we haven't got any more resources, so we are just going to have to make do."

Amanda wasn't ready to give up yet. "What about Alice? She doesn't have a role yet."

"Alice will have a lot to do in support of the project administrator, but to be honest, I don't think that Alice is ready for this yet. I'm worried that she'll focus too much on the costing alone, and worry more about her accounting needs than our project needs." I smiled at her in what I hoped was a friendly, supportive way. I'm sure she interpreted it differently. "See how much I admire your skills? Anyway, that's why you get the job."

"Well, in that case," Amanda said, "I've got things to do. Are we finished here?" We were, but I asked Sheila to stay to discuss the design.

"I spent a lot of time last night thinking about the Design stage," I told her. "I think I'm starting to get a better handle on what it's all about." I told her my idea about the result of the Design phase being an exact description of the final product. "But," I concluded, "I'm a little worried about the process of design. How soon can we get a schedule for it? And how accurate is that schedule likely to be?" I hadn't yet told her about Mr. Graubard's comments at the board meeting about design.

Sheila was way ahead of me. "You know Will, I've been thinking a lot about the design process too, ever since you introduced your consultant's framework to us. You see, design is something that we engineers spend most of our time learning about in school. In fact, I used to think that the project was the design, and the construction was just incidental." I looked at her skeptically.

"I know it sounds strange, but it's true!" she assured me. "Anyway, usually the design isn't complete when the construction begins, so managing the execution has a lot to do with trying to revise the design and build at the same time."

I told her that seemed like a funny way to do it. "Like I said, Will, as an engineer, most of my focus has been on the design. But

I've started to change that perspective since I looked at your framework. In fact," she said, grabbing a pad of paper on my desk, "I think we can work the design process very neatly into your consultant's framework for assignments."

On the paper she wrote:

***Design (Results):*** ***An unmistakable description of the deliverable(s)***

"This pretty much sums up both of our ideas about the results of the Design phase. I've just used the word 'deliverables' instead of 'final product'. To me it seems like a better, more generic word. In this assignment I'm responsible for designing more than tangible products. There are also things like the jobs, the production process, and the information systems." I agreed that the word "deliverables" sounded better.

Just underneath the results of the design, she wrote:

***Design Steps***

1) ***Specify performance criteria***
2) ***Sponsor approves the more detailed performance criteria***
3) ***Preliminary design: problem solving, generation of options, feasibility analysis, proposed 'best' solution***
4) ***Preliminary design sign-off by sponsor***
5) ***Produce detailed design schedule, cost estimate***
6) ***Detailed design schedule and cost approved by sponsor***
7) ***Detailed design***
8) ***Sponsor approves detailed design***

She turned the pad of paper around to me. "I'm proposing that we follow this simple process for design. I'll explain it in a minute, but first, tell me this: when you were thinking about design last night, did you come to any conclusions about why it was hard to predict how long it takes?"

I had indeed come up with an idea. "Because every time you do a design, it is for something entirely new. That means you can't just copy an old design, you have to be creative and come up with new ideas. That creative part of the process is unpredictable.

"It's like a chess game. It's the same game and same rules every time, but playing it is a creative process. It's hard to predict how long it will take to determine the outcome." I didn't bother to explain why I was thinking along the lines of a chess game. My self-esteem wasn't ready for it.

"Exactly!" said Sheila. "That's pretty much how I have been looking at it as well. At some point, the design is a creative process. You start with a large number of possible options for getting the result you want, and you gradually eliminate them until, in the end, you have an exact picture of your particular deliverable." She paused. "The hard part to understand is that each design decision you make has a direct impact on all of the decisions that come after that one. So you don't have a very good idea of what your choices will be for the next decision down the road until you make the current one. That also makes the whole thing hard to predict."

My head was spinning a little. "I'm not sure I follow you, Sheila. Can you give me an example?"

She thought for a moment. "This may be stretching it a little, but let me give you a little analogy. Let's suppose there is this baseball game. Your team is down by one run, there is one out, it's the bottom of the ninth, and there are runners on first and third. The guy coming up to the plate is pretty quick, and he's a good bunter. You're the manager. What are you going to tell him to do?"

As I guess I already said, I like analogies, even when they're not very good ones. I put myself in the position of the imaginary manager. What the hell? I thought, it's not a real game. "I'll go for the suicide squeeze play. I'll tell the batter to bunt the ball up the third baseline."

Sheila made a face. "As the manager, you're facing a situation sort of like the beginning of an assignment." I looked a little puzzled, so she explained. "We have a situation that is unsatisfactory, you're losing the ball game. You want to tie things up. Your constraints are the rules of baseball, the skill of your hitter, and the fact that you have men on first and third, with one out. You have a result that you want to achieve: score a run. In order to decide what to do, you need a preliminary design." She tapped the paper in front of her. "You completed the first step in the process. Tell me, what else did you consider doing?"

To be honest, I hadn't really considered anything else, I had just said the first thing that came to mind. I told Sheila this.

"You would be surprised, Will, how often that is exactly how the preliminary design gets done. But I'll let you go back in time. What else might you have considered before choosing the squeeze play?"

"Maybe a sacrifice fly or a hit-and-run?"

Sheila looked unimpressed. "You have to get off this chess kick, and get your kids into sports! There is only one out! What about letting your batter swing away?"

Sheila was starting to get aggressive about this sports thing, and she was making me nervous. I tried to get her to move on. "So we have some options, now what?"

With a last disgusted look Sheila undermined all confidence in my managerial prowess, and then continued. "You generated possible solutions, you mentally proposed what you thought was the best option, and then, since you are the manager, you also completed the second step. As sponsor, you signed-off the preliminary design. You aren't going to try a sacrifice fly, or a hit-and-run. You are going to try a suicide squeeze. How did you come up with the options and make the decision?"

I thought for minute, still feeling a little defensive. "I suppose I used my past experience and what I know about the current situation to pick what seemed like the best way to reach my goal." I thought for a minute. Saying what I thought Sheila wanted to hear was probably not going to help. "Actually, I just picked a play that I thought would make things exciting. I didn't really weigh the options at all." Some manager, I thought.

But Sheila was excited by my honesty. "That is exactly what often happens during the preliminary design! Especially when you don't have a lot of time to make a decision. Let me illustrate. When you were deciding what to do, information about how well your batter is able to bunt was important. Instead of just making a quick mental assessment of him, don't you think it would have been a good idea to have a quick look through his stats? How many times has he bunted safely? How many times in this particular situation? How many times has he hit safely with men on third? What's his average against this particular pitcher?"

I was becoming a little flustered, since it appeared that my imaginary team was about to go down in defeat because I hadn't done my research. "You didn't give me all that information. And anyway, there isn't time in a real ball game. You just have to make a choice!" I could feel the tension as my batter stood in his imaginary box and waited for the pitch. He probably also needed glasses, and I had probably also forgotten to tell him to wear them.

"That's just it! You didn't have time. In baseball, having to make that snap assessment is part of the game. It makes it more exciting! It's hard to make the right decision all the time, which is why the outcome is unpredictable. But do you have enough time in the real world to make a rational choice? How much information do you collect? How long do you take to decide?"

I left my batter for a moment. "So this is why it's hard to predict how long design takes? Because the preliminary design requires a lot of research and a hard decision at the end?" I was starting to feel like I was talking to Martha. Sheila seemed to have all the answers.

She nodded. "That is a big part of it. Completing the preliminary design takes research and creativity, and that takes time. And if you don't do the preliminary design well, then the detailed design becomes uncertain."

"So how does this help us?" I asked her. "We don't have much time, and we need to tell Ralph how long the preliminary design takes, so we can tell him how long the design will take, so we can plan the execution of this damn thing!"

Sheila frowned. "That is where your designer becomes extremely important. The project team has to rely on the skills of the designer and the feasibility analyst to generate possible options, then briefly examine those and recommend the best one."

"So how do we get a good designer?" I asked, on the edge of my seat.

"What do you think I am?" Sheila asked indignantly.

I back-pedaled quickly. "I was thinking about assignments in general, Sheila. Obviously we have you on this one. But in the future, how do we ensure that we have a good designer?" I thought I had done a good job of turning that one around.

Sheila stared out my window. "That is where I'm stumped, Will. It's like asking how you create a great painter." She turned back to me. "What I do know is that the objective statement provides the general design criteria. A competent designer should be able to take good criteria and turn them into a preliminary design. The greatness of that design depends on the greatness of your designer."

This was getting a little esoteric for me. "Let me get this straight, Sheila. You are saying that the Genesis step provides the groundwork necessary to do the design."

"Not quite," she said. "My experience is that the users are the best possible source of more detailed information about how the deliverables have to perform. As a designer, I want no constraints on what it must be like. I can invent and specify the design features, but I need to start with all of the performance criteria. The best news so far in this assignment is that the users' representative is managing the process that collects and structures that information. Amanda's job is very important to mine. We designers have a bad habit of accepting performance criteria that are far too general."

Suddenly I understood a lot better how the roles fit together, and what a good choice we had made. Amanda loves inventing detailed procedures. Like others who value and understand methods, she never says "methodology" when she means "method." And she honestly wants to make people's jobs easier. The users would not only be well represented, they would see how their needs would be translated for the project team.

I turned back to Sheila's list. "And this simple process you have here should allow a competent designer to produce a preliminary and then a detailed design?" She nodded. "So how long will it take?"

"I'm afraid I can only answer that question in two parts." I guess I looked a little exasperated, because she said, "I'm only telling you how I see it! I can't change the way things are. Anyway, like I said, I can answer that in two parts. First, I don't know how to predict how long the preliminary design takes. It's a brainstorming session to generate ideas, and then the designer and the feasibility analyst have to go away and estimate the potential benefits and costs of each one so that they can recommend the best. You would also have to do that up-front work with the users to make sure that their needs were met. It's hard to predict how long the whole process might take. It would depend on the experience of the designer, how easy it is to work with the users, and what ideas were being investigated. You can put an arbitrary time limit on it, but it takes as long as it takes."

I must have looked a little forlorn, because she said, "The good news is that once the preliminary design is complete, detailing the design is usually pretty straightforward. You can predict much more accurately how long it will take to write computer code or draw up blueprints." I felt a little relief. At least we might be able to predict something.

"How does this work for the baseball analogy?" I asked.

"The analogy starts to get a little weak here," she told me apologetically. "But I'll stretch it anyway. Once you have completed the preliminary design and decided to go with the suicide squeeze, what other decisions do you need to make before execution, I mean, before the pitcher throws the ball?"

I was starting to get into this managing stuff. "Well," I said, taking my imagination back to the ball game, "I'd give the sign to everyone, and then I'd have to look a little more closely at this particular situation. I want the guy to score from third, so maybe I want him to take a big lead off the bag. On the other hand, maybe he's really fast, and I don't want to tip off the other team about what I'm up to, so maybe I hold him close to the bag. Then there's the bunt. Do I go down the third baseline? Maybe the third baseman is a great fielder, so maybe we should bunt toward the first baseman 'cause he's a bit slow, or playing deep. And then there's the runner on first..."

Sheila interrupted me. "I think you're getting the idea. As you can see, our deliverable in this example is the exact situation on the field at the moment of the pitch. Once the preliminary design has been completed, you have to make increasingly detailed decisions about exactly what the deliverable should look like. It's easier to predict those little decisions than the big decision of arriving at the preliminary design. However, your detailed design decisions will be very different if you choose to do a hit-and-run. And if we decide to build a whole new building to manufacture the WindSailor, our detailed design process will be very different than if we just expand some of our existing space."

This was actually starting to make sense to me. Looking at the pad of paper where Sheila had jotted down the steps in design, I said, "It seems to me that having the sponsor's approval as we go will be key to making this work."

"My thinking exactly," Sheila said. "Especially in this case. Al told me about Ralph's preference for a new building, but that decision might be based on about as much reasoning as your decision to go for the suicide squeeze."

I rose above that slight. "I think it's also going to be important to let Ralph know about the design process so he can understand why I can't give him an ironclad schedule. At least, if he wants the best product."

A thought popped into my head about cost. "It would seem to me that most of the cost of design would be in the detailed part. Even if it is hard to predict how long it will take, generating the preliminary design shouldn't take a whole lot of money, should it?"

Sheila agreed. "That's another one of the reasons why getting the sponsor's approval of the preliminary design seems like such a good idea. It's before a lot of money gets spent."

Sheila must have thought that I was looking a little confident about the design process. "We have to keep in mind one other thing, Will. Fundamentally, design is unpredictable, because you are always doing something that has never been done before. Even if something like it has been done, this particular situation has never been encountered. And that means there is always an element of uncertainty. You can set schedules and try to stick to them, but you are dealing with the unknown. We may run into something that we can't deal with, even during the detailed design. Finding a way around those things always takes time, and it may require more than we have allowed." I shrugged. There didn't seem to be much we could do about it.

"I'm going to tell Ralph all about the design process so he'll know what to expect, but it seems to me the best we can do is to try to identify where in the detailed design process we might encounter delays, and keep him informed."

Sheila and I continued to discuss design for a few minutes, and in the end we decided that she and Amanda (the users' rep) and Stu (the feasibility analyst) would get together in the afternoon to start work on the preliminary design. "How long do you think it will take?" I finally asked her.

"I thought we just decided that this was unpredictable!" she said.

"We decided it was hard to predict, not unpredictable. C'mon, I need an estimate: I have to meet with Ralph on Tuesday. He'll want some idea."

Sheila thought hard for a moment. "We have been doing work on possible plant expansions for the last year and a half, which is going to make our job a whole lot easier. I'm guessing at least a week to put this together. Make it two weeks, okay?"

What could I say? "You've got two weeks. I'll probably be in touch daily to see how it's going." I paused. "By the way, what about the ball game analogy? Once the design is complete and everyone is in position, what would be the equivalent of execution?"

"Don't you know anything about baseball?" Sheila asked. "They even call it execution! It's when the pitcher pitches the ball, and everyone now has to do what they're supposed to do. The runner on third charges home, the batter bunts and takes off for first. And if you have the right resources, that is, a runner who can run and a batter who can bunt, then you tie the ball game."

I frowned to myself as she left the office. In Little League, I had always been a terrible bunter.

The evening after my conversation with Sheila, I was back on Martha's porch asking after her health.

"Never felt better!" she declared triumphantly. "Those doctors don't know what they're talking about. It's not the pipe that's killing me, it's time!" She chuckled to herself, took a big pull on her pipe, and blew a smoke ring toward my face. "How's the project coming?"

I couldn't believe my ears. "Don't you mean 'assignment', Martha?"

"Just testing, Willie," she said, chuckling some more. "Just testing. You young people are just a mite too serious."

I brought her up to date on what had happened, including Al's resignation and Sheila's ideas about the design process. "That Sheila sounds like a bright girl!" Martha said. "Sounds like you'll be much better off with her as your designer."

"So what do you think about the design process itself?" I asked. "Does it look like it will work? Does it match your way of doing things?" I felt excited, like a little kid who knows he has 'done good' and wants recognition from his parents.

Martha took the stem of her pipe out of her mouth and pointed it at me. "You see what a little thinking does for you? You don't even need my help anymore. Yessir Willie, I like the looks of your design process. It's right up my alley."

I felt pleased, and then I was instantly on my guard. "What else can you tell me about design, Martha? Some little hints about what to look for to help the process go smoothly maybe?"

Martha rocked and thought for a moment. "There are a couple of things I can add, Willie, but they're more philosophical than what you've got so far." I took out my pad of paper and prepared to write.

"My first suggestion is this: make sure your designer understands the logic of how things must be done before she makes up a schedule for the detailed design. In other words, she must know what has to come before what." That seemed to be obvious, and I said so. "We'll see about that, Willie," she said ominously.

"The second is a question." Somehow, I had been expecting this. "How do you know when your detailed design is complete?" I looked blank, and Martha added, "How do you know that you are done describing the deliverable and are ready to plan how you are going to make it?"

"Isn't there some technical information that the designer has that tells her that?" I asked hopefully.

Martha just kept smoking and looking out over the porch railing. "Not exactly, Willie."

The question had me completely stumped. How do you know when you've fully described the deliverable? Did you have to describe the physical arrangements of the atoms in the material you were building with? I tried to think about a design I was more familiar with: information systems. How did I know when a particular system was fully designed? To be honest, I wasn't really sure, because we were usually implementing the system halfway through the detailed design process, and then completing the design as we went.

I had to admit that I could not figure it out. "It's a tough question," she told me, "and one that you could answer more easily if you understood the whole framework a little better." She puffed on her pipe, then continued. "Mostly it is a judgment call on the part of the designer. When she thinks there is enough detail to go ahead and plan how you would build the deliverable, then the design is complete."

"Don't you mean when there is enough detail to actually build the thing, not just when the designer thinks so?" I asked. "Wouldn't that be when the design is complete?"

"You've hit on just the point I wanted to make, Willie. How do you know that there is enough detail in the design to actually go out and build the thing?"

I thought about my software projects. "I guess the only way to tell if the detail is there is by actually doing the execution." That is how I had done it in the past.

"Absolutely not!" Martha struck like a snake. A moment ago she had been peacefully smoking her pipe, looking like she might have been discussing the pros and cons of mulching versus bagging when cutting the lawn. Now she was sitting forward, with her hands on the rocker's arms, her face red, and a little saliva bubble at one corner of her lips. I sensed that this might be an important point.

"That notion has got more people in trouble than I care to remember! There is real money being spent during the execution. Do you really want to be testing the completeness of your design at that point? What if it is not detailed enough? What if pieces are missing? Is halfway into the execution the time to discover that?"

I mumbled something about how I supposed it wasn't, and she

continued her tirade. "The way to make sure the design is complete is by doing the Execution Plan! In other words, figure out what will happen during the execution, before it actually begins. Don't just start digging holes because you have a shovel in your hand!" She actually reached out and cuffed me on the back of the head. I sat there like a guilty schoolboy, my hair standing up in a cowlick where she had hit me.

As quickly as the storm had begun, it abated. Martha sat back in her chair. "Don't forget. The execution planning process is a test of whether the design is complete. If you come to a point in the planning process where you don't know how you would proceed, because some key design decision hasn't been made, you know that your design isn't complete."

I tried to think of a very simple example. Suppose you were going to build a house, and after the architect had designed it, you made an Execution Plan for how you were going to build it. You would decide when you would dig the foundation, pour the foundation, put up the drywall, wire the lighting fixtures, all that stuff. But suppose when you were planning this stuff out, you came to the task of painting the bedrooms. What if you didn't know what color they were supposed to be? Or even if they were supposed to have wood paneling instead of being painted? Maybe that was an example of an incomplete design. I related the example to Martha.

"Maybe you should have a task that has you buying the paint," Martha corrected me. "Better you should find out at that point that you don't know what color the bedroom is. But yes, that would be an example of a design not being complete. Now, can you imagine what might happen to your execution if you have a lot of these little decisions not made during design?"

The answer was obvious. "The execution takes longer or costs more than you thought."

"Or both," Martha added.

I thought about it for a minute. "That seems pretty obvious, Martha."

She just chuckled. "Good sense is always obvious. Too bad no one pays it any notice."

"So you see, Ralph, this is the design process we are following," I said, pointing to the flip chart I had made up from Sheila's notes. "We are about halfway through the preliminary design. We're hoping to have options and recommendations for you at the end of next week."

Ralph, who had looked a little peeved when I began the explanation of the design process, was starting to look much happier. I had taken him through a condensed version of what Sheila and I had discovered over the past four days, saying it like I had always known it.

Oddly enough, Stu's idea about not treating Ralph like one of the bad guys seemed to be working. "I'm feeling more comfortable with this process," Ralph told me, "but I'm still a little uneasy that we don't know for certain we can be ready by June. Are you sure you can't give me at least a tentative implementation schedule at this point?"

I could appreciate how Ralph was feeling. Intellectually I understood why there would not be any point in doing that, but emotionally I still felt insecure. "I could give you one, Ralph, but I couldn't commit to sticking with it. We haven't even got the preliminary design done yet, so we don't know for sure what we'll be doing." I tried to reassure him. "We're talking to all the 'experts' around the plant to get their very rough assessment about each option, so that we're reasonably comfortable that our 'best' option can be completed in time. But guessing at the details of the schedule now won't change how long it actually takes."

Ralph seemed to want the security of the schedule just as badly as I did. "To be honest Will, the Hyler board is pushing me for some kind of schedule. How soon can I give them something?"

Ralph was obviously trying to work with me, so I tried to hold out some hope for him. "If we finish the preliminary design on schedule, and we can meet with you next Friday to get your approval, we could have a design schedule for you Monday." He looked happy about that, so I added a caution: "But we can't have the implementation schedule until after the detailed design is complete."

"How soon after?"

I had no idea. I hadn't talked to Martha yet about what execution planning involved, so I did what I always do in this kind of a tight spot. I tried to sound confident while I guessed. "About a week after the detailed design is approved, we can have the implementation schedule for you."

Ralph didn't look totally satisfied, but there wasn't anything more I was prepared to commit to. Guessing wouldn't help. "Have you got some cost tracking going?" he asked.

"That was something I wanted to confirm in this meeting, Ralph. Are we going to allocate everything to this project? I mean, all of our own time as well as outside costs?" I was hoping that Hyler personnel time would not be charged to the project, we could be an expensive bunch.

Ralph dashed my hopes on that one. "Everything. We have a new practice of trying to figure out the real cost of everything we do. And in-house personnel are real costs."

I had done a little preparation for this contingency. "I've set up a project number with Alice in Accounting, and everyone on the team is keeping track of their time. I'll have her start accumulating it under the project number." It meant a little more administrative hassle for all of us, but at least I could appreciate why we were doing it.

"When are you going to have this project set up on project management software?" Ralph asked.

I hedged, brilliantly. "Uh, I'm not sure..."

Ralph was adamant. "I want this project run with the most modern and efficient tools we have available, Will. You have my authorization to spend what you need to get a good package. You might want to check with Sheila on that, I know that Al was evaluating packages before he left."

I made a note to do that. "By the way, can we move our next Tuesday meeting to Friday? We're hoping to have the preliminary design complete, and we'll need you to approve it."

That was not a problem, and we ended on a positive note. Ralph told me he was getting comfortable that I had things under control. I didn't bother to tell him otherwise. He also said that he liked these frequent meetings, and I had to admit to myself that they made a lot of sense. He would be well informed and better able to make decisions when we needed them, hopefully starting next Friday. Ralph was not such a bad guy when you let him know what was going on.

"Don't forget about the software," he called as I headed out the door. Before this was over, I would wish that I had.

# CHAPTER 13

Hard as it may be to believe, our son Jake is named after Jake Blues, the character John Belushi played in the movie "The Blues Brothers". I actually wanted to call him Elwood (my son, not John Belushi) after Jake's brother, because without the 'Blues' last name, Jake sounded a little too much like a soap star to me. And anyway, Elwood is a much more unusual name; people remember you if your name is Elwood.

Jenny had a different opinion of the name Elwood, and after many long discussions, I gave in and we named him Jake. Of course now Jake is Jake, and any other name would be ridiculous. I'm holding out for Elwood as the name of our next dog, but Jenny hasn't made any promises.

The reason this whole thing comes up is that the next week and a half sort of reminded me of the movie "The Blues Brothers". We had an objective to achieve, a short time in which to achieve it, and nothing was going to get in our way. Events moved at a frenetic, out-of-control pace, and we had a hell of a good time. In fact, in retrospect, developing the preliminary design was probably the most fun of the whole assignment.

I became much more involved in the process than I had originally intended, but by the time it was all over I was glad I had, because the decisions that were made at that stage determined the details of the rest of the assignment.

While Sheila, Stu and I worked out and assessed options, Amanda began earning her pay as users' rep. By Thursday she came to me with a users' list that was a lot bigger than I had expected. As I went over it with her, I had a number of questions.

"What is the union steward doing on here?" I asked Amanda. "There are no labor relations involved." I have had some bad experiences with unions in the past, so I was a little concerned to see them as users.

"Not quite true," Amanda told me. "We are going to be hiring about 30 new people to work on the WindSailor. Don't you think it might be a good idea to involve the union early? Anyway, our collective agreement says they have to be involved at some point. I think we should get them onside as soon as possible." I had to agree with her. Most of my problems with unions had come because I withheld information. "I also want them to have some input into the training programs for new employees," Amanda continued. "The people on the floor are always saying we never let them help with the thinking."

"I'm sure Mark Goldman will be happy to hear about that," I said. Mark dealt with human resources matters like training, as well as labor relations issues. Sometimes he and our shop steward tended to have a somewhat adversarial relationship.

Amanda didn't seem too concerned. "Like I said, better to get their input now instead of later. This assignment can't afford any delays, let alone preventable ones that happen because we don't involve the union."

I continued down her list of users. "The city? You want to get them involved? We'll be snowed under in paperwork and bureaucracy! I think we should definitely leave them out until the last minute."

Amanda looked exasperated. "You don't exactly have an 'abundance' mentality do you, Will?" I wasn't sure what she meant by that, but I assumed it wasn't complimentary. "The reason we've had trouble with the City of Enderby in the past is that we don't involve them until we've already decided what we want to do. Then it's very expensive for us to change our plans to meet their requirements. As a result, we resent them for just doing their job."

Despite the fact that this explanation sounded plausible, I was still a little suspicious. "So why do we need to involve them so early?" I asked.

"In case you've forgotten, there is the little matter of access to Hyler Lake, for one thing. Do you think that might have some impact on how we conduct major construction here at the plant?" I had to allow as how it might. "There's also the question of sewage. We are on the municipal water system. Do you think maybe that expanding our plant capacity by 25 or 30 percent and adding 30 employees might have some impact on our waste water?"

She was starting to get on my nerves. "Yeah, yeah, you've made your point. So they're a user." The next name on the list was Luigi Delgarno. I didn't bother to ask, but I assumed that since he was going to be in charge of running the process when we were done setting up for it, she figured he should have some input.

I went on to the next person. "Why is Harry Freeman on here?" I was starting to sound like a broken record.

Amanda explained patiently, "We're not just building buildings you know. We are also going to be modifying our payroll and accounting systems. Alice didn't want to be part of the users' group, so she nominated Harry. And," she said, anticipating any further questions I might have, "you'll notice that Mark is on there from Human Resources, and Les French from the warehouse. Don't forget, revamping the plant is going to have an impact on most areas of our existing business. Wherever people are going to be directly affected, I've tried to get some representation."

I was glad that it was her and not me dealing with this bunch. I had to admit, to myself at least, having all of these people involved up front was bound to make life easier for us down the road. I could see why it made sense to have one person acting as the users' representative. It looked like it was going to be a lot of work. I could see even more clearly why we would not want all those diverse interests showing up at every meeting of the assignment team. We would never get anything done with that group sitting at the same table!

I scanned the rest of the list and handed it back to Amanda. "I am starting to think that you may be able to cure me of my hesitancy to share information," I told her. "This list is nothing if not comprehensive. I'll be counting on you to keep all of these people in touch with what is going on."

That wasn't quite enough for Amanda. "And I'll be counting on you to listen to me when I tell you their concerns, Will. Don't forget that this is a two way street. We want their input so we can make the project work better for them, not just to pacify them!"

"That's assignment, not project," I corrected her. "And yes, of course we will listen to their input. In fact, I want to you to run all of our potential preliminary design options past them before we recommend one to Ralph." If that didn't make me sound like the visionary, participative, focused, quality-oriented team leader that I wanted to be, I didn't know what would. And anyway, I knew that we wanted to get the users' acceptance of the preliminary design.

As Stu and Sheila developed alternative ways of expanding Hyler's manufacturing capacity, I helped them guess what the implications of each might be in terms of how much they would cost, how long they would take, and how well they would serve our needs now and in the future. Although there were many variations, the decision about manufacturing space boiled down to two alternatives. The first was to construct an entirely new facility; the second to build onto our existing space. Each option had to be detailed to a reasonable extent in order to make what we considered to be semi-intelligent guesses about its implications. Fortunately, for some time before Al made his sudden departure, he and Sheila had been looking at a possible expansion of the plant, so a great deal of the legwork had already been done.

We also had some tough choices about our payroll and inventory systems. Our current payroll program didn't have the capacity to handle the extra staff we would be bringing on board. In fact, the whole accounting system was old, and in my opinion, in need of replacement. Like the accounting system, our inventory control system would require significant modifications to take on the new product. The question in both cases was: modify or replace?

And so it went. Options to consider, implications to determine. All I can say is, thank God for Amanda. Between Sheila, Stu and I, we had no problem coming up with what we thought were viable options, but many times our scenarios contained flaws, of which we were totally unaware, that would have sunk the assignment if we had gone ahead.

Fortunately, as soon as we had described an option, Amanda would run it by the users for their comments. In this way we discovered that the shop floor workers were unhappy with the current trend in training. They felt that there was not enough hard information being imparted, because too much time was spent during the training sessions playing "games." This information had come from Sue Coleman, the union shop steward.

"When we take time off work," she had told Amanda, "believe it or not, we really do want to learn something. But it seems like we spend all our time in training doing funny exercises that don't have anything to do with our jobs. We need to see a little more practical information."

This was particularly surprising for Mark Goldman, because the "games" that Sue was referring to were team-building simulations which were all the rage in human resources circles. He adjusted his expectations accordingly.

By far the biggest break we got from Amanda's organized approach related to the City of Enderby's opinion about our expansion. Based on our preliminary work, it was starting to look like Ralph's preference for building a new building to house the WindSailor was going to be the best choice. Although the most expensive, it appeared to make the most sense in the long run. We were all quite surprised that the city did not approve of our plans.

"They'll shut us down, starting with denying us the building permit," Amanda reported. "They don't like that option at all. In fact, they are pretty much opposed to us expanding."

"That doesn't make any sense!" said Stu. "We've been here for 50 years! We provide jobs! We pay taxes! Why are they coming down on us?" We all felt apprehensive. Here was a potential stumbling block that had been completely overlooked until now.

"We are zoned for industrial use," Sheila said. "How can they stop us from doing what we want on our land?"

Amanda had obviously heard an earful from the city planning people. "They can deny us building permits, they can refuse to let us hook up to the municipal sewage system, and they can tie us up in bureaucracy from now until it's too late."

Stu was suddenly adamant that we should move the whole plant. "We should talk to Ralph. If the city doesn't want us, well then screw them. We'll go somewhere that does."

I sighed. "That's hardly practical, Stu. Apart from the fact that it would be horrendously expensive to move, I have a feeling that it would affect our ability to have the WindSailor to market next summer." I turned to Amanda. "Did you get a feel for why they are doing this?"

"I got a lot more than a feel," she told us. "As you all know,

Enderby is becoming a bedroom community of Portland. More and more people are moving out here and commuting. That means that more and more land is being zoned residential. As it turns out, the city has just approved an 80-lot subdivision for the 50-acre parcel of land behind the donut shop."

"So?" asked Sheila. "Why does that matter to us?"

Amanda continued. "The city is becoming very concerned about noise pollution, air pollution, and all of those negative things associated with industry. They don't want us to expand because they're worried that our new facility is going to disturb the neighbors."

"And drive property prices down," added Stu. "I wonder how many city councilors have invested in that subdivision?"

Sheila was getting more frustrated by the minute. "But that is bullshit! We're not testing jet engines or tanks here! We're making fiberglass boards! We make less noise than a few lawn mowers!"

"Doesn't matter, Sheila," Amanda told her. "I've been over it a dozen times with them. We are industry, and the town doesn't want us putting up a brand new building right now."

"What's the bottom line, Amanda?" I asked her. "Are you saying that we are dead in the water, or is there a way around it?"

We all held our breath for a minute while Amanda thought. "To be honest, they didn't give me any indication that there was anything we could do to get their approval." She grinned ruefully. "I guess sometimes being a little secretive helps."

"Why is that?" I asked her.

"Well, I gave the city planning people an overview of our assignment, including the part about the tight time frame. I thought it might help to give them an appreciation of why we might want to move things quickly through their department. Anyway, they know that we can do what we want on our own land, given enough time, but I think they're planning to slow us down enough that we just don't bother with the expansion at all."

Everyone looked glum. Stu seemed particularly depressed. "I can't believe this! We've had such a good relationship with them over the years." He paused for a second. "What I really can't believe is that I didn't check into this before I got everything in motion."

Sheila had been scribbling furiously on a sheet of paper, and now she looked up. "Hang on folks," she said, "We're not dead in the water yet. All we have to do is provide something to the city that offsets their perception of us as heavy industry, in exchange for them not blocking our expansion."

Stu looked disgusted. "Then we are just allowing ourselves to become the victims of blackmail! Why don't we just pay them off with cash?"

"It's not quite the same, Stu," said Sheila. "We just have to negotiate a little. Look," she told us, "from a home owner's perspective, the city does have a point. Who wants to have a factory in their backyard?" She held up her hand as Stu was about to comment. "I know, Stu, I said it myself. We aren't like what most people think of as a factory, but that doesn't matter. To your average person, a factory is a factory. It has big smoke stacks that belch pollution, and it makes a lot of noise. So what we need to do in order to get the city on our side is be prepared to change our plans a little." She paused and looked around the room. "What can we offer to them that would seem to make this area a nicer place to live?"

We all stared blankly at her. "Free windsurfing lessons?" Amanda offered.

"No!" Sheila said with mock disgust. "Are you people blind? What would you say is one of the favourite recreational attractions for families in Enderby?"

I started to see what Sheila might be getting at. "Hyler Lake," I said.

"Exactly! Our little lake is a very popular spot for people in this town to windsurf, sail, swim or just picnic. As you all know, the lake is technically ours, and Hyler has agreed to maintain public access to it. But what is the main problem with the public access to the lake?"

"It runs right through the plant," I said, sure now of where she was going.

"And what do people complain about most about that access?" Sheila asked us.

"The fact that it runs right through the plant!" Stu said. "The city has been after us for years to build a new access off Ascot Street so people won't have to drive through our plant site. Of course, we've never done it, because we haven't had to."

Everyone was getting in on this. "It has been a pain in the butt for us, too!" Amanda said. "It means having security on site 24 hours a day, and we still have some vandalism and theft."

We turned back to Sheila. "So what are you proposing?" I asked her.

"Simply this," she said. "We offer to construct a new access off Ascot Street, complete with a parking lot and maybe even public washrooms. In return, the city fast-tracks all the paperwork for our expansion."

"What about the cost, Sheila?" Stu asked. "We've suddenly increased our scope considerably."

"In that scenario, we don't go for the new building. It was only marginally better anyway. Instead, we go the less-expensive route of expanding our existing space, and building the new access. It will still be cheaper than the new building. Then the city feels like they win two ways: they don't get a big new 'factory' next to their subdivision, and they have a better, more convenient access to the lake."

I still get a cold chill when I think about how close I came to running across that little difficulty with the city much farther along, and how it would have affected the schedule and the assignment.

By scrambling hard, we managed to pull together a presentation for Ralph by the following Friday. We had even received tentative approval from the city for the expansion with the new access. By the time the meeting rolled around, there really was only one choice to make, but we figured that we would show Ralph all the reasoning that had gone into our final recommendation.

I was elected to make the initial presentation, although Sheila, Stu and Amanda were also in attendance to help me answer questions. I tried to keep it brief, so at the end of half an hour I was winding things down.

"And so, Ralph, here are the specifics of our recommendation. We will expand the existing manufacturing space. We will construct a new access for Hyler Lake, and we will build a new security fence between the plant and the lake. That, plus the fact that we won't have people driving through the plant all the time, should cut down on our security problems. In addition, we're recommending a new payroll and inventory control system to help cope with the new situation. The training programs will include some new-employee initiation sessions, and we're recommending some exciting new computer-based training for the operators of the new machines. We are also recommending a new supervisory seminar about performance management, for all new supervisors. If it works well, we'll expand it to include existing supervisors." I paused. "Once we have your approval on the preliminary design, we'll proceed with detailing it."

Ralph was busy taking notes, and didn't say anything for a few minutes. Finally he looked up. "How much do you estimate the recommended option will cost?"

I took a breath. Honesty had worked well so far. "Our guesstimate is now $1.6 million." Ralph scowled, and I continued hurriedly. "Like I explained to you before, we don't have enough detail to commit to a firm price. We will know better once we have detailed the design. But for now, $1.6 million is our best guess."

"What about time frame?" Ralph asked. "Can we complete this option by June?"

"Once again, Ralph, based on our best guess, yes, we believe so. We'll know better when we have completed the detailed design and the Execution Plan."

"And how long will that be?" he asked.

I hoped we had all guessed right about design. "Three months for everything to be complete," I told him. "Some things will be done sooner, but three months should do it for everything."

"Does that $1.6 million include design costs?" he asked me.

I was impressed with the question. Ralph seemed to be catching on to Martha's process. "All design costs are included in that estimate," I told him.

"Have you got a revised objective statement for me to sign?" I couldn't believe I was hearing this. In fact I had brought one with me. As soon as we had the new estimates, and the preliminary design information, I had revised the original statement. I had brought it along, thinking that I would have a devil of a time getting Ralph to sign the thing again.

"Give it to me now, but I can't sign it yet." He paused. "But you may as well go ahead and begin to detail the design for this option." We all smiled. "I can't promise anything," he continued. "I will have to get this increase approved by the board. But the way you've laid it out for me, it doesn't appear that we have much choice, at least if we still want to proceed." He turned to Stu. "I assume that you have rerun the numbers already?"

Stu nodded. "I've re-projected everything based on this new cost. Our projected five-year return on investment drops from 35 percent to 22. It still makes sense to proceed."

"Get me a copy of the new feasibility report by this afternoon. I want to have it when I talk to Henry Stanton." Stu agreed to have it to him before lunchtime.

Ralph then addressed all of us. "Except for the fact that you won't commit to a final cost, or a schedule, I like the way things have gone so far. But you must recognize the pressure I'm under. I'll continue to explain things to the board as we go, but they're my sponsors, and all they want is a commitment on final cost and schedule." He gestured toward me. "Will says that you'll be able to give me a final implementation schedule a week after the detailed design is complete. I need to have that as soon as possible." We all nodded, and I hoped that I wasn't off-base with my estimate.

As we got up to leave, Ralph asked me casually if I had chosen a software package yet.

I couldn't lie about it and say I had, because Ralph might ask me what it was. "Ah, we're just narrowing down the options," I said. "We should have our final choice by next week."

"Good!" He said. "I'm looking forward to getting regular reports from the package. In fact, I was thinking of having it installed on my own machine here. It should save you a lot of work."

I nodded as I walked out, although I wasn't sure that I was ready to have Ralph playing with our plans. And anyway, what were we going to use software for? We were three weeks in, and all we had needed so far was a word processor. I supposed that I would have to ask Martha.

# CHAPTER 14

I was sitting at my desk, staring at the page that Sheila had just put in front of me. The sheet was a regular $8^1/_2$ by 11-inch piece of paper, turned sideways. Along the top was a time scale starting on September 15th, and ending in December. At the left of the page was a list of what looked like all the activities we had talked about at our detailed design planning meeting yesterday. Next to each task, placed somewhere along the time scale at the top of the page, was a solid bar. The bar length was different for each of the different tasks. It looked something like this:

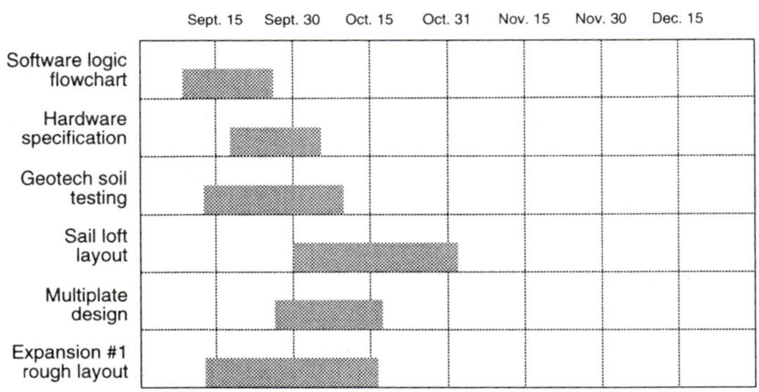


"It's a Gantt chart printout from our project management software program," Sheila told me. When I looked blank, she prodded, "You know, a Gantt chart. Otherwise known as a bar chart? The most important planning tool we have?" I started to recognize what I was looking at.

"Of course," I said. "To be honest, I was just a little fooled by the layout. I'm much more used to seeing really messy ones that have been drawn by hand."

"Well, then this one should look pretty good to you." She was not impressed that I was not impressed. "See," she said, pointing to the left-hand side of the page, "there are all of the activities in the detailed design. And the bars show when each activity is scheduled to start and finish."

This was something that Ralph was going to be happy to see: a schedule at last! On the Monday after our meeting with him, we had had a detailed design planning meeting. Sheila, Mark and Amanda, along with Les French, Harry Freeman, Luigi and I had identified what we thought was a complete list of all the tasks that had to be done for the detailed design to be complete. The tasks included the design of all of the building expansions (there would be three), re-layout of existing manufacturing space and layout of the new space, the hiring process, the training programs, the new payroll and accounting software, new parking lots, the new access off of Ascot Street, all of the detailed design steps.

Listing all of the tasks had taken the better part of the morning, and when we were done, I was a little concerned. "Okay gang," I told them, "we now have a list of tasks to do to complete the detailed design. But that is all we have, a list. How are we supposed to turn this into a schedule?"

"Don't worry about that," Sheila said. "That's one thing I am very familiar with. I did a lot of these for Al Burton. We'll just turn this list into a Gantt chart schedule. I can have that for you by tomorrow morning."

Sure enough, here she was with the schedule in hand. "How long is the detailed design going to take?" I asked her.

"Good news, Will: it looks like about nine weeks."

That was good news; we had told Ralph that we thought it would take 12 weeks. "Have you got contingencies built into that schedule?" I didn't want to commit anything to Ralph that wasn't well padded. If there was one thing I had learned from projects in the past, it was that they always take longer than you think.

"We've planned it out as carefully as we can, Will. You were in the meeting. I think we've accounted for everything."

Sheila didn't sound too convincing. "Stretch everything out a little so that it takes 12 weeks. I want to have a cushion in case something does go wrong." I didn't want to take any chances. "What about the cost?" After listing all of the tasks, we had figured out the resources required to do each . Sheila was supposed to estimate a cost based on the total time required of each resource.

"About $125,000, if we include all the Hyler resources." I was still getting used to the idea that we were going to charge all of our own people's time to this project. It sure made the whole thing a lot more expensive.

"That's a little more than we originally estimated," I told Sheila. "Where is the extra cost coming from?"

She looked defensive. "Like I told you before our meeting with Ralph, I was just guesstimating. There wasn't any extra cost. When we figured out all of the tasks and resources, it just came out higher than I had guessed."

"I'm not trying to blame you," I told her. "I was just wondering why the first guess was low."

"It seems pretty obvious to me," she said. "The first guess was just that: a guess. When we figured everything out in detail, we just had a lot better information." That made sense, although I knew a lot of people who liked to think that their guesses were good enough without any backup.

"Fair enough," I told her. "We are about $35,000 higher now on our cost estimate for the detailed design. Do you think we should get Ralph's approval of the new cost?" I had already made up my mind, but I wanted to get Sheila's reaction.

"We didn't actually tell him how much the detailed design was going to cost; we just gave him the total project cost. Personally, I wouldn't bother him. An extra $35,000 out of $1.6 million isn't much. Who knows, maybe the execution will cost less than we're estimating." That jibed with my thoughts. Why bother the sponsor over a mere $35,000?

"Ralph told me that he'll have the extra costs on our objective statement approved tomorrow. Why don't you start getting all of our ducks in a row so we can begin the detailed design as soon as I have the signed objective statement."

I looked again at the Gantt chart printout in front of me. "Let's get back to this project management software package for a minute. Ralph has been bugging me to do something about it for a while, but I've been putting off making a decision. Are you telling me that this package you are using is going to be our choice?" I was quite happy to leave that decision to Sheila. I was planning to stay as far away from the software as possible.

Sheila looked a bit like a child who had taken a cookie without asking. "Well, actually, Al and I had been evaluating project management software packages for about a month before he left. I just bought the one that I liked the most. But you can go through all of the demo packages if you like, and we can switch to the one you want."

I just smiled. "Sheila, I am extremely happy that you have already picked a software package." She looked relieved. "In fact, I wouldn't have known where to begin. We'll go with the program you've already selected."

I asked her to leave the Gantt chart printout behind, as I wanted to show it to my "consultant." She left after I told her that I would contact her the next day, as soon as I heard from Ralph, and I went down to the coffee room for a refill of Irish Mocha. Somebody in Accounting was married to a woman who owned about six gourmet coffee shops in Portland. As a result, we always had unusual, and good, coffee in our communal coffee pot.

I returned to my office and sat back down at my desk. Sipping my coffee, I looked over the bar chart. Not only did it show when each task was scheduled to take place, it was also simple and easy to understand. Give me a nice, simple tool any day over some complicated, mathematical chart that is confusing to read and hard to decipher. I expected that our Gantt chart was going to impress our "consultant."

I was a little nervous about going to see Martha that night. I guess I should say I was nervous in a different way, because seeing Martha always tended to make me nervous. I put it down to the tuna casserole we had for dinner, because I have never gotten along too well with tuna, but I was probably worried that Martha might pick some holes in what seemed to be the smooth fabric of the success we had achieved so far. As I expected, she wasted no time.

"You didn't listen to my advice did you, Willie?" She blew a smoke ring my way, and rocked back in her chair. I thought quickly. Hadn't I been listening to all of her advice? I tried to recall something she had told me that I'd decided to ignore. I came up blank.

"Martha, as far as I know, I've been doing everything you told me to do. And," I added, partly as proof of this statement, and partly to try to soften up the old girl with a little praise, "things have been going extremely well because of it."

Martha took her pipe out of her mouth and leaned forward in her rocking chair. With the stem she tapped the Gantt chart that lay on the little table between us. "This is your schedule for your detailed design, is it?" I nodded. "Let me ask you a question then, Willie. What happens to your finish date if this task here takes two weeks longer than you expect?" She was pointing to a task labelled 'Geotech assessment of base stability'.

I pretended to cough to give myself time to think. I could see from the bar chart that the task was supposed to start in three days and run for a week, but what was it? I tried to remember our detailed design planning session. I seemed to recall that Sheila said something about the soil on which one of the building expansions was going to be constructed being a little unstable because it was close to the edge of the lake. Yes, that was it! And in order to design the foundation properly, there had to be some kind of engineering assessment of the soil. I felt relieved. I hated looking stupid in front of Martha.

My relief was short-lived, however. Now that I knew what the task was, how was I supposed to figure out how a delay in this one little item would affect the finish date of the whole detailed design? I casually took my handkerchief out of my pocket to blow my nose and cover my confusion.

"You don't have a clue, do you Willie?" Martha asked me smugly. My handkerchief was halfway to my nose at this point, but since she was obviously seeing through my little ruse, I put it back in my pocket.

"This is complicated engineering stuff, Martha," I told her. "How am I supposed to know how a delay here will affect the finish date? I'm sure my designer could tell you." I hoped it was true.

"I'm not so sure, Willie. But if that is the case, how about this task?" She was pointing to one of the software design steps, something I did know about. "What happens to the finish date if this task is delayed two weeks?"

I hemmed and hawed for a few seconds, but couldn't come up with an answer. "There is an important lesson here, Willie, one that will be vital to understand when it comes time to plan the Execution. I won't tell you what it is just yet, though. I think you'll appreciate it more if you knock your head against it a few times. But I will repeat my hint: don't ignore the logic!"

The old bat wouldn't say anything more about it, even when I pestered her. All she would tell me was that learning the hard way might help me remember it. To make matters worse, she started having one of her coughing fits.

Tuesday night turned out to be a bad night all-round. After I helped Natalie put Martha to bed, I returned home to find that Jake had some kind of coughing sickness of his own. The poor little guy couldn't stop hacking. We ended up running the hot water in the shower to fill the bathroom up with steam, then Jenny and I took turns sitting with Jake in the steam bath until he finally fell asleep at about 3:00 a.m.

By 6:15 the next morning I was 2,000 feet beneath the surface of the ocean, collecting specimens of deep-sea plant life for the U.S. Oceanographic Survey. Suddenly an electronic beeper went off in my diving helmet, and I knew that I had less than six minutes of oxygen remaining. As I struggled to reach the surface, I faced a terrible dilemma: come up too quickly and die from the rapid decompression, or drown on the ocean floor. I was paralyzed until a voice spoke to me. It said: "Turn off the damn alarm!"

By the time I got to work I was starting to wonder if I shouldn't have just taken the day off. I am frequently thankful that I have never been captured by the 'enemy' (whoever they are these days) and tortured via sleep deprivation. I would happily tell them all I know inside of about 10 minutes. Since I don't know anything that they would likely want to hear, they would probably kill me anyway, but the point is that my sleep is important to me. Without enough of it I just don't function well.

Luckily there was a pick-me-up waiting for me on my desk. It was the revised objective statement, signed by Ralph. He had attached a note asking me to bring him the schedule for the detailed design as soon as I had it.

I ended up leaving work at about three in the afternoon, but it was still a very productive day. I met with Ralph to present him with Sheila's Gantt chart (after she had lengthened the schedule to 12 weeks), and to let him know that he could expect regular reports generated by our newly selected software package. On the spur of the moment, and against my better judgment, I also told him about our increase in the detailed design cost. To my surprise, he was fairly reasonable about the whole thing. I suppose I had prepared him well for the uncertainty of guessing at design in the early stages. We decided not to revise the objective statement yet, as it was a small increase relative to the overall budget, most of which was still a guess anyway.

I also got Sheila started on completing the detailed design. She told me that she was contracting for some of the engineering design, and putting Hans Schmidt, one of my people in Information Systems, in charge of all of the software work. Hans would be reporting directly to her for work on the assignment, and she needed my permission for this. It all sounded good to me, so I told her to charge ahead.

I arranged for Amanda, as the project administrator, to take over the software from Sheila. We got a copy of the program installed on her PC, and she started to read through the instruction manual. Sheila agreed to help out until Amanda was comfortable, but I was confident that it wouldn't be long. Amanda learns software very quickly. All she needed to learn from Sheila was what to use it for. How tough could that be?

In the end, I forgot all about what Martha had told me the night before. It didn't come back to haunt me until about four weeks later.

# CHAPTER 15

One of the nicest things about computers is that they provide you with the ultimate scapegoat. They are particularly effective in this role because of two characteristics:

1) Most people don't understand how they work.

2) They can't deny your allegations.

Because of this, you are free to place final blame on the damn things, and not many people will disagree with you.

People like me who work with computers tend not to appreciate this attitude for a couple of reasons. The first is that, due to our close relationship with the machines, people think of us as the 'human masters' of this alien race of creatures, one of which happens to be sitting on their desk attempting to cause them trouble. This means that computer users can transfer some of the blame onto us, or at the very least, have the satisfaction of yelling at something they know can hear them.

The second reason is that computers very rarely make mistakes. They do exactly what we tell them to do, and it usually turns out that the mistake is in our commands. As I am fond of telling people, all computers can do is add.

But systems people like myself are still far from perfect, and when the computer kicks out something I can't understand, my first instinct is always that there is a problem with the software. And so, four weeks later, I was hovering over Amanda's work station, trying to find out what was wrong with our project management software.

"Explain this to me again please, Amanda."

"Like I told you, Will, I've been keeping our plan up to date on a daily basis. Every time one of our detailed design activities starts, I put the actual start date into the program, and every time something finishes, I put that in too. I want to make sure that we stay right on top of this schedule."

"That's good," I told her. "I really do appreciate your efforts. But why is this a problem?"

"That part isn't the problem. The problem happened here." She pointed to the screen, which was displaying the Gantt chart schedule. Her finger was on one of the inventory control system design tasks. "Hans told me that he is having this task done by a local consultant because we don't have the expertise. It just finished now."

I looked at the screen, and noticed for the first time that there were two bars for every task. The top one appeared to be the planned start, duration and finish of the task, and I guessed that the bottom one would represent how long the task actually took. The task she was pointing to should have finished two weeks ago. "What does this do to our completion date for finishing the detailed design?" I asked, trying not to sound panicky.

"That's where the problem is," Amanda told me nervously. "I don't know! When I put in the actual finish date, the finish date for the whole schedule didn't change. That's when I suspected that we might have trouble. I went back and looked at the other design tasks that have finished. Look here and tell me what you see."

As I ran my finger down the screen, it appeared that there were several instances where the second bar (the actual) for a task was a little longer than the first. None were as late finishing as the software task, but several extended beyond their planned finish dates.

"It looks like most of our tasks are taking a little longer than planned." I told her.

"Bingo! Now don't you think that would have changed our scheduled completion date?" I told her I thought it would. "Which is why I think that we must have a problem with this software," she continued. "It doesn't seem to be calculating correctly. If it was, we'd have a new completion date with all of these delayed tasks."

I stepped back from the machine and tried to put my Information Systems hat on top of my project manager's hat. It didn't fit very well. "Let's call in Sheila. Maybe there is something about the software that we don't understand." Amanda looked doubtful, but I picked up the phone and dialed Sheila's local. Luckily she was in, and five minutes later she was looking over Amanda's other shoulder.

She couldn't figure it out either. Since we weren't about to check the code of the project management software program, I decided that we had better eliminate human error first. I asked Sheila to describe what she had done when she had put the design tasks into the program.

"I started by typing in the names of all the tasks. Then I typed in all of the resources we had planned to have on this project, and I included their hourly costs. Then I went back and assigned the resources to the tasks, just like we did on the flip chart in the initial planning session. After that, I went down the list of tasks and scheduled each one, based on my best guess of when it would take place."

"So how did you come up with a completion date for the detailed design?" I asked her.

"I got it from the finish date of the latest task that I had scheduled," she told me.

It appeared to make sense, but I was not yet ready to believe that the software program was the problem. Suddenly, my conversation with Martha from four weeks ago started to come back to me, and I could feel little beads of cold sweat forming on my back. I turned to Sheila. "What would be the impact on the completion date of the design if this task," I gestured to the one that had touched off this whole discussion, "finishes two weeks late?"

Sheila looked hard at the screen and chewed her bottom lip. Finally she said, "I can work it out, but I think it will change the completion date by about three weeks."

"Three weeks?" I said, just a little too loudly. "We don't have three weeks! I told Ralph 12 weeks for the whole thing."

Sheila gave me an exasperated look. "Don't forget, Will, I padded the schedule by three weeks, like you asked. Besides," she added, "you said it yourself: the design is a little unpredictable. That's all. Don't worry, we'll get it done."

"The fact that it's going to take longer is not what is bothering me," I told her. "It's the fact that we've been taken by surprise. And this software doesn't seem to be telling us what the new completion date is. Any ideas?"

Sheila continued to stare at the screen. "I guess I'll have to go through each task and give it a new start and finish date to make a new schedule."

"That's stupid!" Amanda interjected. "Why can't the software do the adjustments? I mean, what's it good for?"

Sheila was starting to get a little defensive. Not only did it appear that I was coming down on her for the design delay, now Amanda was criticizing her choice in software. "How will the software possibly know about new start and finish dates for each task unless we enter them?" she snapped at Amanda.

Amanda wasn't sure. "I don't know, Sheila. It just seems like there should be a better way."

I thought there should be a better way too, but Sheila assured us that this was how it was done on other projects, and that she would spend more time helping Amanda update the status.

"How long before you can give me a estimate of the new completion date?" I asked.

"About an hour," Sheila told me.

As I went back to my office, I couldn't help but wonder if maybe we weren't doing something wrong. An hour to recalculate the schedule! Not exactly lightning quick. I did not know how, but Martha had understood that we would run into problems at this point. I would have happily suffered a lung full of smoke rings to find an answer, but she was off visiting her son, Jenny's uncle, in New Jersey. She had a habit of going East in the fall to see the leaves change color. Personally, I figured there couldn't be too many trees left in New Jersey, but never having been anywhere in the state except Newark, I supposed I was in no position to judge.

The next eight weeks were some of the most stressful of my life. Not because things went wrong, they didn't. And not because things were out of control, they weren't. It was just a feeling that I was unprepared for any surprises. Every time something changed, and believe me, there were a lot of little changes, I had to yank Sheila off whatever she was doing to help Amanda figure out what the new completion date would be.

I tried to get Sheila to show Amanda or myself how to recalculate the schedule, but she had so much information in her head that we just couldn't seem to get the hang of it. All the while I cursed

Martha for being so cryptic, and for letting me learn whatever lesson I was supposed to be learning the hard way.

Halloween came, and Jenny and I took the kids around the neighborhood so that they could collect candy for me. It is tough to be a parent at that time of year, but I believe the sacrifice is worth it in the long run. It's just not healthy for kids to eat all of that junk food!

Consequently, I was at the health club riding a Life Cycle to rid myself of the caloric sacrifices I had made for my children, when one of the women who worked at the front desk approached me.

"Mr. Campbell?"

"Yes," I said, turning my head a little too suddenly. You would think that people who work in health clubs would be used to this kind of thing, but maybe she was new.

"There is a phone call for you at the front desk," she said, as she grabbed a towel and wiped frantically at my sweat on her face. I guess Wagon Wheels don't smell so great when they come out of your pores.

I hopped off the bike and headed for the front desk, giving the attendant a wide berth. I suddenly had a tight little knot in my stomach, and believe it or not, I was hoping it was some kind of home emergency and not my project.

The voice at the other end of the line said: "I've got some good news, and some bad news." It was Amanda.

"Can't you come up with something original?" I asked her. "If I had a nickel for every time I've heard that cliché..." I trailed off. After a few seconds of silence I said, "It's a good thing I don't pay you for your sense of humor."

"That was a joke?" she asked, a little too innocently.

"Just tell me the good news and the bad news," I said impatiently. "I'm in the middle of my workout."

"I just came out of a meeting of the Enderby City Council, and they've changed their minds about our new plant."

This made the tight little knot in my stomach even tighter. "Changed their minds?" I echoed.

As the users' representative, Amanda had done an excellent job in getting the city engineers to agree to all of our proposed changes at the plant. In fact, we were proceeding with the detailed design on the assumption that the city approved of our plans.

The one hitch was that the whole thing had to be passed by the city council. The engineers who worked for the city had assured us that whatever they recommended, the councilors would agree to, and that the approval was just a rubber-stamping process. Apparently, this was not the case.

"Remember Bud MacDonald?" Amanda asked me. I didn't. "He's one of the councilors, and he is also a retired civil engineer. He used to work for the water department in Portland." I slumped against the wall. Engineers did not seem to like me. "Anyway," Amanda continued, "he considers himself an expert on water and sewage systems, and he wants us to build a small on-site waste treatment facility to process all of our water before it reaches the municipal system."

I don't know about other people, but when I hear phrases like 'on-site waste treatment facility', I see dollar signs floating before my eyes. I slumped even harder against the wall I was already slumping against. "You said you had some good news," I said weakly.

"The good news is that we have the town's approval as long as we do the on-site waste treatment!" Amanda actually sounded excited. I decided to calm her down a little.

"Amanda, do you have any idea what this on-site treatment is going to cost? And how much time it will add to our schedule?"

"I don't know about the schedule," she said, "but I talked to Bud after the meeting..."

"Bud?" I interjected. "This guy is the enemy, and you're on a first-name basis?"

Amanda gave an exasperated huff. "He is not the enemy, Will. He is simply doing what he feels is his job. And anyway, as users' rep, I want to be on friendly terms with the users." She was right of course, so I didn't say anything. "Bud talked to me after the council meeting, and told me about a self-contained treatment system from ERMASCO that he figured would be large enough for our plant, and that would meet the city's requirements."

"How much?"

"About $50,000. And according to Bud, about four and a half weeks to do the extra design work for the installation."

I had mixed feelings about this information. When I heard $50,000, I was very relieved. I had been imagining a price about five times that figure. But the four and a half weeks for the design brought back my out-of-control feeling. I had no idea how much time that was going to add to our design schedule.

"I guess we'll have to get together with Sheila first thing tomorrow morning and figure out the impact of that on our detailed design schedule. And then I'll go in and see Ralph about the increased cost." I paused for a minute. It was important to give credit where credit was due. "And by the way, Amanda, I think you're doing an excellent job as users' rep. It's a good thing that one of us gets along well with the city."

I could tell she was pleased by the way she said, "I just hope you appreciate all the work I've put in."

When I hung up the phone, the guy at the front desk tossed me a towel. "What's this for?" I asked him.

"To wipe off the wall where you were slumping. Otherwise we'll have to charge you for repainting."

It's a good thing that Halloween comes only once a year.

For some reason that Sheila was never able to adequately explain, the extra four and a half weeks for design work on the onsite sewage treatment system did not make the completion date of the whole design process any later. I thought it would, but she said, "It has to do with how all the tasks interrelate. It's kind of hard to explain."

When things are 'kind of hard to explain', I tend to feel nervous. In the heat of the moment, I guess I had forgotten what I had learned from Martha: Any plan that is unexplainable is not really a plan.

In the end, I didn't exactly get burned by our poor plan for the detailed design, just a little singed. Our detailed design work was completed on the 18th of December, just a little more than 13 weeks from when we started. This was only one week over the estimate, so Ralph was quite pleased.

I had a different feeling. It was as if I had been dozing at the wheel of my car, and awakened to find that the car had driven off the road and then come to a stop at the edge of a cliff, all of it's own accord. Right up until the end of the eighth week, Sheila had been predicting that we would be finished in nine weeks. Then she discovered a few things that hadn't been done that needed to be done before a few other things. And some of those other things also had tasks that came before them that hadn't yet been done. When we finally finished only a week late, I felt that we had been saved from disaster by luck more than anything else, and I vowed not to let the same thing happen during the execution. In other words, I vowed to visit Martha a little more frequently.

Fortunately, that would be much simpler with the approach of Christmas. The old girl had been having such a good time watching leaves change in New Jersey that she had decided to stay out there for the whole fall, and wouldn't be arriving back in town until December 22nd. Things pretty much shut down at Hyler over the Christmas week, so I had not planned for anything to happen on the WindSailor assignment until after the 28th. I figured that this would give me plenty of time to find out about Execution Planning from Martha.

# EXECUTION PLANNING

# CHAPTER 16

"Would you like some eggnog?" Natalie asked me, temporarily interrupting Martha's cross-examination.

"Yes, please!" I answered gratefully. Anything to stop the heat for a few minutes.

I am one of those unlucky people who has an allergic reaction to milk. I've tried the Lactaid pills, but they don't help. I still get an upset stomach, and my sinuses are clogged for about two weeks after I have anything cow-related.

This is hard on me, because my favorite food in the whole world is cheese. Before I found out about my problem, I used to eat about two pounds of cheese a week. Jenny always tells me that with that rate of consumption, it is no wonder I have a problem.

All of this is by way of saying that I should have refused the eggnog, but didn't. About four times a year, usually Christmas, Easter and two other random occasions, I break down and have some type of milk product. Of course I never do it in moderation, so it generally takes me about two weeks to recover, during which I swear that it was the last time. But when the next special occasion rolls around, I'm ready to punish myself all over again.

I happily accepted the glass from Natalie, and looked over to see Jenny glaring at me. She is the one who has to put up with my complaining after every binge. I raised my glass to her, and took a sip.

It was Christmas Eve, and we were all at Jenny's parents' place having our annual Eggnog Fest and Present-Opening Celebration. Jenny's sister and her family were down from Seattle, and all the kids were playing noisily together on the living room floor, never straying far from the presents under the tree. This was going to be Jake's first Christmas as a 'conscious' participant (he was almost three now), and we were all looking forward to it.

"So go on, Willie," Martha prodded me. "Finish up your story."

I had been giving her a summary of what had happened during the detailed design process, and I was just about finished.

"In the end we managed to wrap it up in a little over 13 weeks, despite, or maybe because of, all my worrying." The relief of having finished, along with the eggnog, was making me a little sentimental. "Everything is done. All the design for the training, new systems, org charts, blueprints, the works! We had a team meeting. Everyone was there, including Ralph and Stu. Leslie brought some champagne, and we all toasted when Ralph signed-off on the detailed design. It was a great way to break for Christmas."

Ralph had pulled me aside after our little party to ask when I would have the schedule complete for the execution. Apparently some of the board members were still impatient with our process and wanted to be assured that we would have the assignment completed on time. I had promised it to Ralph the first week in January. I hoped that was enough time.

"Did you manage to figure out what was causing your uneasiness during the detailed design?" Leave it to Martha not to savor the success, but to look for what we did wrong.

It was Christmas time and all, so I figured that I might as well be truthful. "To be honest, no. I just had this feeling that we weren't on top of what the implications of the changes were."

Martha shook her head and said, "Take a little stroll with me out to the porch."

"It's about 35 degrees out there!" I protested. Thirty-five degrees isn't very cold, especially when you've grown up with East Coast winters, but it's amazing how quickly you get soft when you move to a warmer climate. Besides, I knew that the only reason Martha wanted to go outside was so she could smoke her pipe. Pipe smoking did not justify freezing, at least not in my book.

"Don't be a wimp, Willie," she said as she got out of her chair and tottered toward the front door. "A little brisk weather is invigorating. How do you think I got to be 89?"

Bad luck? I thought to myself, but I didn't say it out loud. Sighing, I got up from my nice warm chair, helped Martha on with her coat, took mine off the coat rack and followed her onto the porch.

It was actually quite a nice night. Darfield is small enough that the city lights don't outshine the stars, and this Christmas Eve was clear and beautiful. As I looked up at the sky, savoring the clear night, a smoke ring drifted past my nose, sort of like a warning shot across the bow. It was Martha's way of saying that it was time to get down to serious business. I looked over and she was in her accustomed place, rocking chair rocking, and pipe burning.

"I'm a little disappointed, Willie," she told me. "I thought you might have worked out your problem before I got back from New Jersey." She blew another smoke ring in my general direction.

"Believe me, I tried," I said. "But with everything else I had to think about, it wasn't easy."

As always, Martha didn't see it my way. "On the contrary, Willie, it is not only very easy, but also very obvious." I could tell by the way she was over-using my nickname that it must be something she thought was particularly simple. "Tell me again why it was you felt out of control."

At times like these I always hope for brilliant insight. I hate being browbeaten, especially by elderly women. Of course nothing came to me, so I resigned myself to having Martha lead me through the maze. "I felt out of control because I wasn't able to see how changes in some activities affected our whole schedule. Every time something changed, I had to get my designer to tell me what it meant. And even she didn't always know for sure how to rethink the schedule. Right up until the end, she thought we were going to finish in nine weeks, and then she discovered she had forgotten about something, and it took us an extra five weeks to complete. Luckily, I had padded the schedule a little, and the sponsor was still quite happy."

I guess I sounded a little too smug when I said this last part, because Martha jumped on me. "If you depend on luck to get you through assignments, you're in for a lot of pain," she said crossly. "Whenever you don't understand something as fundamental as how all of the activities go together, it's time to think hard about the problem, not just press on and hope it doesn't matter!"

Sure, easy for her to say. She didn't have the President of the company breathing down her neck, asking when things were going to be finished. Of course I didn't say any of this to Martha. Instead I said, "Don't you think adding a little slack to the schedule is a good idea?"

Martha took her pipe out of her mouth, then hawked and spat off the porch. Sometimes the old girl can be a real charmer. "Understanding the fundamentals of the situation is paramount, Willie. Padding schedules that are based on guesses is not a very useful way to try to make up for this lack of understanding. You got lucky this time. Do you want to be asking yourself 'Do I feel lucky?' during the Execution Phase as well?"

I decided I had better sit on my ego and try to figure out what Martha was telling me. "No," I said. "Just explain to me how to get an understanding of the fundamentals of the situation."

Martha looked away from me, up at the stars. She took a long pull on her pipe and held the smoke in her lungs until I thought she would explode. Finally she let it out. "Let's leave the detailed design for a moment, since it sounds like it's pretty much complete, and let's think about the Execution Plan. If you had to draw me a picture of the assignment as it sits right now, what would it look like?" She looked over at me expectantly.

"Martha, that is a bizarre question! What would it look like? I have no idea. I don't see how you could even think of drawing a picture."

She picked up a pad of paper that had been sitting beside her rocking chair and held it toward me. "Humor me, Willie. Just draw it."

I took the paper from her and stared at it. Draw what the assignment looked like? To kill time I reached inside my coat for a pencil. Some people might think it looks nerdy, but I always keep a writing implement or two inside my coat. As I took out the pencil, I was inspired. On the pad of paper I drew something that looked like this:

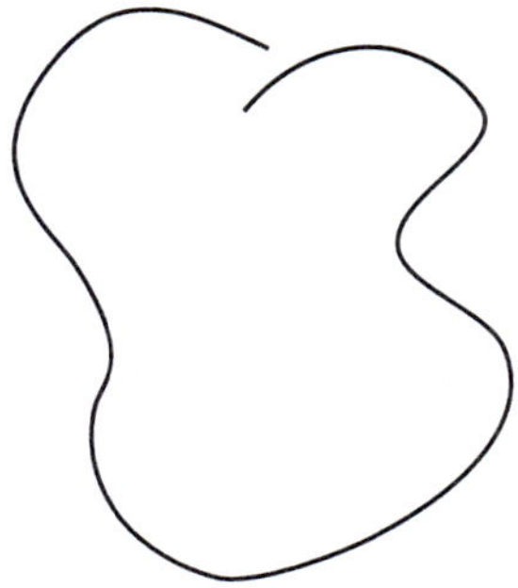

If my last name was Picasso, it probably would have been worth about $400,000. Being a Campbell, I turned the pad back toward Martha for her comments. All she said was, "Explain it."

"This big blob represents all of the work that has to be done during the Execution: all of the construction, all of the hiring, all of the training, everything. There are probably several hundred tasks that have to be done, and right now they are all jumbled up in this big blob of work." I felt as if I had just done a Rorschach ink-blot test.

It must have been the answer Martha was expecting, because she went right on with her questions. "Why have you drawn it as one big blob instead of as a bunch of little blobs? Say, one for each task?"

"Because," I told her, "you wanted me to draw the project as I see it now. We haven't figured out what all of the individual tasks are yet. Right now it's just one big mess, and by next Monday we have to have a schedule and a cost for this blob."

Martha surprised me by saying, "Very good, Will. You have a pretty accurate picture of where you stand. Or," she added, "where you sit." She chuckled to herself, although I have no idea why she found this funny. "How will you be able to take this big blob and put a cost on it, and figure out how long it will take?"

Why do you think I am here, Martha? I said to myself. To act as a human smoke ring target? Out loud, I described what we had done for the detailed design plan. "We'll try to break the blob down into individual tasks, assign resources to them, and then schedule them." I wasn't too confident about this, since it hadn't quite worked the last time.

"And what will you need to know about each individual task?" Martha asked.

I rattled off the information we had collected last time: "What the task is, how long it takes, and the person or people who are going to do it."

Martha's questions continued. "And how will you use this information to schedule this task along with all the others?"

I opened my mouth to answer, and then closed it again when I realized that I didn't know. With the detailed design, I had just let Sheila work out the schedule. She had tried to explain to me how she had done it, but I couldn't understand. "I'm not really clear on that part, Martha. In fact, that's where we had most of our problems with the detailed design."

"I'll give you a hint, Willie," she said. "You are missing one piece of information about each task."

Missing information? What else was there to know? "I don't know what you mean, Martha."

"I already told you a little bit about this, back when we were talking about the detailed design. Don't you remember?" Without waiting for me to answer, she went on. "Let me try to give you a better hint." I almost asked her why she couldn't just tell me, but I knew by now that this was not her way. She picked up the pad of paper and tore off my Impressionistic blob. "Tell me, Willie, what do you have to do in the morning to get ready for work? And give me your pencil." She reached out her hand.

I handed her the pencil and looked at her questioningly. "To get ready for work?"

"Trust me, simple examples make complicated truths simple. Tell me."

I played along. "Well, I get out of bed, I shave, I have a shower, I get dressed, eat breakfast and read the paper, and then drive to work." I paused and then said: "That's not strictly true. I also help Jenny get the kids up, maybe change a diaper, help make the kids some breakfast, have some mashed bananas spilled on my tie, change my tie, notice there are also bananas on my shirt, change my shirt..."

"Enough, Willie!" Martha interrupted. "Let's keep it simple." She turned the paper toward me. On it was written:

**Shower**
**Shave**
**Get out of bed**
**Eat breakfast**
**Get dressed**
**Drive to work**
**Read the paper**

"Is this what you do in the morning?" she asked me. I allowed as how it was close enough. She continued, "Let's suppose that we are doing an Execution Plan for what you do in the morning, Willie. We have a list of the activities. What do we need after that?"

This seemed like a stupid exercise to me, but I said, "We need to know who is going to do each task, which will be me, and we need to estimate how long each one takes."

"Let's do just that," Martha said.

When we were done, the list looked like this:

| | **Who?** | **How long?** |
|---|---|---|
| **Shower** | **WC** | **8 minutes** |
| **Shave** | **WC** | **7 minutes** |
| **Get out of bed** | **WC** | **10 minutes** |
| **Eat breakfast** | **WC** | **25 minutes** |
| **Get dressed** | **WC** | **8 minutes** |
| **Drive to work** | **WC** | **15 minutes** |
| **Read the paper** | **WC** | **25 minutes** |

"It takes you 10 minutes to get out of bed in the morning?" Martha asked me, rather overdoing the incredulity, in my opinion.

"I like to listen to the news on the radio," I said defensively. "Anyway, you're supposed to be illustrating a point, not critiquing my bedroom habits."

Martha turned the pad toward me. "Would you say that this is an adequate Execution Plan for your morning routine?"

"You don't have them in the right order, but otherwise that just about says it all."

"You've just hit on something, Willie," Martha said, and she looked at me as if she expected to see a lightbulb over my head any minute.

"The fact that they are not in the right order? Anyone can see that. What's the big deal? You just rearrange them until they make sense. For example, getting out of bed should be first, then shaving, then showering, and so on." I paused. "What's your point?"

Instead of answering my question, Martha handed me the pad of paper and started to load up her pipe again. "Put the sequence in a column on the right-hand side." When I was done, the page looked like this:

| | Who? | How long? | Sequence |
|---|---|---|---|
| **Shower** | **WC** | **8 minutes** | **3** |
| **Shave** | **WC** | **7 minutes** | **2** |
| **Get out of bed** | **WC** | **10 minutes** | **1** |
| **Eat breakfast** | **WC** | **25 minutes** | **5** |
| **Get dressed** | **WC** | **8 minutes** | **4** |
| **Drive to work** | **WC** | **15 minutes** | **7** |
| **Read the paper** | **WC** | **25 minutes** | **6** |

I handed the pad back to Martha. She glanced at it and said, "Does it take you an hour and 38 minutes from the time you wake up until the time you arrive at work?"

"No," I said, "it takes more like an hour or an hour and 10 minutes. Why?"

She tapped the page. "That's what it says here."

I took the pad back and added up the times listed in the How long? column. Sure enough, the total was 98 minutes. I stared at the list for a second, unsure of where the extra time was coming from. "I see the problem, Martha: I read the paper and eat breakfast at the same time." I handed the list back to her again. We were getting into a serious game of hot potato with that list.

Martha looked at it again. "This still tells me that it takes you an hour and 38 minutes." She handed it back. "Do you understand what this list is telling us now, and it's not doing a very good job, that it didn't tell us a few minutes ago?"

"Sure," I said. "The order you are supposed to do the tasks in." Suddenly, a lightbulb did start to go on over my head. "Wait a minute! This is where the problems started for us in the detailed design! We had a list of activities, but we weren't really sure of the sequence. At least none of us except Sheila. And that meant we couldn't tell what would happen if certain tasks went long." I stopped for a minute and thought. "Come to think of it, Sheila wasn't really sure of the sequence, since she kept making mistakes."

Martha looked pleased. "I would be a little more precise than the word 'sequence', Will. In fact, the information you need to collect about each activity or task is: what it is, how long it will take, who will do it, and how it relates to all the other activities. Not exactly the sequence, but how all of the activities fit in with each other."

She paused and puffed on her pipe for a few minutes. When she continued, she was quite somber. "Will, this is something that I don't expect you to grasp right away. Not because you are stupid...this isn't that complicated...but because it is an idea that seems to elude most people. The idea is this: the logic of how the activities must go together to produce the desired outcome of your assignment determines the schedule of your project, not the other way around. Most people are guilty of what I call 'Gantt chart thinking'. When it comes time to plan the Execution, they figure out what the tasks are, and then simply decide when they ought to take place, using nothing more than a calendar and a sketchy, intuitive grasp of what the interdependence among the tasks may be. The result is a schedule that is not based on cause-and-effect logic." She looked at me and smiled. "Sort of like what you handed me, back in October."

Everything she said rang true, especially with this assignment. Sheila had taken all of our tasks for the detailed design and scheduled them directly on a Gantt chart. But without the logic of how all of the tasks were connected, she had to guess at what would happen when things went wrong. The results were pretty inaccurate, and I supposed that the more complex the plan, the greater the chance of a mistake.

Martha continued on, and began to wax philosophical. "When you are figuring out how to execute an assignment, you are not creating something new. You are simply revealing the underlying structure of the 'best' way for things to go together. Let me give you an example, Will. The human race did not invent the elements on the periodic table. They were always around, waiting to be discovered." She pointed her pipe stem at me. "It is the same with projects. Your job during the Execution Planning stage is to reveal the logic of the best approach. And that logic is what determines how long your project will take. A must be done before B, and B before C and D. If you want to do things otherwise, and compromise the logic, your chances of achieving your desired outcome decrease dramatically."

She was getting a bit far out for me, and I began to suspect that the drink she was sipping had a little too much Christmas cheer in it. "This philosophical stuff gives me a headache, Martha. Can you give me an actual example of when the logic was ignored?"

She glared at me a little and puffed on her pipe. Obviously she thought philosophy was important. It's not that I don't, it's just that I relate to the real world a little more easily. "I don't have to," she told me. "You can give me one from your detailed design process."

As soon as she said it, I knew that she was right. It was one of the reasons why we took 13 weeks instead of nine to complete the detailed design. Sheila had scheduled the layout of the new manufacturing and warehousing space independently of the design of the new inventory control system. In fact, it happened that they were both supposed to be done in the eighth week. What Sheila forgot was that the inventory control system was going to identify specific inventory locations around the plant. So we were missing a bunch of information on where and how big the various storage and holding spaces would be throughout the plant, and it delayed the completion of the plant layout until the inventory control system design was done. In essence, we had tried to do two activities simultaneously when they had to be done in sequence. I related the story to Martha.

She nodded her head and stared out at the night sky. "You would be amazed, Will, at how often a schedule is derived not from the logic, but from someone's guess. Of course the fact that it was a guess shows up during the execution. Unfortunately, that is when it's most expensive to correct it."

I was not all that amazed. In the past, I never thought consciously about the logic of an assignment when putting together schedules. I suppose it must have been in the back of my mind, as I'm sure it was in the back of Sheila's mind, but I never thought of it as determining the schedule.

I looked down at the pad in front of me. "I have one problem with all of this, Martha. It looks like it gets really complicated. Even our detailed design plan had about 50 tasks on it. How do you show all of the logic on this list without boggling your mind?"

Martha looked back at me and smiled. "You don't."

"You don't? Then how do you do it?

"Let's just say," she said, "that a picture is worth a thousand lists."

Santa was kind to everyone that Christmas. Jake and Sarah both received toys too numerous to mention. Jenny gave her mother a beautiful handknit sweater, and was given a pair of top-quality leather hiking boots. Fred got the handyman's usual assortment of tools for his workshop, where his gifts to everyone else had been handmade: a toy box for Sarah, a rocking horse for Jake, a spice rack for Jenny, and some lovely lawn animals for Natalie. I've always wanted wooden skunks on my lawn. Maybe Fred will make me some one day. I can only hope.

We all chipped in and bought Martha a brand new pipe and a large supply of her favorite tobacco. Pipe paraphernalia has become a regular Christmas gift for Martha. Thank God she smokes that pipe, or we wouldn't have a clue what to get her.

And as for me, I received the usual assortment of things a young father and son-in-law receives: new ties, socks, underwear and aftershave. But I got something even more valuable, from Martha. Something that I couldn't wait to try out at work the following week.

# CHAPTER 17

I had the feeling that my personal popularity was at an all-time low with my teammates. I could tell this by the expressions on people's faces as they sat around the conference table and stared into their coffee. It was December 28th, the Thursday after Christmas, and not even our now-traditional box of donut holes was making a dent in the black cloud that hung near the ceiling of the conference room. I had been expecting a little bad feeling, but as the Californians like to say, the reality of all the negative energy was getting me down.

At Hyler our business is quite seasonal. From January to July we are frantically busy preparing for the summer season, while the rest of the year is quite a bit more relaxed. As a result, it has become somewhat of a tradition for everyone at Hyler to take a holiday from December 23rd until after the New Year. In fact, that period is not even considered part of our regular holiday time. The factory shuts down, and only keeners and losers – those with nothing else to do – show up during the Christmas break.

Right now I wasn't sure whether my project team considered me a keener or a loser. Maybe both. However, we had a WindSailor to deliver, and we didn't have an Execution Plan. I had been worried since the beginning of the assignment that we wouldn't be ready for this coming season, and now I wanted to find out for certain. I had been on the phone the previous day convincing everyone to sacrifice some of the Christmas break.

Mark Goldman started us off, with a rousing round of, "How long do you think we'll be here?" which immediately got everyone's attention.

I began with my team-building address. "Thanks for coming in today, folks. I apologize for breaking in on your holidays, but Ralph wants to see an Execution Plan right after the New Year, so this is our only time to get it done. As to your question, Mark, I expect we'll be here until about 2:00 p.m. or so." Everyone groaned. "We may be finished a little sooner, but I want to get the first cut at our Execution Plan done today."

At this point Sheila piped up with, "I've loaded the project management software onto my laptop, Will. I was thinking that, to save time, we could plan the execution right on the computer." This drew a lot of nods from the crowd. People often think that if there is a computer involved, things will go faster.

Fortunately, Martha had warned me about this. "Actually Sheila, I want to approach this Execution Plan in a slightly different way. I've been in touch with the project consultant again, and she has suggested some new ideas that I want to try."

"She?" said Luigi. "The last time I heard about that consultant, she was a he." Trust Luigi to pick up on something like that.

"Sorry." I corrected myself. "He. I've had a little too much eggnog and it's rattled my brain. Anyway, I want to try his process." I turned to Sheila and Amanda. "He also seems to have solved our computer software problem." Of course, after Martha had explained things, it was obvious that it wasn't a problem with the software at all, but I thought I would save that until later.

I stood up and walked over to the wall of the conference room. Like a lot of companies, we have an erasable whiteboard hanging on one wall of the room, although at four feet by eight feet, Hyler's board is a little bigger than average. Martha had assured me that I would need all the space I could get.

I turned to address the group. "We are going to use something called a dependency chart to help us develop our Execution Plan." I had thought hard about how I could briefly summarize Martha's ideas for them. "Our assignment now looks like this." On the whiteboard I drew a reasonable facsimile of the blob I had drawn for Martha. "The Design phase is complete, and there is now a whole bunch of activities to be done so that we can be ready to produce the WindSailor this year.

"What we have to do to create the Execution Plan is to break this huge blob of stuff into discrete tasks that we can assign resources to, cost, schedule, track and eventually accomplish." I took the marker and drew lines across my blob, sectioning it into little pieces to illustrate how the blob was just a bunch of activities.

"Our job today is to identify each of those activities. But to do our Execution Plan properly, we need to know four things about each one of these bits of work: what it is, how long it takes, who or what is needed to do it, and how it relates to all of the other tasks." I stopped and wrote the four things on the whiteboard.

***Description***
***Duration***
***Resource(s)***
***Predecessor(s)***

"The first three are easy to figure out. We do it all the time, and we did it effectively during the planning of the detailed design. The fourth item – how each task relates to all of the others – is not so easy.

"If there were only a few activities, we could just number them from one to the end. Our assignment is much more complicated than that, and most of the activities will not be sequential. In other words, we'll have several tasks going on at any one time, and we will need to be aware of all sorts of complicated relationships among them.

"So instead of writing all that information down in a big table or a list, we are going to draw a picture." I took a three-by-four-inch pad of sticky notes from my pocket and held it up to the group.

"We are going to put each of our tasks on one of these yellow stickies – name, resource and duration." On the top sticky I wrote out a sample task:

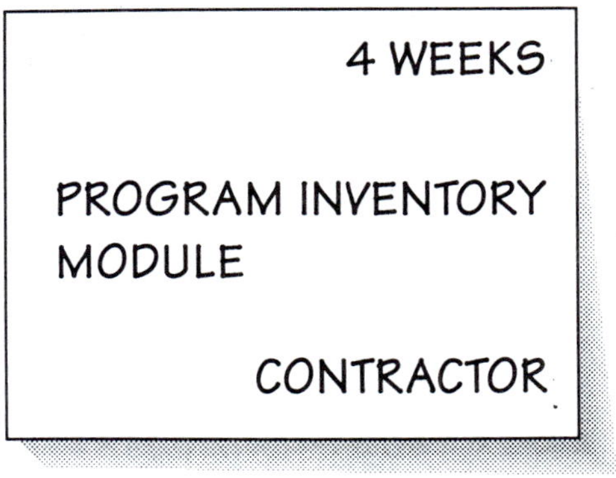

"As you all know, some of our tasks will relate to upgrading our existing information systems. For a sample, I've picked one of those." I read the information on the sticker. "Once we identify a task, we stick it on the whiteboard." I stuck the note in the middle of the board.

"Now comes the tricky part: how does this task relate to all the other tasks? Since we don't have any other tasks up there, we can't really show any relationships, so let's make another task." On another sticky note I wrote:

2 WEEKS

INSTALL AND DEBUG
INVENTORY
CONTROL SYSTEM

CONTRACTOR

I read off the information to everyone, then turned to the whiteboard. "Now we have a second task. Anyone care to guess how it relates to the one we already have up here?"

"It comes after it," Amanda volunteered.

"Exactly," I said. "It comes right after it. So now I stick this task up to the right of the first task." I did this, and uncapped my marker. "The final thing we need to do is show that the two are related. Any idea about how we are going to do that?"

"With a line," Sheila said, and without waiting for me to draw it, she continued: "Now I understand the problem we had with the software! It was missing information. I had all of those lines inside my head, but not in the machine." It was the same revelation that I had had while talking with Martha, but I didn't want to spend a lot of time on it now.

"Precisely, Sheila." I drew a line from the first task to the second, and put an arrow on the end, pointing to the second. The whiteboard looked like this:

"This picture is called a dependency chart because it shows how all the activities depend on each other, and according to my consultant, it is the simplest, best way to plan the Execution."

People were starting to buy into this idea. Leslie said, "This makes a lot of sense! It's big and visual so that the whole group can get involved in the planning. I was expecting that we would all have to be hunched over a computer screen."

I tried to capitalize on what Leslie said, by mentioning a couple of other advantages that Martha had demonstrated. "Using these sticky notes and the erasable whiteboard means that we have a lot more flexibility during the planning. Anytime we don't like what we've got, we can move the stickers somewhere else, erase the lines and draw new ones. And according to Marth–" I had to catch myself, "–Martin, the consultant, once the dependency chart is finished, the whole thing is ready for computer input." Only Amanda and Sheila seemed to care about that one.

At this point, both Mark and Alice were looking at me with that I-don't-really-believe-what-you're-saying-have-you-been-drinking look. Martha had warned me to confront the skeptics early, otherwise the planning process could fall apart, so I said, "Mark, Alice, something seems to be bothering you two."

They looked at each other, and Mark spoke up. "Isn't that dependency chart thing going to be awfully complicated? I mean, wouldn't it be simpler to just draw a bar chart or work from a list?"

"That's what I was thinking too, Will," Alice chimed in. "I may not have gotten along with Al Burton very well, but he was a project management expert, and his project plans were always simple bar charts, and very easy to understand. How come he didn't use something this complicated?" I seemed to recall that the last time we talked about it, Alice didn't think Al knew what he was doing. It's funny how our memories can be so selective.

"Let me ask you both two simple questions. Do you think it is important to know the logic of how the tasks relate?" I waited for their answer. Finally they nodded their heads, and gave me a grudging "yes." "Okay, we need to know the logic. Now, how can we best keep track of the logic?"

After a pause, Mark said, "I see what you're getting at. Even a small project has lots of links to remember. Keeping them inside your head would be a disaster, and anyway, you would have no way of showing anybody else how the tasks fit together."

Alice still wasn't convinced. "But it's still going to be pretty complicated."

"It will only be complicated if you try to conceive of the whole thing at once. At the individual task level, it will really be quite simple. You'll be able to look at one of these stickers, see what the task is, how long it takes, who or what is going to do it, then look at the lines to see how it relates to other tasks." I hoped that this was getting through.

"I guess I'll go along with it for now," Alice said finally. "We'll see what the final product looks like."

Sheila said, "Don't forget, Alice, once we have all this information, we can produce a bar chart like you would normally see. Only this time it will be based on something other than guesses."

I was anxious to get going, so I continued, "Martin also suggested two other things. The first was that we plan the project from the end to the beginning. He called this objective-driven logic."

"You mean start at the end of the project and work backwards?" Luigi asked. "Why do that? It's only going to make the whole thing confusing."

Personally, I agreed with Luigi, but Martha had assured me that it would give us a better plan. "According to the consultant, looking at it from the point of view of 'It is finished, now how did we get here?' will give us a different perspective on the plan, and help us create a better one." I gave them Martha's example verbatim. "Think of a jig-saw puzzle. When you dump it out of the box onto the table, the first thing you do is look at the picture on the box so you can see where you are supposed to end up."

Alice said, "Well if your consultant does it that way, we should probably give it a try."

It always amazes me that people can be so accepting of so-called 'expert' opinions. In the future, whenever I have a good idea, I'll just claim that some consultant suggested it.

"What was the second thing, Will?" Mark asked, getting us back on track.

"We are going to put this plan on a time scale." I turned to the whiteboard and began drawing vertical lines, about a sticker-width apart. "The space between the lines will represent one week. This way, when we are done, we'll immediately have a rough idea about how long this should take." When I finished the time scale I turned around to face the group once more.

"I'm afraid that there are two more things that I need to introduce about dependency charts: float, and the critical path."

This brought looks of dismay. "Does this have to do with PERT or one of those fancy mathematical models?" Sheila asked. "That stuff is impossible to work with. Too much math!" Suddenly one of my leading supporters was dragging me down. At the mention of the word 'math' I could see dependency charts losing favor in everyone's eyes.

To be honest, when Martha had explained it to me, the same thoughts crossed my mind. I had done some work back in college with PERT charts and the critical path method, as well as with arrow and network diagrams. At the time, I didn't even understand what they were for; I thought they were just complicated mathematical models. No one had explained the underlying principles to me.

"Relax. There is no math involved! And the two ideas are very simple. Let me illustrate them for you with an example." I turned to the planning board and picked up the pad of sticky notes. I said a silent prayer that I would be able to make this look as easy as I had in practice. "I'm going to plan a very simple project to illustrate how dependency charts work, and also to show you float and the critical path. I won't even use real task names, just letters of the alphabet. Now, what is the last task in any project?"

Everyone looked back at me with a blank expression. After several long seconds of silence, Luigi asked, "Why are we starting with the last task?"

People's ability to forget what you have just told them is impressive. I suppose it's just another selective-memory phenomenon. "Remember, team, we are using objective-driven logic. That means starting from the end and working backwards." When no one said anything for several more long seconds, I decided to help them out a little. I wrote on one of the stickers, and said, "The last task in any project is this task," I held up the sticker so they could see it. It looked like this:

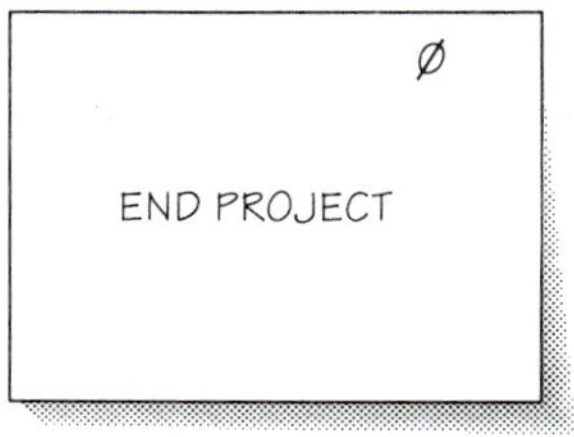


"This is a milestone. It has a zero time duration, and it just marks the event of the end of the project." I turned and stuck it on the planning board. "The next-to-last last task in the alphabet project is task **Z**. Task **Z** takes two weeks." I wrote this on a sticker and peeled it off the pad. "Task **Z** must be done before the end of the project, and we have to show its duration on the time scale. Believe it or not, it's really quite simple." I turned to the whiteboard and, sticker in hand, counted back two weeks from the end project sticker, and put the sticker down. Then I drew a line from the task **Z** sticker to the end project sticker and put a little arrow on the end of the line. The whiteboard looked like this:

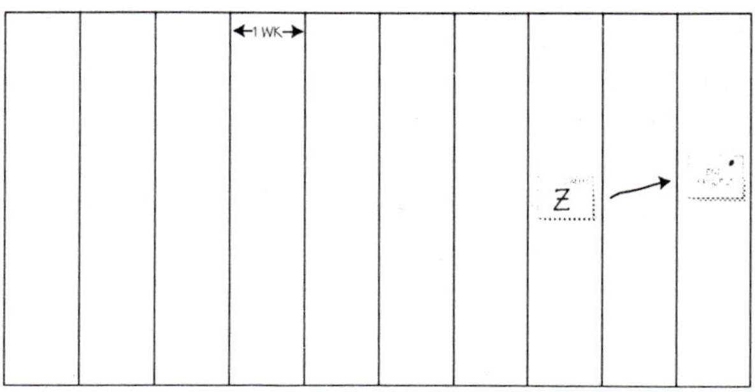

"I changed my mind," Mark said. "This is too frigging simple. We'll be here forever if we have to do this for the whole project!"

"Just give me a chance, Mark! I haven't finished yet." I tried to hurry things along. "Now I just ask myself a simple question: What has to be the case before we can start task **Z**? And as I answer that question for each task, we generate more tasks, we stick them on the chart, and very quickly," here I looked pointedly at Mark, "we generate a plan. In this case, task **M** must be finished before task **Z** starts." I had been going to use most of the alphabet for the demonstration, but I decided to cut to the chase.

"Task **M** takes three weeks." I wrote the name and duration on the sticker. On the board I counted back three weeks, put up the sticker, and drew a line from **M** to **Z**. The whiteboard now looked like this:

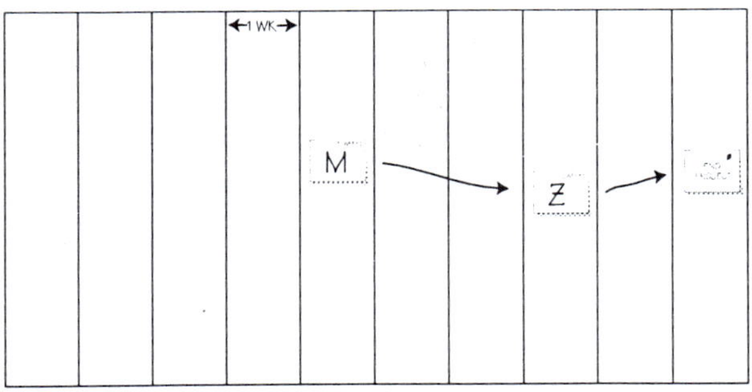


"Is there anything else that comes before task **Z**?" I asked the group. I had intended it as a rhetorical question, but Alice said, "I have the feeling that you are going to tell us."

Ignoring her, I continued. "In fact, there is! Task **L** also comes before task **Z**. Task **L** takes two weeks." I wrote this on a sticker, put it on the board and drew the line. This is what the whiteboard now looked like:

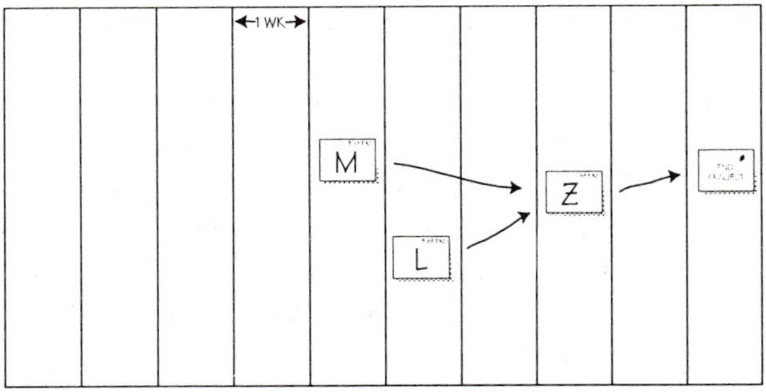


"If you can hang on for three more tasks," I said, "all will be revealed. There is nothing else preventing us from starting task **Z**, so now we have to pick either **L** or **M** and work backwards from there. Any preferences?" They say that effective speakers try to get their audience to participate as much as possible, but my audience seemed to feel like they were at a New York crime scene; they did not want to get involved.

"Well, then," I continued, after more silence, "Let's pick task **L**. What has to be the case before we can do task **L**? As it turns out, we need to have completed task **D** before we can do **L**. Task **D** takes two weeks." I wrote this on a sticker and put it on the board. The picture now looked like this:

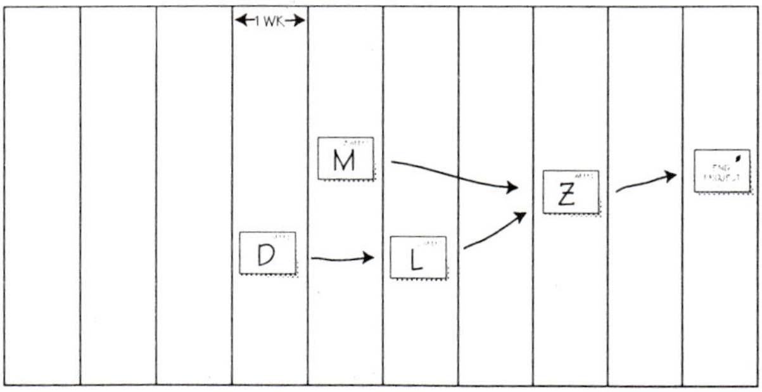


"Anything else before task **L**? In this case, no. So let's move on to task **M**. What has to be done before task **M**?" I paused to let the team ponder this question. Before they went to sleep, I gave them the answer. "In fact, before task **M** can start, task **D** must be done. In other words, task **L** has the same predecessor as task **M**. That's okay, it happens all the time in projects. But we do have one problem. Can anybody see what it is?"

Amanda finally spoke up. "Task **D** isn't finished before task **M** starts."

"Exactly!" I said enthusiastically. "Because we are doing this on a time scale, we can see right away that **D** has to start a week earlier than we thought, so that it can be done before **M**. Luckily, we are using an erasable board and movable tasks. I'll just move **D** and erase the line, then connect it to **M**." When I was finished, the board looked like this:

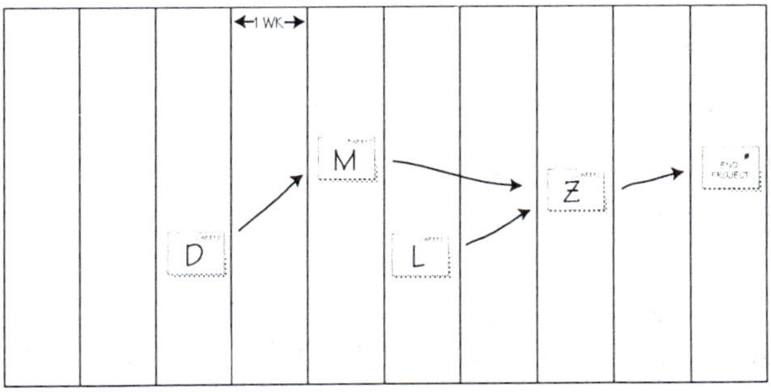


"There is one problem, though. Can anybody see what it is?"

Mark pointed it out. "**D** used to be linked to **L**, but now it isn't."

"Good!" I said. "And that is where the concept of float comes into play. Float is the slack time between when **D** ends and **L** begins. We show it on the dependency chart with a squiggly line." I drew in the dependency relationship on the board, so the picture now looked like this:

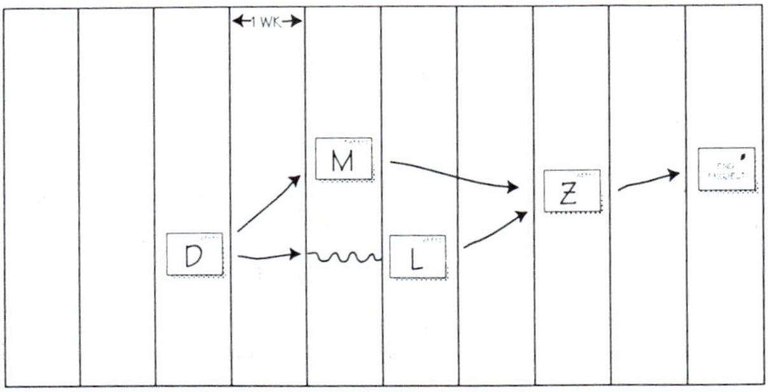

No one seemed too impressed by the concept of float; it seemed so obvious when you used a time scale.

"Next, we ask ourselves what has to be done before we can do task **D**. The answer is, task **A**, which takes two weeks." The board now looked like this:

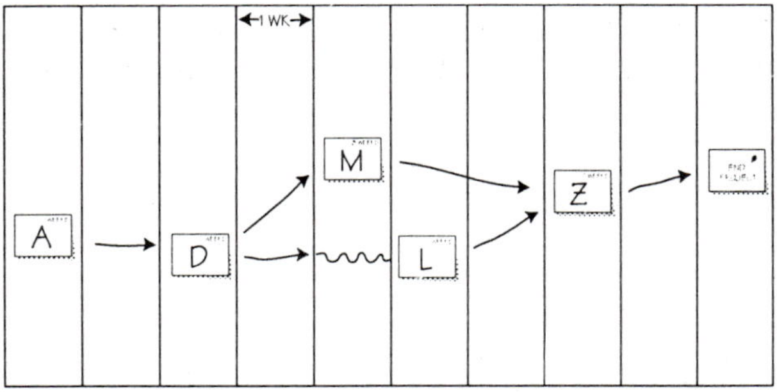


"Finally, we ask ourselves what comes before **A**. The answer in this case is, the **start.** This is another milestone, and like the **end**, every project has one." I stuck up the **start project** sticker to complete the plan.

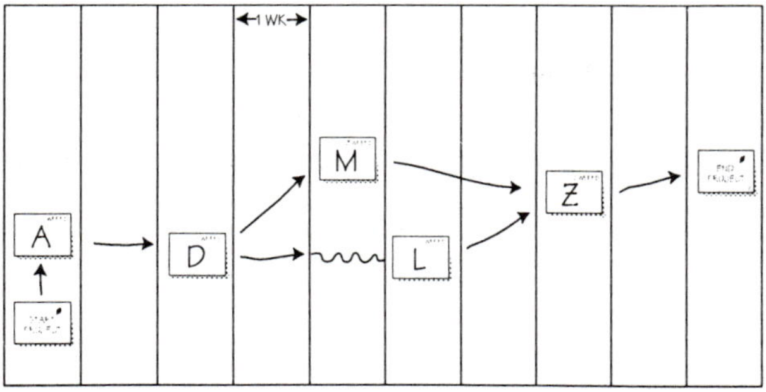


I surveyed the group. By now they were no longer openly hostile. I could tell that they thought this technique wasn't all that hard to use. "What about the critical path?" Alice asked.

"First, let me make one more point about float, Alice," I said. "Let me ask you a question about the float around task **L**. What happens to the completion of this project if task **L** is delayed by one week?"

Everyone stared at the board for a moment, then Mark said the obvious: "The finish is delayed by one week – assuming nothing else changes."

"Exactly. Now what happens to the end of the project if task **D** is delayed one week?"

Luigi spoke without thinking first. "The float gets used up, and the project completion doesn't get delayed."

Sheila was quick to correct him. "Look at it again, Luigi. If task **D** gets delayed, it delays **M**, which delays **Z**, which delays the completion."

"That's right, Sheila. If **D** is delayed, the completion gets delayed again."

"So what is the point of having the float?" Alice asked. Finally, the audience was going where I wanted them to.

"That's a good question, Alice. The point is, as much as possible we want to have the float come after the particular task or activity with which it is associated. That way, if something goes wrong, we have the float as a cushion. So," I turned to the board, "if we just reschedule the task, without changing the logic, we can make use of the float." I picked up the task, erased the line, put the task in its new position, and redrew the line. The whiteboard looked like this:

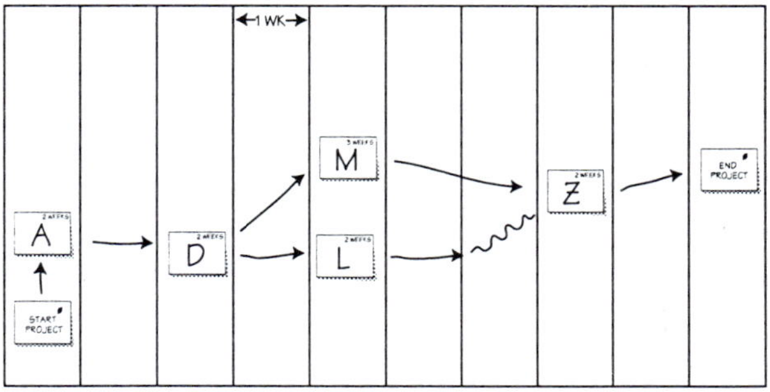


"So that is all we need to know about float." In fact, I had learned a great deal more about float in college when I learned about PERT charts. Martha had assured me that this was as far as we needed to go.

"The last thing is the critical path. The critical path is just the path with the least amount of float." I looked around the table. "Can anyone tell me where the critical path is on this project?"

Instead of answering, Alice asked, "What is a path?"

Oops! "A path is any way of getting from the start to the end without going backwards. In this project there are two paths: **Start-A-D-M-Z-End**, and **Start-A-D-L-Z-End**. So which one is critical?"

I could tell that everyone knew by the way they mumbled the letters of the path, but no one jumped to volunteer. Even by the time we reach mid-life we are all afraid of getting the answer wrong in front of the class. To help them out, I put my pen at the start and said, "Call out the letters of the path as I go, and I'll mark it with a double line." This worked much better. When we were done, the chart looked like this:

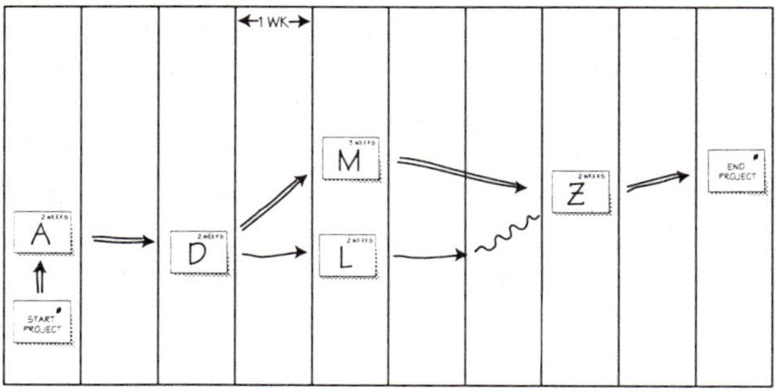


"As you can see, finding the critical path is simple – no math required. You just find the path with the least amount of float. Now why would we care about the critical path?"

"Because it's critical?" Mark said, only half jokingly.

"Why is it critical?" I asked the group again.

Finally Sheila spoke up. "Because it's the path that takes the longest to complete."

"Exactly! Does everyone see that? It's the longest path, and therefore it determines how long the project will be." Everyone nodded in agreement, making me feel that perhaps I had over-simplified things a little. In fact, as Martha had explained, there was no simplification involved. There wasn't any complication involved, either. I had just shown my team everything we needed to understand about putting together the Execution Plan.

Alice raised her hand like she was still in school. "I have a question: what's the difference between a task and an activity? And how big is a task, anyway? I mean, what kind of ground rules are there for defining one? Is it cost? Or duration?"

As it happened, I had asked Martha the same questions myself, so I answered them for her just like my 'consultant' had done for me. "A task and an activity are the same thing; a bit of work that we have to get done. As for how big to make one, what kind of ground rules do you think we should use?"

Everyone jumped in to answer that one. "Use a dollar limit"..."How about a time of between one week and one month?"..."A combination of duration and cost...." Finally someone said something useful: "Why not define each one in as much detail as we need to to be able to control it?" We all turned to Amanda, the profferer of this advice. "What I mean is, putting some arbitrary dollar figure or time limit on what makes a task seems pointless. Why don't we just make tasks based on our own judgment?"

That was exactly the answer I was looking for. Martha had harangued me for quite some time about this one. "That is what the consultant recommends. In his words, we should 'define the tasks in a way that makes sense'. For example, a task like **hire and train workers** is 'way too broad to be of much help to us in managing this thing. But **tie shoelaces** is probably a little too detailed." As Martha had put it to me, we were supposed to "make the task as small as the dependency logic or the resource requirement demands."

We spent a little more time talking about tasks, critical paths, dependency charts and the depleted state of the donut holes before we finally got down to the task at hand.

"Okay kids, we're ready to start on this plan. We will start at the end and go backwards." I pointed to the **end project** sticky note that I had put on the far right-hand side of the whiteboard, then I paused and surveyed the room in what I hoped was a commanding manner. "So what did we do just before the end?"

Everyone looked around at each other, but no one said anything. I couldn't blame them, I felt the same way. This planning backwards stuff was going to be hard work. I decided to try to get us started. "How about a task called **hand over facility to production**?" I wrote this on a sticky note and put it up on the board, drawing a line from it to the **End** task.

"That should be the last thing we do, for sure," said Luigi. This interested him, of course, since he was in charge of production.

"What about **Move retail facilities**?" suggested Alice. "As you know, the new design calls for the retail store to be moved to the other end of the plant so that it's by the new public access."

"One of the last things we do should be the **Paving for parking at the new retail outlet**," chimed in Mark.

As this discussion was going on, I was frantically writing things on yellow stickies. Finally I said, "Just give me a minute, people! I can't keep up. Look, let's work on one thing at a time. If you think of a task that doesn't relate to whatever we're currently working on, just jot it down and bring it up at the right time. It's important for all of us to focus on the same part of the Execution Plan and not get scattered!"

Four hours later we stood back to admire our work. Mark said, "It looks like a spaghetti dinner." Luigi disagreed. "Too messy," he said.

In fact, our final product did look a bit like spaghetti dinner. We had more than 80 tasks with all of their logic relationships stuck on the board. As well, we had identified the resources required to perform each task. It was quite a significant amount of information in one place. Best of all, at least in my eyes, our time scale was telling us that we would be finished during the third week of June – barring surprises, of course.

"I don't think Ralph is going to like it," warned Alice.

I reacted a little defensively. "Why wouldn't he like it? That's our Execution Plan right there – all the information we need to know. What's not to like?"

Alice wouldn't be drawn into an argument. "All I'm saying, Will, is that it looks pretty complicated. Ralph doesn't like complicated things. And neither does the Hyler board."

I should have paid a little more attention to Alice's comments, but I was just a little too high on our plan. "Look, does everyone agree that we now have a real handle on this project?" Everyone nodded their heads vigorously. "And is there any information on this plan that you think we could do without?"

Sheila was adamant about that. "Absolutely not, Will! This is like a lightbulb going on for me. Everything is there in one place.* Sure it looks a little complicated, but once we put it into the computer we'll be able to clean it up quite a bit."

I felt satisfied. "There you go, then. This is only as complicated as it needs to be. I expect that both Ralph and the Hyler board will appreciate that." I turned to Amanda. "I am meeting with Ralph on January 3rd at 2:00 p.m. Any problems having this in the computer before then?" She shook her head. "Great! And look, it's only 1:30 p.m. I'll see you all back here after the New Year!"

On the whole, I felt very good about the day. We had put together what was undoubtedly the best plan I had ever seen, and we had done it without a single disagreement. With a few simple rules from Martha, the plan had almost built itself. Looking back, the only thing I would have done differently would have been to listen more closely to what Alice had to say.

* The apparatus developed specifically to support this technique and instructions to reliably input the plan to project management software are contained in our Project Planning Kit. See back of book.

# Chapter 18

"Daddy, why is your smile turned down all the time?"

Jake was starting to talk a lot now, and sometimes it could be really annoying. How do you explain to your almost-three-year-old kid that your damn Execution Plan is screwed up because all of the resources are overloaded, the cost seems to be about $1 million more than your original estimate, and the thing won't finish until November, which is five months too late? I guess the answer is, you don't.

"Daddy has a lot on his mind right now Jake, and sometimes all of this thinking makes my head hurt."

"Play with me and it makes your head better, Daddy." He wasn't talking like a graduate of Harvard Medical School yet, but I supposed that he was doing all right.

"Okay Jake, what do you want to play with?" I knew what he would say.

"My blocks!" What else. His great-grandmother, none other than Martha herself, had given him blocks for Christmas, and since then he seemed to spend all of his spare time, something you have a lot of when you're three, building things with those blocks. Jenny kept saying it meant he would be an architect when he grew up. I pointed out it could also mean he was destined to be a bricklayer. Jenny thinks I'm a wet blanket.

As Jake laid out his blocks on the floor and got ready to create another sky-scraper, I pondered my situation and prepared to assist him (okay, I admit the blocks are fun). It had only been a day since the high of completing our Execution Plan. At that point, everything had seemed under control.

Amanda and I had gone into the office this morning to put the plan into the project management software program. We had both planned on spending no more than a couple of hours getting it set up. Instead we had been there until six in the evening, and our difficulties still weren't resolved.

When you came right down to it, our problem was that the software program was telling us things that we didn't want to hear. In fact, it was telling us things that we didn't even believe to be true. For example, according to the program, the completion date was November 18th. But because we had done the plan on a time scale, we could see that it finished in June. We had also done a rough estimate of the costs from our plan on the whiteboard (we could do this because we had identified all of the resources on the tasks), and found that our cost was going to be about $1.4 million. We were all pretty comfortable with that for a rough cut. But now the software was telling us that it would cost $2.5 million!

It had taken us much longer than expected to input the plan from the whiteboard, and by 6:00 p.m., after spending two fruitless hours trying to find out why we and the software disagreed, we had decided to call it a night.

"No bump, Daddy!" Jake said, startling me out of my reverie. I had been knocking my elbow against one of his just-constructed spires.

"Sorry son," I apologized. The little guy was getting pretty testy about his blocks. When I was a kid I always thought that knocking things down was the best part.

A few minutes later I was watching Jake trying to stack a group of single bricks as high as he could. He was getting frustrated because after about the sixth brick, the whole thing kept tumbling down. Try as he might, he couldn't make it stand.

As I watched, I could see his problem: he was not quite stacking the blocks squarely on top of each other. The second block was just slightly off kilter from the first one, and the third block was only slightly off as well, but when the two mistakes were added together, it spelled collapse by the fifth or sixth block. Just to prove my theory, and to show Jake how a master builder does things, I stacked a single pile 10 blocks high.

Jake stopped what he was doing and looked at my pile very closely. He examined it up and down, looking for the secret, and then he went back to his own pile. This time, he placed the blocks very carefully so that all the sides lined up squarely, and he was able to get up to eight blocks before he accidentally knocked the whole thing over when he was turning to pick up another block. This started him crying, and since it was half past eight, I picked him up and took him upstairs to bed.

Later, as I sat in the living room playing with the blocks on my own, I started to think about our software problems. And because I like analogies, I started imagining the inputting process as block stacking. It was done piece by piece, each bit of information depending on the rest. If mistakes were made stacking the blocks, the whole thing fell apart. If mistakes were made inputting the data from the whiteboard, it seemed to me the result would be the same.

In fact, when I thought about it, we hadn't really been all that systematic about inputting the project information. We didn't set out to make mistakes, but we had tried to do it in a bit of a hurry. And when we were trying to find mistakes, we spent more time staring at our original plan and then staring at the computer screen, than we did looking for simple data entry mistakes. We had been hoping to find a big error in planning, or some obvious error the program was making in calculation. It never occurred to us that the cause of the problem might be much simpler.

The next morning, I found that I was right. We had made no less than 17 different mistakes in entering the plan into the computer. We had about six different logic links entered incorrectly, as well as several task durations that were wrong. In one case we had accidentally typed "4m" (four months) instead of "4d" (four days). When we corrected those errors, our schedule suddenly had a completion date of June 28th.

Our costs had decreased significantly as well, but I checked all of that information just to be on the safe side. Sure enough, we had the hourly rates wrong for several resources. I resolved that in the future, I would be much more careful about getting the data from the planning board into the computer. After I thought about it, I could see that was where mistakes were most likely to slip in. For her part, Amanda resolved to devise a foolproof method of transferring the data quickly and accurately.

When we had completed all of the corrections, we were confident that what the software was telling us was correct. I was also confident that I didn't really want to be at work any longer. It was Saturday, after all.

"That looks nice Will, but where is your Gantt chart? And I need to see a work breakdown structure. Have you got those?" Ralph sat back in his chair. "You did do those didn't you?" he asked.

I had just finished presenting our plan to him, proudly displaying our dependency chart of the Execution Plan. Apparently Ralph was not as impressed as I had been. "Well, uh..." I mumbled, incoherently.

Ralph turned to Stu, who was sitting beside him, watching the presentation. "I thought I made it clear that I wanted a Gantt chart and a work breakdown structure!" He turned back at me and glared. "I've been giving you a free rein with this project so far. Is it too much to ask to give me the plan in the format I requested?"

"Um, I, ah,.." My speaking abilities always desert me in pressure situations.

Ralph stood up. "There is a board meeting next Monday in Portland. At that session I will be expected to provide an update on this project, which means that by Friday I want to see a Gantt chart schedule and a detailed work breakdown structure. Is that clear enough for you?"

I nodded yes, not trusting myself to say anything intelligent, and Ralph strode angrily out of the board room.

"Nice going, sport," Stu said as he put his feet up on the conference table. "You really showed him that you know what you're doing."

"But Stu, why does he want to see a Gantt chart, or a work breakdown structure? All the information is right here!" I tapped the dependency chart that was taped to the wall. "This is the basic tool for execution planning." Besides, I thought to myself, I'm not even sure what a work breakdown structure is.

Stu took his feet off the table and leaned forward over it. "To be honest, Will, I'm quite impressed with the planning work that you've done so far. And that dependency chart, although it looks a little complicated at first, really does provide a good picture of the project. There's only one problem."

"What's that?" I asked.

"I'm not the sponsor. Ralph is, and if he wants to see his plans a certain way, then you've got to present them that way."

"Even if his way is wrong?" I retorted.

"Even if his way is wrong. Look Will, Ralph pays the bills. He is like your customer, and he is always right. If you feel that a dependency chart is the tool you need to manage the execution, then great, use it. But if Ralph wants to see things in a different way, then you have to accommodate that too." He paused and leaned back in the chair. "It seems to me that right and wrong may not be good words to use here anyway. And besides, if your dependency chart is such a great tool, it should be no problem for you to produce whatever arrangement of information Ralph wants."

Stu was making a lot of sense. Ralph had a different perspective than I did. And it didn't matter to him that "Gantt chart thinking" had gotten us into trouble during the detailed design. I was supposed to take care of the details, and give him his information in a nice, neat format. One that he could understand. And, as Stu said, if the dependency chart had all the information we needed, doing a work breakdown structure (whatever that was) should be no problem.

"There is one other thing that you should know, Will. There is a rumor of some kind of trouble at Mantec. The company's stock is down on Wall Street, and there is talk of changes being made within the organization. Ralph's future is a little unsure, and it's making him nervous."

I was not impressed. "So he takes it out on me and this project?"

"Yes, he does. That's the reality of having to work with other people. Their problems become your problems." He stood up to leave. "Remember, Ralph is not against you, he just needs to have some things his way. I think he has done his job as sponsor pretty effectively so far. Get him his Gantt charts and work structures, or whatever, and he'll continue to do a good job."

Thirty minutes later I was with Sheila in Amanda's office, briefing them on the meeting. "The upshot is that we have to produce a Gantt chart and a work breakdown structure for Ralph before Friday so that he can be ready for Monday's board meeting."

"And so we can get going on the Execution," added Amanda. "Don't forget why we're doing this. We need Ralph's approval to continue."

"Yes, of course," I said testily. She was right, naturally, but it was easy to get caught up in doing things to keep your sponsor happy, and forget about why you were really there. I supposed that this had probably doomed many assignments, along with their project managers, especially if they weren't clear on just exactly who their sponsor was. "I guess Ralph isn't going to trust us about dependency charts, and that means lots more work for us, reporting things in the way that he likes."

I guess I was overdoing the martyr stuff, because Sheila said, "Give me a break, Will! It isn't going to be very much work at all. Our dependency chart has all of the fundamental information that you need for the Execution Plan, so any variation, like a Gantt chart, is easy to produce. Here." She punched a couple of keys on Amanda's computer and pointed at the screen.

"It looks like a Gantt chart," I said.

"It is, Will. It's created automatically when we enter all of the project data. We just have to print it out."

"Well, why didn't you tell me we had one? Why didn't you print it out for my presentation?"

"As you may recall, Will, you specifically did not want anything but the dependency chart. I asked you about other things, but you told me", her impression of my voice sounded very sanctimonious, " 'the dependency chart has all of the information, why would I want anything else?' "

I felt a little sheepish. I guess I had been somewhat righteous about the whole thing. "So what you're saying is we just have to print, there is no extra work?"

"Exactly," Sheila said. "The Gantt chart is already there. The work breakdown structure, however, will be a little more work."

"How much?" I groaned. Inwardly, the martyr side of my personality was happy. I wanted Ralph's requests to turn into some extra work, otherwise how could I resent him for it?

"It should take us about 15 minutes."

"Really," I said as my martyr hopes were dashed. "Fifteen minutes? Maybe we should start by you telling me exactly what a work breakdown structure is."

Sheila was happy to comply. "Until we did our dependency chart, I used to think of work breakdown structures (or WBSs) as a planning tool. Now I would call them just alternative ways of arranging the project information."

"That's a bit cryptic, isn't it?" Amanda asked.

Sheila tapped the computer screen. "Look. All we have here is a big database of information about the project, task names, durations, resources, links, etc. The dependency chart is the best tool we've got to help assemble those data, but once the project is together, we can arrange it in as many different ways as we want. And that is where the software comes in very handy. It allows us to produce new and different arrangements of the project information at a moment's notice. A Gantt chart is an example of a new arrangement of data. It shows the task, the duration and the schedule, but it doesn't show the logic. For it to be correct, of course, it has to be based on the logic."

"So the work breakdown structure is just another arrangement of the data?" I asked hopefully. If we weren't going to have to do a whole lot more work, which would have satisfied my martyr instincts, I wanted to do no extra work, which would satisfy my lazy instincts.

"Not exactly," Sheila said cautiously. "The work breakdown structure has come to mean a little more than that. It has to do with grouping the tasks in the project into different categories."

"For example?" Amanda prompted.

"Well, the most common choices are to group the tasks based on the functional area within the organization, sub-categories of scope items, or by the phase of the project."

"For example?" I prompted.

"Well, in this project, we might group the tasks under the headings Systems, Human Resources, Operations, and Construction. Under Systems we would put the tasks like **Program new inventory control module**, and **Debug accounting module**. Under Human Resources we would put all of the training and hiring-related activities. Operations would get tasks like **Equipment purchase**, **Warehouse racking**, and so on. And Construction would get all of the construction tasks. The final picture looks something like this." She scribbled on a pad of paper beside Amanda's computer. When she was done, this is what her picture looked like:

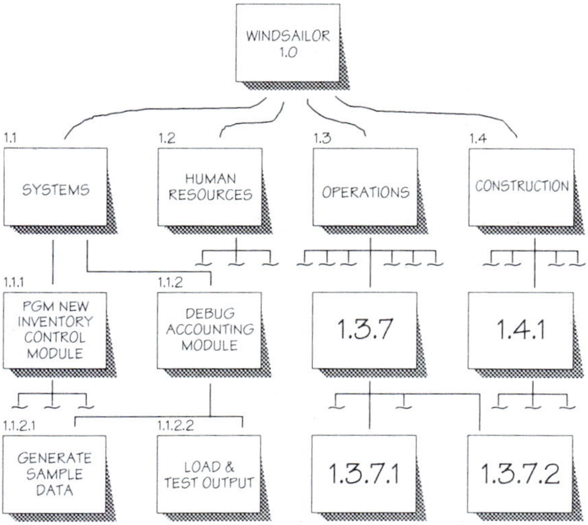


"It usually comes with it's own hierarchical numbering system to identify the tasks," Sheila told us, explaining the numbers she had jotted on the chart.

"Great," I said. "We have something like an organizational hierarchy for the project. Why would we want to do this? It doesn't seem to have any practical application for managing the execution."

"Don't snap at me, Will, I didn't invent them. In fact, they mostly get used for costing purposes, so different departments can budget for projected work. They are kind of a throwback to the days when organizations were much more hierarchical than today."

"Throwback?" Amanda asked. "That implies that organizations today aren't. Hierarchical, I mean."

"You know what I mean! Anyway, that's a work breakdown structure. All we have to do is decide how we're going to group the tasks, then input that new information to the software, and it will print a chart for us. I've checked, and it has that function."

"Great," I said without too much enthusiasm. "I can hardly wait. By the way, how do we decide how to group the tasks?"

Amanda is always full of good ideas. "Why don't we just use an old structure that Ralph has seen before?"

"Good idea!" said Sheila. "Al used to think of them as the way to plan a project. He even had a generic one that he wanted to make standard throughout Hyler. I think it was based on functional area. I'll go and check his office."

As it turned out, Al did have a nice, standard work breakdown structure based on functional unit. We spent the next hour and a half forcing our project into that mold. When we were done, we had picture that would satisfy Ralph. I had also gotten used to the idea that giving the sponsor what he wanted, so long as it didn't greatly interfere with doing the assignment within the constraints of the objective statement, might not be such a bad thing after all.

The Friday meeting was a much happier one. I suspected that Ralph was in a better mood to start with, and I had what he wanted to see. I got accidental vindication of my belief in dependency charts when Ralph had a question about one of the tasks.

As we were staring at the Gantt chart he asked, "How come the training on the new forklifts takes place so much earlier than all of the other new equipment training?" We were purchasing special forklifts to transport the WindSailor hulls from the manufacturing space to the warehouse for curing.

"We'll be using existing staff to operate the new forklifts, but we will be using new hires to run most of the other new equipment," I told him.

"In that case, why don't we buy them right away and get them used to them earlier?"

"Because we need to have the new warehouse space constructed and laid out before we purchase the trucks. Otherwise we'll have no place to conduct the training, or to store them. There's no point in spending the money before we can use the equipment."

"Well, what about storing them in the new dinghy manufacturing space?"

"We won't have access to that site at that time, our old access road is being torn out and moved over, to accommodate the other warehouse expansion."

Ralph had one last question. "How do you keep all of this information in your head?"

Unable to resist, I pointed to the dependency chart that was sitting off to the side of the Gantt chart, next to me and out of Ralph's direct line of sight. "You can see here that the dependency relationships show why we had to plan things as we did. I don't need to remember them, they're all here."

Ralph looked from the dependency chart to the Gantt chart, and back again. His only comment was, "The Gantt chart sure is easier to read."

I resisted saying anything to the effect that ***Spot Goes Splash*** was easier to read than the ***Encyclopedia Britannica***, but that it didn't give you quite the same information.

By the time we wrapped things up, Ralph was very pleased to sign-off on our Execution Plan. The extra costs didn't bother him, I assume because we showed him where they came from, but he did have yet another question.

"Why aren't your contingency costs the standard 10 percent of the total project costs?" he asked when he saw how much we were budgeting.

"We did it a little differently this time, Ralph. We tried to think of what might go wrong, and planned how we would respond to it. We then attached a cost to our response plan and estimated how likely we thought it was that we would have this particular thing go wrong. After that, we multiplied the probability by the cost for each contingency, and added them all up. We felt that that would give us a better estimate for contingencies."

That wasn't strictly true. It had been Martha's idea to cost contingencies in this manner, and I wasn't completely in agreement, especially since our contingency costs were 16 percent of the total Execution cost instead of the usual 10 percent. She had been good to me so far, however, so I was willing to go along with it.

Apparently, Ralph was not. "Drop your contingency costs to 10 percent, and I'll sign-off on the plan." I didn't fight very hard for Martha's idea, although when I thought about it later, it really made pretty good sense, more than an arbitrary 10 percent, anyway.

Just as he was leaving the conference room, Ralph said, "By the way Will, I've decided that I would like you to attend the board meeting on Monday. I think the board should see your presentation of the project." As he walked out into the hall, he said, "It starts at 2:00 p.m. sharp at the Four Seasons. Don't be late."

Stu stood up and chuckled. "You're getting to be a real popular guy."

# EXECUTION

# CHAPTER 19

I had always suspected that our neighbors, Harlan and Eileen Kilbrew, were freaks. The way he had his hair cut (as if he went to a soup bowl dealer, not a barbershop), the way she always fixed her glasses with tape instead of glue, the fact that they gave haircuts to their golden retriever, Chunky (fortunately they didn't use the same bowl…).

My worst fears were confirmed when I noticed the two of them coming out of the video store. Under Harlan's arm was the classic Tim Conway video, Dorf on Golf. I had serious reservations about living next door to anyone who watches Dorf on Golf of their own free will.

I was just getting out of my car when I noticed them. I had stopped at the video store to pick up something for the kids to watch with the babysitter while Jenny and I went out to dinner. The Execution phase of the WindSailor assignment had been underway for three weeks, and things had been going well. I thought a little celebrating was in order.

I tried to hide in a casual manner, but Eileen saw me crouched down behind my car. "Hi Will! Did you drop something?" She rushed over to help me find whatever it might be, while I frantically took my keys out of my pocket and pretended to pick them up.

"Oh hi Eileen, Harlan. Didn't see you. I was just looking for my keys." I held them up. "Here they are! Don't trouble yourself." I was trying to head her off before she got too close, but it was too late. Eileen caught her skirt on the bumper of the car somehow, and fell heavily into me. The frame of her glasses crunched against the bridge of my nose, and the tape gave way.

"Honey bun," she called to Harlan, "I've dropped my glasses. Come help Will find them." I reached down and picked them up. She must have been really nearsighted, because they felt as though each lens weighed about a pound.

"Thanks Will," she said, pulling a roll of tape out of her pocket and fixing her frames on the spot. This kind of thing happened to her often.

"So, Will, I hear you've got a little competition," Harlan said while Eileen taped.

"Harlan, would you mind not leaning on my car with your keys in your hand?"

"Oh, sorry," he said. "It's just a little scratch. It'll buff out." Dorf on Golf was probably serious drama to these people.

I've often wondered how they get by in the world. What's even more incredible is that Harlan and Eileen own the sporting goods store in Enderby. Somehow they seem to do okay, although I've never met a less-athletic couple.

Of course their store sells windsurfers, aluminum fishing boats and day sailors, as well as all manner of other sporting gear, so Harlan feels that he and I have some kind of special bond. I always try to put him off by telling him that I just deal with computers, and know nothing about the sailing end of things. He never seems to hear me.

"Like I was saying, Will, your competition is getting the jump on you. I just got a flyer from California Water Sports introducing their new product. It's called the WindWalker. It's kind of like a cross between a windsurfer and a small sailboat."

For the first time since I had met him, I was very interested in what Harlan was saying. "You just got this flyer in the mail?" I asked, a cold sweat forming on the small of my back.

"Yessir," Harlan said happily. He was obviously pleased to have someone who cared about what he had to say. "Just got it this morning. They're claiming they'll have it available for us dealers by July. I'll tell ya, it looks like they've got a real winner with this product. It should be a lot easier to sail than a windsurfer, yet much more portable than a sailboat. I mean, you can put it on the roof of your car. And the best part is, once they sail the WindWalker for a year or two..."

"...the customer will move up to either a new windsurfer or a daysailer," I finished the sentence. I couldn't believe what I was hearing. Direct competition for our product so soon? As I recalled, all of our projections were based on having at least a year's head start on the competition. How could we have lost our jump so quickly? Something twigged in my head. "Harlan, what did you say the name of the company was?"

"California Water Sports. You know them, they're based in San Francisco. They make the Wind Ripper and the Weasel and the..." Harlan proceeded to give me a list of every product the company made, but I stopped listening very quickly. I knew at least part of the reason we had lost our head start. California Water Sports was the company that Al Burton had gone to last fall.

Two days later, Ralph, Stu, Carrie Starblanket (the Vice-President of Marketing) and I gathered in the conference room. Carrie had done a little digging with sales reps and agents, and had come up with a synopsis of what had transpired at California Water Sports. I felt as if we were at a military debriefing after an ambush.

"As you all know, California Water Sports manufactures a product line similar to ours, except they don't make the aluminum fishing boats or the trailers." You could tell by the way she said 'aluminum' that Carrie didn't think of our trailers and aluminum boats as glamour products. "They are a smaller company, with about $30 million in sales, and until recently they were owned by a guy named Bob Wickwire. Just after Al left us to join them, Darnell Holdings Ltd. purchased the California company. Is everyone familiar with Darnell?" No one else volunteered their ignorance, so I did. "No? Darnell is a medium-sized corporation similar to Mantec. It has holdings in shipping, trucking and manufacturing. We're not sure why they acquired California Water Sports, but they certainly appear to be ready to provide it with all the support that it needs.

"Soon after Al arrived down in San Francisco, and soon after the company was purchased by Darnell, CWS did a product development tour of Europe. When they were over there they spent some time in Eastern Europe, and apparently they hooked up with a company in Odessa."

Everybody looked at her in disbelief. "Yes, the city on the Black Sea that was behind the former Iron Curtain. I guess the new economic reforms have been working for somebody. Anyway, this company has a new product, very similar to ours, that they are planning to bring to market this summer. With Darnell's backing, CWS has purchased the right to manufacture and sell it in North America. With the money that their new parent company is providing, CWS plans to have the product on the market by August to catch the end of this season. And here's the kicker: my sources tell me that they are planning to outspend us on advertising by about two to one!"

"What about patent violation?" Stu asked hopefully. "Any chance they could be infringing on the WindSailor?"

Carrie shook her head. "I talked to the legal people, and they don't think there is much chance. Just from the advance marketing information I've received, you can see that the design of the craft is quite different. However, the use is the same, and the target market is the same."

"You're the marketing expert, Carrie," I said, "where does this leave us?"

"If CWS holds to their schedule, their boat will arrive at almost exactly the same time as ours. If that is the case, and they really are outspending us in advertising, we'll lose a significant edge in terms of product differentiation and recognition. Off the top of my head I can't tell you what that is going to mean in long-term sales, but obviously we are looking at a different picture than before." She paused and made a few notes on the pad of paper in front of her. "Being first to the market is so important with a new product. Even if we could have a few months we would have a heavy-duty advantage."

Ralph had slowly been coming to a boil as he listened to Carrie. "Damn!" he finally exploded. "And we've already spent more than $250,000!" Thanks to my diligence with project costing, Ralph knew exactly how much money we had spent. He looked around the table for someone to blame. His eyes stopped on Stu. "You said that the WindSailor was the only product of its kind, Stuart. Didn't you do some investigation to confirm that idea?"

Stu was not ready to be the scapegoat. "As you know from my reports, we surveyed the other European and even Asian manufacturers extensively to try to determine their plans. Look Ralph, we did the best we could. Like I said in my original report, there was some risk in proceeding with this, not the least of which was that someone could copy us more quickly than we thought."

Ralph did not want to let Stu off the hook. "But you practically guaranteed us 18 months without competition! Now we don't even have 18 days!"

Ralph could be a great guy when things were going well, but he tended to turn pretty nasty when things were not. Carrie decided to step in and change the direction of the conversation before things got even more unpleasant. "We shouldn't be throwing in the towel yet. The market for this product is large, and our projections allow for us to make money even with competition. Granted, we didn't think it would be for two to three years."

Ralph turned to vent himself a little on Carrie. "Those first two years were going to be the payback for our up-front investment! Without them, why make the investment in the first place?"

Like Stu, Carrie was not about to let Ralph shoot her down without a fight. "What about all those strategic reasons, like being on the cutting edge of the new product market...maintaining our name as a leading manufacturer...positioning ourselves for the future? Do you want to throw all of that out of the window?"

From the expression on Ralph's face, I guessed that he would if it would improve his next quarter's results. "Look," he said, "all that future crap is nice, but if we don't get our payback in the first two years, our performance looks like dirt." And there goes your promotion, I thought. Too bad.

I decided to throw my hat into the ring. "Carrie, you keep coming back to the idea of being first into the market. What if we could be ready for the beginning of this season instead of the end of it? How much of an advantage do you think that would give us?"

Carrie's face brightened. "It wouldn't be as good as a season and a half, but it might be 70 percent as good."

Ralph immediately seized on this possibility of salvation. "Seventy percent? If we have the product to the dealers by June?"

Carrie nodded. "It would mean changing the focus of our marketing campaign. At this point we've got everything set to go for June, not April. We would have to refocus our efforts, but if I had a half-season head start, I could establish a significant advantage for

Hyler over any other competitor."

Ralph turned to me. "The question is, Will, can we have the product by April?" Everyone else turned to look at me, too.

To be honest, I wasn't feeling as uneasy with that question as one might think, and certainly not as uneasy as I would have without Martha's help. At that point we had a pretty coherent plan that was specified in such a way as to make it easy to do a little sensitivity analysis. Since we knew how all of the tasks went together, we could quickly see the results of shaving off some time off here and there.

"Ralph, the answer is: I don't know. However, I can find out very quickly if it is possible."

Ralph stood up. "Then do it. We'll meet again tomorrow at 10:00 a.m. sharp. Carrie, I want you to make sure that the marketing campaign can be shortened as well. And people, " he said to both Carrie and me, "try to keep the cost down. We're already at the limit of our budget. Spending more money for less of a competitive advantage than we thought will not go over well with the board."

"Don't worry, Willie," Martha said as a smoke ring went by my ear. "If you're willing to spend a little more money, you can always make the execution a little shorter."

I wasn't so sure. Amanda, Sheila, and I, and various other members of the project team, had spent the rest of the afternoon after the meeting with Ralph trying to tighten up our plan. We had found a few places where we were able to save time, but not enough to bring our finish date from June 23rd to April 15th.

"But, Martha, we've already been over the plan several times, and we ended up saving about a week and a half. We need to cut almost two more months!"

That didn't seem to bother Martha. "Like I said Will, it can be done. It's just a question of money."

"That's another thing," I said dejectedly, "Ralph doesn't want us to spend any extra money."

Martha picked up my pad of paper and a pencil, and drew something. When she was done, she turned it toward me. It looked like this:

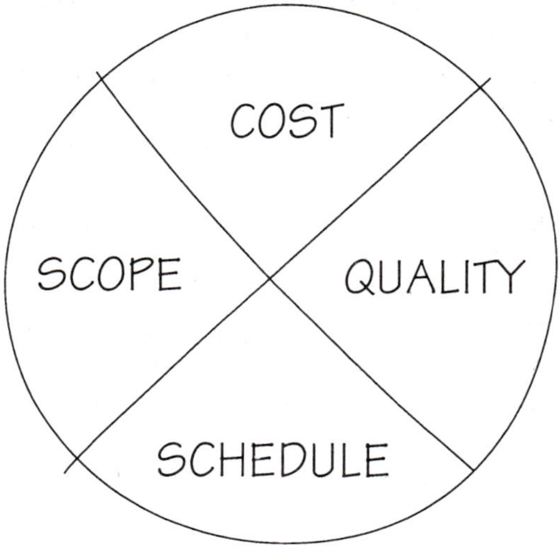


"This is a picture that both you and your sponsor need to learn about, Willie," she said, tapping the diagram. "I've simplified things a little, but these four components roughly represent all the aspects of an assignment." She tapped each in turn as she elaborated. "There is scope. That has to do with how much is in the assignment.

"There's schedule, which has to do with how long things are going to take.

"There's cost, which has to do with the price of disposable diapers versus cloth." I looked up at her quizzically. "Just seeing if you were awake, Willie." What a weird lady. "Actually cost has to do with how much the whole assignment is going to cost.

"And finally, there is quality, which has to do with the standard to which the work is performed.

"Every assignment is a system that operates within the constraints of all four of these components. And each one affects one or more of the others in a very predictable way. For example, if the scope of work to be done in the assignment increases, what kind of an effect do you think it will have on these other variables?"

I looked at the page. "Well, an increase in scope might increase the cost, or it might take longer."

"Or both," Martha added. "Exactly. Now what about cost? What if the budget for your assignment were suddenly cut?"

I had had a great deal of personal experience with that one. "Easy. You might have to decrease your scope and compromise your quality, or even take a little longer." Before she could say it, I added, "Or a mixture of all three."

"You're getting the picture, Will. Now let me ask you another question. Can you picture a situation in which one of these variables changes without affecting one or more of the other three?"

The way she said it, I thought it might be a trick question, so I didn't answer right away. Instead I did a couple of 'mind experiments', as Einstein called them. I tried to visualize a situation where cutting the budget didn't affect something else. I found that I could.

"Actually Martha, there was an assignment I worked on when I was still back East that had the budget cut. We still did the same amount of work, with the same quality, and relatively on schedule." The part about the schedule wasn't true, but that was pure disorganization, and it was already in place before the budget cut.

Martha didn't seem fazed. "Let me ask you, Will: was your time charged against the assignment?"

"Well, actually, no. None of the inside employees' time was. Why?"

"Did you find yourself working more hours than you had expected to?"

Had she been there and I had not noticed? "Yeah, I did. A lot more. You see, we had planned to contract out a bunch of stuff, and when the budget got cut we had to do it ourselves...." Suddenly I could see what she was getting at. "What you're saying is, we spent at least the same amount of money. It's just that our time wasn't charged to the project like a contractor's would be. We really only cut costs on paper, not in reality."

Martha nodded. "That's exactly it. Having employees work unpaid overtime is a cost, whether you choose to account for it correctly or not. Now I ask you again: can you think of a situation where one of these variables changes without affecting the other three?"

The picture was clear now. "No," I said.

"Will, understanding the interaction of the components in this picture is to assignments like understanding the law of gravity is to designing buildings. You simply can't cheat. However, once you recognize the relationships, you can deal with things more effectively."

"So what you're saying is that Ralph's dream of not spending any more money is just that, a dream." Somehow reality never seems quite as good as a dream.

Martha didn't agree. "Not necessarily, Will. However, if Ralph wants to shorten the schedule, there will have to be changes in one or more of the other three."

I started to see what she was getting at. "So you're saying that we could also cut the scope a little, or lower the quality, and not just spend more money."

"That is exactly right, Will. All the possibilities must be examined. Now," she took her pipe out of her mouth, "we need to talk about crashing."

"Crashing?" I echoed. "Is this another test to see if I'm paying attention? I thought we were talking about projects here."

Martha chuckled as she stuffed more tobacco into her pipe. "Crashing the project just happens to be the name given to the process of doing what you have to do now, make the project shorter." She studied her tobacco-stuffing job, and continued. "The rules are simple, but important. As always, I'll start with a question: if we want to decrease the duration of the project, which activities should you focus on making shorter?"

I felt like I was behind the play. "Which activities?"

"Yes," Martha said impatiently. "You want to make your schedule shorter. That means that you have to shorten some of the activities that make up the schedule. Which ones?"

I thought for a minute. "I guess the ones that you can shorten for the least money." That sounded good to me.

"Only partly right, Will. The activities that you want to focus on all have a certain characteristic. What is it?"

I had no idea until I visualized our dependency chart. "They are the critical activities. You focus on making them shorter because they are the activities that determine the length of the project.

Otherwise you might spend money or cut tasks that don't affect the completion date at all."

I got a smoke ring in the face as a reward. "Oops," Martha said. "But you are correct, Will, you must focus on the critical path. And then you have to make those activities shorter. How?"

I thought about a simple activity like spreading topsoil on the place where you want your front lawn to be. If I wanted to do it faster, I would just add more people. Or I could change the scope by deciding to make the lawn smaller. Or I suppose I could change the quality by spreading the topsoil thinner. Or I could hire a bulldozer to do it for me, instead of doing it by hand. "To shorten activities you could add resources, or reduce the scope of the task, or not do it as well, or even change resources to more productive ones."

"Close enough," said Martha, "although you have to remember that changes you make in each task affect all of the others. If you choose to do less during a particular task, you better make sure that it doesn't cause you problems down the line. Now what do you need in order to add more resources?"

That was easy. "Money. Something that I don't have a lot of."

That didn't bother Martha. "Yes, well, you still need to understand how to do it. Remember, you only have to tell your sponsor how to make the schedule shorter. It's his decision about the extra money, or decreased scope, or whatever."

Martha puffed on her pipe and looked out over the lawn for a few minutes without saying anything. Finally she turned back to me. "I think you understand what you need to do now, and I don't want to keep adding details that may confuse you, or that you may not need. However, there are two things to keep in mind about crashing projects. The first is that there is something called the ultimate crash point. It is the shortest time in which a task can be done. Adding resources at that point only costs you more money; it doesn't save you any time."

I tried to apply the idea of the ultimate crash point to my topsoil example. I visualized adding more and more people to the picture. As I reached 15, lineups started at the dirt pile. People started to get in each other's way. At 20, they needed a supervisor just to direct traffic. At 25, they formed a union and went on strike. I got the picture.

"The second thing is, as you shorten tasks, remember that the critical path may change. You must check the critical path each time you crash a task. You don't want to be spending your money to shorten tasks that are suddenly non-critical!" That seemed pretty obvious, but I made a mental note to watch out for it. Martha had yet to steer me wrong.

I looked at my watch. It was 9:45 p.m. I thought the chances of getting my project team together that night were slim. I'd call them at home and settle for an early-morning meeting. I got up to go.

Martha said, "One more thing, Will," and hesitated.

"Yes, Martha?"

"You're doing...I think...It's nice that you listen to me." Before I could say anything, she got up and tottered inside. I was not sure, but I thought she might have been paying me a compliment.

# CHAPTER 20

The crashing process turned out to be more tedious than anything, despite the fact that the name made the whole thing sound quite exciting. We rolled Amanda's computer into the conference room, taped a printout of the dependency chart to the wall, and went to work. I made sure that everyone on the assignment team was there, as well as some of our 'technical' experts like Mark and Luigi.

The necessity of focusing on the critical path made the choice of where to start very simple. The tedious part was inputting the results of any changes we made, recalculating the schedule, finding the new critical path, and starting all over again on a new activity. We also had to save every combination and possible shortened schedule, to keep track of them for evaluation purposes. Once we added in potential scope changes, we created a myriad of combinations.

By 9:30 a.m. we stopped creating new scenarios and started evaluating the ones we had already created, because at 10:00 a.m. I was supposed to have an answer for Ralph. By the time Ralph and the others showed up at the door, I was sure I had an option that he couldn't turn down.

The silence in the conference room told me that we had pulled off an upset. I don't think anyone, most especially Ralph, had expected the scenario that I had just presented.

"Could you explain that to me one more time?" he asked in a puzzled voice. "You mean to say that we can have the WindSailor facilities ready to go by April 15th, and it's going to cost us less money?"

Clearly he had been expecting my cash requirements to go up, but I was quick to qualify his statement. "That's right, Ralph, but as you can see," here I gestured to the dependency chart on the wall, "we have decreased the scope of the project a little. We won't be paving the new employee parking lot this season. The same is true for the new public parking lot and access road, which will have to be approved by the city council. We also won't have the entire assignment finished by the 15th of April. The new fencing between us and Lake Hyler won't be done until our original date in June, and the same goes for the new retail facility." I looked back at Ralph. "We shortened up the delivery of part of the project, the production facilities, but not all of the other components will be ready by then."

This didn't seem to concern Ralph very much, which is what I expected, and Carrie seemed pleased as well. Stu wasn't quite clear on things, and he said: "You didn't really answer Ralph's question, Will. Why is this new plan costing less than the original one?"

"Two reasons," I told him, as if I had understood this all my life instead of having figured it out 10 minutes before the presentation began. "The first, and largest, has to do with the decreased scope. You see, we have to speed up the construction, machine installation, and worker training activities to get the production facilities done on time. That actually increased our costs. As you can see on the plan, we're now doing installation and training on three different shifts instead of one, and we're doing construction on two shifts. That means more money in shift differentials, instructors, insurance premiums, equipment, all kinds of things. The net result is that, while we cut a lot of time off the completion date, we need more money to do it. In order to make up for that extra money, we went looking for scope changes we could make that wouldn't significantly affect the end product. We happened to stumble on paving, which, as you may or may not know, is horrendously expensive. We figured that we could cut the paving for this year and do it some other time when we had more money. As it turned out, dropping the paving saved more money than it cost to crash the other activities." I made it sound like we had planned this little loophole into the assignment from the beginning, but in fact, it was just blind luck. Nevertheless, having a plan was what made it easy (even possible) for us to discover this.

"You said there were two reasons why the cost went down, Will," Stu said. "What was the other one?" Leave it to Stu not to miss a trick.

"In fact, the second reason was fairly minor in this case, and it had mostly to do with the construction activities. As they got shorter, the overhead costs associated with them actually went down instead of up."

"What do you mean by overhead?" Ralph asked.

"Things like supervision and clerical support. They didn't have to be provided for as long, and therefore that portion of the cost went down." I had almost not noticed this decrease in cost, but I thought it was important to mention.

"Wait a minute, Will," Ralph said. "You're telling me that contracting companies actually lowered their bid prices when you told them to do the job more quickly?" Ralph was a suspicious kind of guy.

"No Ralph," I conceded. "You're right, the contractors haven't agreed to lower prices at this point, although we are going to try to get them to reduce that portion of their cost. In fact, the savings I calculated come from the reduction in our staff hours supervising the contractors." Everyone seemed impressed that I had gone to that level of detail, but in fact the savings had been minor. Money is money though, and because of the way we had specified the contracts (we required dependency charts and costs by activity), I was confident that our contractors would not get the better of us.

Ralph looked at me, then at Carrie and Stu. Finally he looked back at me again. "I can't see a problem here. Can anyone point one out for me?"

Carrie had a question. "You're sure that you will be ready for production by April 15th?" I nodded. "How many days to produce the first 400 boards?"

I shook my head. "I hate to abdicate responsibility, but that is not part of my assignment, so I can't give you any firm production rates. Luigi Delgarno is the person to talk to for that." Carrie looked a little annoyed, so I told her: "Luigi tells me that he'll be ready with that number by May. But you better confirm that with him; it ain't my job."

"I don't see how I can turn this down, Will," Ralph said. "My only question might be why the original plan didn't look like this?"

When we had discovered the possible savings, I had figured out the answer to this one. "The constraints have changed, Ralph, and that changes the plan. Here, let me show you something..." I drew Martha's circle with scope, cost, quality and schedule in the quadrants. After my explanation of how all the things interrelated, Ralph grunted.

"Seems pretty obvious, really. Anyway, all that theoretical stuff aside, I like the new plan. I want you to proceed." Ralph got up to leave.

"Uh, there's one more thing, Ralph," I told him. "This changes the objective statement, and I'd like to get your signed approval before we go any further." I handed him an objective statement that we had revised by hand just before the meeting.

Ralph looked a bit annoyed. "I'm beginning to feel like you don't trust me, Will." He stared at the paper. Finally, he put it down on the desk and signed it. "I suppose you want to make sure it's my head on the block, not yours." That was not exactly the point, but I didn't bother to correct him. He pointed his pen at me when he finished writing. "You just make sure that you are ready for production by April 15th."

Things were frantic over the next couple of days. Amanda worked hard to secure the city council's approval of the delay in paving the parking lot and access roads. In the end we had to commit to the paving by the beginning of next season. We agreed readily, but I admit to thinking that it wouldn't be my problem by then, which was a bit selfish of me. I did, of course, let Stu know about the deferred costs so he could recalculate the company's return on investment.

Sheila and I worked hard with the contractors to get their agreement about completing the work in less time without charging us an arm and a leg more. Fortunately, we had their dependency charts as a base to work from, which meant that they could only charge us extra where they showed us it would cost extra. It was lucky we had taken the time we did when we wrote the contracts.

The biggest crisis occurred because of Leslie Frame (and I suppose Carrie Starblanket) in Marketing. After I had promised to deliver in less time for less money, they had felt obligated to promise the same. As it turned out though, all of the promotional literature for the July rollout to the dealers had already been printed. With the revised dates, most of it would have to be redone, and four-color brochures are expensive. Ralph blew his stack over that one, but in the end the money we saved was simply transferred to the Marketing budget, and everyone came out of it okay.

By February 10th we were officially on a "crash" course with the 15th of April. All of the contracts had been renegotiated, the city had agreed to the lack of pavement, and even Marketing had promised to come through with the product name, logos and decorative styling to meet our accelerated schedule. All that was left was to actually do it. As I discovered then, and many times since, that part turned out to be a lot simpler than I expected. Of course, the execution wasn't without its share of difficulties.

"Look, Will, I think you're going to have to get out there. He doesn't want to deal with me anymore. He wants to talk directly to you." Sheila's tone was insistent. I cowered behind my desk.

"I'm awfully busy right now..." I started to say, but Sheila cut me off.

"Will, he's halted construction! He says he isn't going to start again until he speaks with you. Now stop fooling around and get out there!"

Slowly I stood up. "Well, I suppose if that's the only way...." Sheila rolled her eyes and headed out my office door in front of me.

I followed Sheila out of the building. As we walked toward the site of the biggest of our building expansions, I could see what was waiting for me. It hung near one of the on-site cranes like a black cloud from one of my bad dreams.

"It" was Bud Zalansky, the prime contractor for our construction work, and prime for just about all of the work that went on around Enderby. If there was a building going up in this area, you could bet that old Bud had a hand in it. He had been a fixture on the commercial and residential construction scene for almost 30 years, and right now I had a feeling the fixture was going to let go from the ceiling and crash down on my head.

"If you don't get your candy-ass people off my site and let me get this Goddamn job done, I'll pull my men out of here and let you build it yourself!"

"'Afternoon Bud," I said. I wasn't being cute, I just couldn't think of anything else to say.

"Don't 'afternoon' me, young fella," he growled. "You've got people all over me trying to tell me how to do things, and it's driving me crazy!" He hawked and spat on the ground as he tried to wrestle his pants up over his huge gut. He gave up quickly. "I been in this business since before you wuz weaned, so I don't need you telling me what to do!"

Until today, I had not dealt directly with any of the construction contractors. That was no accident; in fact, I had avoided them because they intimidated the hell out of me. Besides, I felt I didn't have a solid enough grounding in what they did to be telling them when they were doing it wrong. So I left that to Sheila.

I looked up into Bud's flaming face. "I'm not sure I understand the problem, Bud." I looked back down at his chest. The view was less disturbing.

"Aren't you listening, son? You got a bunch of know-it-alls running around here telling me my business, and I won't stand for it." He produced a pack of cigarettes from somewhere in his jeans and shook one out. "Let me tell you, Hyler was a much better place when Al Burton was here. Now there was a man you could deal with."

The mention of Al's name irked me. "Look Bud, we've got a plan for the work you're doing. My people jump all over you when you don't stick to the plan."

"That's exactly the problem, Will," Sheila said, "he's not paying any attention to the dependency chart!"

I could tell by the way he looked at her that Bud wasn't a feminist. "You know as well as I do that the plan is just for general reference," he told me. "Things change when you're working on the site. My experience is my guide." He lit his cigarette and tossed the match over his shoulder.

"I'm sorry you feel that way Bud," I said, "but I don't agree. And if you check your contract, you'll see that, like it or not, you'll stick to the plan or you won't get paid. If you deviate from the plan, you're supposed to tell us why, and what the impact will be."

Bud just stared at me in silence as he took a drag on his cigarette. Finally he said, "If I had known that, I woulda looked a little closer at the damn thing."

"Looked a little closer?" I echoed.

"Yup. I didn't think you meant it about the planning part." Bud had the ability to smoke a cigarette without actually touching it with his fingers. As he talked, it just kind of bobbed along on his lip. I couldn't take my eyes off it.

"Who did the plan for you then?" I asked.

Bud gestured toward Sheila. "She did." I turned to look at her. She didn't say anything.

"Well?" I prompted.

"Well what?" she asked defensively. "After we crashed the project Bud didn't want to be bothered with redoing his plan, so I just did it for him. We didn't have a lot of time, you know."

I shook my head and turned back to Bud. "And you didn't look too closely at the plan she produced?"

Bud laughed. "'Course not. Never heard of anyone being so picky as you about stickin' to some stupid plan. Anyway, what's your problem? We'll get your stuff finished on time. Don't worry."

I laughed too, trying to get the same snarly, sarcastic sound Bud produced, and turned back to Sheila. "Forgetting for a moment how the plan was arrived at, just what is Bud doing incorrectly?"

"I ain't doing nothing incorrectly," Bud interrupted before Sheila answered.

I corrected myself. "What is Bud doing that is not according to plan, that will cause the construction to finish late, and," I turned to look into Bud's simmering face again, "that will cause Bud not to be paid?"

Sheila gestured toward the trailer that was serving as the construction supervision office. "I can show you better if we go and look at the plan." The three of us walked over to the trailer in silence.

Inside, Sheila pointed to the dependency chart on the wall. "Bud's got a third of his crew out there working on getting the base prepared for the fencing, and he's planning to pour the concrete and set the poles in two days."

The dependency chart logic showed a number of things that needed to be completed before that took place, including the removal of most of the heavy equipment from the expansion site. A glance out of the window confirmed that that, at the very least, had yet to be done.

I looked at Bud. "Well?"

Bud sniffed arrogantly. "You wanted this project speeded up, I'm speedin' it up. I'm getting going on the fencing now so we don't have to do it at the end."

I looked back at the dependency chart. "Fencing isn't even on the critical path, Bud. Why are you wasting people on that?"

Bud's arrogant sniff disappeared in a hurry. He leaned over and stared nearsightedly at the chart. "Well, uh..." I wasn't sure that he even knew what a critical path looked like, but he seemed worried.

"And," said Sheila, "when you go to take out your heavy equipment, you're going to have to make a hole in the fence to do it."

Bud stood back from the plan. "No we won't. We'll just walk it out the main entrance of the plant."

"Only if you pay for the damage," Sheila shot back. "That road will be paved by then. If you walk your equipment over it, it'll wreck the pavement."

Bud wasn't out of answers yet. "Then we'll bring in a flatbed and truck it out."

Apparently Sheila wasn't finished either. "Did you notice that you didn't bring your equipment in that way, Bud? The road through the plant is short and twisted, and there are overhead electrical wires. You can't get your truck through there, and you can't get it back out with equipment on it."

Bud went back to peering at the plan and not saying anything.

I decided to sum up the situation. "Let me see if I've got this right, Bud. By ignoring the plan, you were about to spend a bunch of money crashing an activity that wasn't going to affect the completion of the project, and by having done it at the wrong time, you were then going to spend even more money getting your equipment out, either by knocking down part of your newly constructed fence, or repaving our road. Meanwhile, resources are diverted from critical activities. All of which would have cost us our completion date, and therefore cost you a lot of money." Bud continued staring silently at the plan.

I softened my tone. "Look Bud, I'm not trying to play some kind of macho game of right and wrong. I just want to get this thing finished on time and looking something like it is supposed to look. We have every confidence in your abilities as a contractor, but we're dealing with a very tight deadline and a complex situation. It's just too complicated to keep inside someone's head, even one as experienced as yours." Bud finally looked up at me. "Can you work with the plan?" I asked. "And," I added as an afterthought, "with Sheila?"

Bud nodded silently. "Thanks. I'll leave you and Sheila to go over the details." I walked out of the trailer and back to my office.

Sheila told me later that Bud couldn't get over the fact that we actually wanted him to work from a plan. According to him, that kind of behavior just wasn't part of the construction business. She figured that she hadn't converted him to dependency charts yet, but that he would at least stick to the one on this job. "I think when you made the point that it would cost him money to not follow the plan, you really got his attention, Will."

By the evening of March 25th, I was sitting on my in-laws' porch, enjoying the spring that was already well underway, and remarking on the (to me) surprising smoothness of the execution. Martha just chuckled. "Just like everyone else, Will, you probably expected that the execution would be the most stressful time of all."

"That's how it has always been for me in the past! Now I'm nervous all the time because everything is going so well." It was ironic. Before this one, I always found assignments stressful because they seemed to be constantly slipping out of my grasp as new things got added and problems cropped up. Now I was stressed because none of this was happening, but I expected it to start at any moment. I felt like I was waiting for the other shoe to drop.

"That's an attitude you're going to have to change, Willie," Martha told me as she crammed some tobacco into her pipe. "With proper preparation up front, the execution should be boring, with no surprises. It's better that way, because the execution is where most of the money gets spent." Martha paused for a moment and got that faraway look in her eyes. I braced myself for something philosophical.

"You know Will, I have never been able to get over how difficult it is for people to understand what you are experiencing right now: a clearly defined assignment, followed by a well-specified design and a detailed, useful Execution Plan resulting in a boring, as-planned execution. No one seems to understand that. Why do you suppose that is?"

I started to answer. "Well, I suppose..."

"I'll tell you why that is, Will," she continued on as if I wasn't there. "It's because our civilization doesn't reward people for thinking long-term and preventing crises. It rewards those who are incompetent enough to create crises, and then lucky enough to muddle through them and solve them, or at least survive them. Our society doesn't want to see planned success, it wants to see lucky success. We want the quick fix, the lucky break, the Slim-Quick-Easy-Diet Solution!" Martha was almost starting to foam at the mouth by this point, so I thought I should jump in and try to calm her down.

"That may be true, Martha, but I'm getting nothing but praise from the higher-ups at Hyler about how we're running this assignment. I think they are very impressed by what your ideas have allowed us to accomplish."

"Humph!" Martha grunted, but I could see that she was pleased with the compliment, so I continued.

"The interesting thing is, we've had lots of little crises during the execution, especially after we had to crash the thing, but having the detailed plan has allowed us to deal with them quickly and effectively." It was true. Problems that would have seemed insurmountable before I knew about dependency charts were now easy to solve, and caused me very little stress.

"Well," Martha allowed, "I suppose I shouldn't give up hope yet. But I don't see a lot of encouraging signs." I couldn't disagree with her there, so I decided to change the subject.

"We're still on schedule to have our production facilities in operation by the April 15th, and I'll be finished everything by about June 1st. I'm looking forward to getting back to my regular job."

Martha turned to me and said, "You know, Will, you've done a good job so far with this assignment, but it isn't over yet. If I were you, I wouldn't be thinking ahead to June 1st as the end of your involvement with the WindSailor."

I swallowed. "Why do you say that?" Did she know something I didn't?

Martha smiled at my discomfort. "No particular reason, Willie. It's just that in my experience, people who have success at certain things are thought to have special abilities. And they are often asked to use their special abilities to perform similar assignments." She paused and puffed on her pipe. "Just remember, you do have some special abilities now, and if the situation is similar, you can apply them with the same success."

I didn't really like the sound of that, but Martha wouldn't tell me any more. By 10:00 a.m. the next morning I was starting to think that she might be psychic.

# Chapter 21

"I'd like to start this meeting off by saying how pleased I am with the way this project has gone to date." Ralph was talking, and Stu and I were listening. "You've kept the whole thing on track, and you've kept me up to date with regard to the schedule, as well as the cost, extremely well. Frankly, I'm a little surprised. When we lost Al Burton, I thought this project might flounder." I glanced quickly at Stu, but resisted the urge to smirk openly. "Anyway," he continued, "Marketing now tells us that they believe Ms. Starblanket's prediction is correct about our early entry into the market. So despite getting caught off-guard by California Water Trends, things are definitely looking up."

"Now, I didn't call you in here just to compliment you on your success so far. In fact, I have what I believe you would call a scope change. Or maybe even a whole new assignment." My heart sank. More work, just like Martha said.

My sinking heart must have shown on my face. Ralph continued: "Don't look so glum, Will. This isn't punishment, it's a reward! Your project management skills have impressed me to the extent that I don't want to trust this to anyone else."

Resignedly, I asked, "Just what is the 'this' you're talking about, Ralph?"

"Marketing has decided that they want to rollout the WindSailor to the dealers in a grand way, something they've never tried before. Instead of the original 'take it to the dealers' approach, they want to bring the dealers here and make a big splash." That Ralph, always the card. "They want to organize a kind of boat show and regatta on Hyler Lake for the weekend of June 6th and 7th, and bring in all of the major dealers on the West Coast for a look. The dealers can see how the product is manufactured, and sail it themselves."

That sounded like a good plan to me. Only thing was, I didn't see how I fit into the picture. "This all sounds great, but what do you need me for?"

Ralph smiled and said, "I want you to organize it."

"Me? Why me? It's Marketing's show! Why aren't they organizing it?" This did not sound like good news to me.

"The people in Marketing have a lot on their plate right now, whereas you are now in the final stages of your project. You'll have the time available, and you've demonstrated that you have the skills as well." In his usual manner, Ralph stood up to leave. "Stuart will be the sponsor of this project. Don't worry," He held up his hand to cut off my question, "he has all of the necessary spending authority. Believe it or not, I have learned a few things over the last eight months about being a sponsor. As I'm sure you recognize, time is short on this one, so I recommend that you get started as soon as possible." With that, he left the room.

I turned to Stu with an accusatory glare. "This is all your fault."

Stu held up his hands. "Not me, buddy," he said. "This is 100 percent your own fault. Believe me, if your assignment hadn't been going as well as it has, you wouldn't be in this position. That, and the fact that Marketing has been screwing up big time on their part of the WindSailor. Notice how I'm the sponsor, not Carrie? Believe me Will, I'm about as happy with this as you are."

"Your unhappiness doesn't really help me much, Stu. I don't know anything about arranging boat shows! I can't even book a hotel room for myself! I get confused when they ask for a credit card number."

As usual, Stu wasn't interested in excuses. "You didn't know anything about production facilities or construction work did you? And I'll bet you still don't, do you?"

I had to admit it was true. I had only helped organize the work. I did learn a little bit in the process, but nowhere near enough to set up a factory without a lot of specialized help. "But I had technical people who did know about those things."

"And you'll have technical people to help you on this one too. Ralph's line about the people in Marketing being busy is mostly bull. What else do you think they have to do right now except get ready for this show? You'll have all the specialized resources you need. All you have to do is organize this thing like you did the last one, and everyone will be happy."

I sighed. "I suppose I don't have a lot of choice, do I?"

"Of course you do," Stu told me. "You could quit." He gave me his exasperated look. "You spend more time and energy trying to weasel out of things than getting down to work."

"I can't help it," I said. "I'm superstitious. If I actually do something willingly I'm afraid it will bring me bad luck, and everything will go wrong."

Stu passed me a piece of paper across the table. On it were a list of names. "You don't have a lot of time, and I know you don't know many people in Marketing, so I took the liberty of suggesting who you might want on your project team. I've slotted them into the roles that your consultant suggested. You can make whatever changes you want. Like Ralph, I recommend that you get started right away."

And that is exactly what I did. We had the first team meeting that day, and following Martha's process, produced our first objective statement. I met with Stu the following morning, and he signed it.

As it turned out, most of the design process had already been completed by the Marketing folks. Mind you, it wasn't in a very presentable format, but that was not a problem. Now that I understood a little about how the design process worked and what it was supposed to produce, we had no difficulty generating a good, detailed design inside of three days. It looked a lot different than the blueprints, job descriptions and process flow diagrams that came out of the first assignment, but what we had did the job. Our deliverable for this assignment was like the suicide squeeze play from Sheila's analogy. Our design described exactly what the situation would be like the moment before we opened the show.

Stu signed-off quickly on the detailed design as well.

Next we created the Execution Plan, which turned out to be every bit as complicated as the one for remodeling the plant. I was amazed at the number of activities that go into organizing something of this nature. I was also concerned: all those activities, so little time. Through it all, I simply acted as facilitator to ensure that the process flowed smoothly. Once my new project team got used to the idea that I wanted, – make that ***needed*** – their input, things went well.

When we had the first pass at the dependency chart on the planning board, I borrowed Amanda from the first project team to help input the plan to the project management software. I figured that time was of the essence, and she was by far the most familiar with it. After our horrendous first experience with inputting the plan to the computer, she had developed a very slick, two-person procedure for transferring the information from the planning board.

After all of the activities and resources had been input, we discovered that we could be ready to go by June 5th, as required, but that it was going to cost us more than Stu had in his budget. Happily, I knew that this was going to be Stu's problem, and his decision to make, not mine.

Seven days after the assignment had been passed to me, Stu signed-off on the Execution Plan, approving the increased budget, and we were off and running.

By the time April 15th rolled around, things were getting a little uncomfortable for me. I was managing two fairly large assignments, and still trying to juggle the work of my regular job, as well as attempting to eat dinner with my family occasionally.

Like all momentous occasions, the 15th was a day of both joy and sorrow. There was joy because we handed over the newly completed production facilities over to Luigi and his crew. There weren't any champagne bottles broken over the bow of the new buildings or anything like that; we didn't have time for a major ceremony. In fact, there was no ceremony at all. The crews simply went on regular shift at 8:00 in the morning, and began producing WindSailors.

I was around to watch for a while, until Luigi shooed me away, saying that he had everything under control. Even despite the lack of pomp and circumstance, I felt good. We had completed the big deliverable when we had to. There were still other activities to finish before my responsibilities were completed, but they were less important in the bigger picture of getting the WindSailor to the market for the summer.

The sorrow came in the form of more complications with the

boat show and regatta, which were rapidly approaching. The news sailed into my office with Leslie Frame.

"Will! Great news! We've got Buster McKay!" Leslie told me breathlessly. She looked as if she had run all the way from her office.

"Wonderful!" I said. "Who is Buster McKay?"

"He's our celebrity endorsement! You remember."

When she put it that way, I did remember. In fact the whole idea of the celebrity guest selection had made me very nervous when it went into the project plan.

The Marketing people had thought it very important to have a role model or "opinion leader" who would recommend our product. When I pointed out to them that the WindSailor was supposed to appeal to the novice, or to people who weren't very good, and that there probably weren't too many famous sailors or windsurfers who fell into those categories, they weren't interested. According to them, it didn't matter if the opinion leader actually used our product, the person simply had to be well known, and "in vogue."

From all of this I deduced that someone like Tom Cruise would be a good celebrity to employ, since he would meet both criteria, whereas Ted Bundy, who might fail the second test, would not.

The fact that we didn't have a celebrity, and the fact that my project team wanted to build the finding of one into the Execution Plan did not please me. My brief experience with systematic planning of projects seemed to indicate that there shouldn't be a lot of uncertainties by the time the Execution Plan is created. To me, selecting a celebrity endorser was uncertain at best, and a design decision.

However, it looked like Leslie was telling me that I had worried for nothing. "So is this Buster going to meet our needs?" I asked.

"Absolutely! In fact, he is better than we had hoped. He's a local boy, from Crescent City, California,"

"That's local?"

"It's West Coast, and that's close enough. Anyway, he's been the Windsurfing World Cup champion for three of the last five years. He even does color commentary for ESPN for some events. And he's had bit parts in a few beach movies, so his recognition factor is quite high!"

"Sounds like his ego is probably getting bigger along with his recognition," I mumbled.

Leslie didn't seem to hear me. "The best part is he's got a six-year-old son."

"So?" I am obviously not a Marketing person at heart.

"Don't you see?" Leslie exclaimed. "His boy is still too small for a regular windsurfer. We'll get Buster teaching his son how to sail the WindSailor! It gives his endorsement a real ring of truth!"

"I thought that whether or not the celebrity actually used the product was unimportant."

Leslie gave me an exasperated look. "You really can be a wet blanket, you know that, Will? No, it isn't an absolute requirement that our endorser use the product, but it doesn't hurt. Anyway, you should be happy. We've got our celebrity, ahead of schedule."

"Does Buster fit into our budget?" I wasn't ready to start celebrating just yet.

Leslie got a guilty look on her face. "Well, not exactly, Will. In fact, that is what I'm here to talk to you about. We need to sign Buster right away. Coppertone has a promotion that they want him to do that same weekend. We need to decide this today."

After a hasty meeting with Stu, we increased our budget again, but we all slept better knowing that Buster was on board.

And so it went. Little crises presented themselves, were resolved, and we continued. On the whole, things went pretty smoothly, especially when I compared my current situation to my past experience with assignments during Execution. The difference reminded me a little of an experience I had with push-ups.

In my wild and crazy youth, a friend got me interested in Tae Kwon Do, a Korean martial art like karate. I really enjoyed it, and decided that I was going to become the next Bruce Lee. That was not to be, but I learned something interesting that didn't have a lot to do with kicking people in the head.

Every day during the warm-up, the instructor would have us do push-ups. I wouldn't have expected this to be a problem for me because I was reasonably fit at the time, but I found doing push-ups in the class to be extremely hard work. The difficulty, it seemed, was that we did so many of them. We would do push-ups until I felt ready to drop. I frequently did, before the instructor was finished.

After about three days of this, I thought something would have to be done, so I decided that I would start practicing at home to build up my endurance.

During the fourth class, I counted the number of push-ups that we did, so I would know my goal. I was quite surprised to discover that we did only 20! In fact, in every class we did between 15 and 20 push-ups, which I would normally have no trouble completing. But not knowing how many we planned to do meant that I had been unable to pace myself and allocate my resources to last for the whole time. Each push-up became a major chore, and I was constantly prepared for the current one to be the last. Once I had an expectation of how many we were going to do, I could prepare myself accordingly. It wasn't a piece of cake, but I knew what to expect and could mentally prepare myself.

My experience with executing a project was similar. There were variations from the plan, and the whole thing wasn't a piece of cake, but knowing what to expect meant that I was better prepared to get the job done.

"Would the owner of the lime-green BMW, licence plate SAIL4U, please return to your vehicle. Your car is blocking the entrance to the hot dog stand." The public address system seemed to be blaring right in my ear, so I took the children by the hand and led them away to a quieter spot.

It was the afternoon of the second day of our WindSailor extravaganza. I was getting very tired of public outings in general, and of this one in particular. The only thing that kept me going was the knowledge that today marked the end of my project-related responsibilities. My work on the first assignment had ended the previous Thursday, when we finished our new retail facility next to Hyler Lake and closed the temporary access to the employee parking lot. Technically, my responsibilities for the product launch were finished too, but I had to be around to the end to make sure that everything went off okay.

Suddenly a large bald man wearing too much cologne was

pumping my arm like I was attached to a well that had gone dry. "Will Campbell!" he said effusively. "Damned glad to meet you! My name is Biff Flagstaff! I own the Sports Trends chain of stores. I think this WindSailor thing is the best damn idea you folks have ever had, and the best damn way to tell people about it I've ever seen. I just had to congratulate the man in charge. I was talking to Stu Barnes over there, and he said you were the man responsible."

I looked over to where Stu was standing with his wife, and he gave me an elfish grin. "Thank you, Mr. Flagstaff," I said modestly. "I'm glad you are enjoying yourself." I thought I'd put in a mild sales pitch. "I hope that the WindSailor will be one of your top sellers this summer."

"I'm sure it will, Will. I'm sure it will." While I tried to sort out the repetition, Biff switched his attention to Jenny and the kids. "And this is your fine family, I assume?" he asked me. I guessed that it was a rhetorical question, because he introduced himself. "I'm Biff Flagstaff, Mrs. Campbell. Very pleased to meet you."

"Likewise," said Jenny with more than a hint of sarcasm in her voice. I gave her a be-nice-to-the-customers look, but Biff didn't notice. He was kneeling down in front of Jake and Sarah.

"Watch my hand closely," he told them. He waved his hand around, and then reached behind Jake's ear and pulled out a piece of bubblegum. Biff handed it to Jake, and with his other hand he pulled a chocolate coin out of Sarah's nose. Both kids smiled shyly.

"What do you say?" Jenny prompted.

"Thank you," they replied almost in unison.

Biff stood up. "Fine family you have here, Will. And a fine new product. You can tell your salespeople that I am very impressed with everything, from the manufacturing process on. The WindSailor is going to be a big part of our summer plans." He shook my hand again and strode off toward another knot of people.

We all stared after him. " 'Biff'?' What kind of a name is that? You know, Will," said Jenny, "I'm glad you're not doing this marketing stuff full-time. It can be very tiresome. That guy," she pointed at Biff's retreating back, "is an idiot." My wife does not believe in beating around the bush.

"He also happens to own 43 retail sporting goods outlets that specialize in sailing and boating products."

"So he's a rich idiot," Jenny said.

"I like him, Daddy," Sarah said. "He's nice."

By half past seven that evening, things had pretty much wound down. All of the hot dogs and hamburgers had been eaten, and most people were regretting their last three. The barbecue pits were nothing but smoking embers, the beer was all gone, and most people would be regretting their last three of those later.

Ralph, Stu, Carrie, Leslie and I stood together at the edge of the lake as Carrie gave us her assessment of the event.

"It was unbelievable! The dealers loved it! No one has done anything like this before, and it was unquestionably the edge we needed."

"Sure, everyone had a good time, Carrie," Ralph said, "but how do you think this will translate into actual sales?"

"I don't think, Ralph, I know." Carrie paused for a little dramatic effect. "As of right now, we have verbal commitments for 2,700 WindSailors for this summer."

"That's more than 100 percent of our capacity!" Stu pointed out.

"That's not my problem. I just sell 'em. I let you folks worry about delivering them."

"That is good news, Carrie," Ralph congratulated her. "You're right, we'll worry about the extra capacity. You just keep selling them."

Carrie turned to me. "We really should be thanking you, Will. To be honest, I had my reservations about having a non-Marketing person organize this whole event." Apparently it was getting to be a regular thing for people to have reservations about me. "But you surprised me! It was fantastic. Except for Buster McKay twisting his ankle on that beer can, it could not have run more smoothly!"

"Well," I said, trying to sound modest, "it was nothing, really. It was your concept, I just helped put the idea in place." I could see that Carrie appreciated my giving some of the praise back, especially in front of Ralph. It was easy to do, because it was the truth.

It was her idea, and all I did was organize it systematically. I was beginning to learn that those two facets of planning were very different.

"Will," Ralph said, putting his hand on my shoulder in what I guess he thought was a real man-to-man gesture, "Good job! You've really come through for Hyler. In fact, we've been talking about trying to make better use of your project management skills. That's something we'll talk about next week. For now though, I guess you are officially finished both assignments."

But as Martha pointed out the next day, that wasn't quite true.

# The Review Process

# CHAPTER 22

"Not done? What are you talking about? Everything is finished! We got the production facilities online, everything is operating normally, I even finished the extra assignment. Why are you saying that I'm not done?"

Martha was used to my outbursts by now, so she just sat there calmly, smoking her pipe. Finally she took the stem from between her lips and said, "Apparently you've forgotten all about the framework of an assignment, so let me ask you a question: How do you improve your ability to do something?"

I thought for a minute. "You mean like how do you improve your ability to play golf?"

"Or do assignments, but yes, that's what I mean. How do you improve?"

"Practice," I said. "You do the thing over and over again until you get good."

"That's right," said Martha. "You do something again and again, each time changing how you do it so that you improve, because, as we agreed some time ago, you can't do something better unless you do it differently." She paused to send a smoke ring out over the railing of the porch. "What is it that you need to have frequently during an experience to help you improve?"

"Success?" I ventured. I really had no idea where she was going with this line of questioning.

"Not necessarily, Willie. What you need is the thing that tells you whether you're having success. What's that?"

I shrugged. "I don't know, your boss?"

"It can come from your boss, but it doesn't necessarily have to be verbal at all. Think!"

I felt as if I was playing a little kids' What am I? riddling game: 'I can be wide or narrow, I have no legs but I never stop running, and factories like to use me for their effluent. What am I?' "You're going to have to tell me, Martha, because I have no idea what you're talking about."

Martha made a dissatisfied grunting sound. "I guess all of your short-term success has gone to you head, Willie, leaving no room for common sense. Not that there was a lot of room to begin with." She regarded me from her rocking chair for a moment before she finally told me. "Feedback! Feedback is what you need in order to improve. How can you tell if what you're doing is the right thing, if you don't get any feedback? And therefore, how can you improve how you do something without feedback? You can't!"

I gave her what I hoped was a condescending stare. "Feedback? Of course you need feedback! Don't you think that is a little self-evident, Martha? No wonder I didn't understand what you were talking about. I was looking for something that I didn't already know."

Martha was not impressed by my condescension. "You know all about feedback do you, Willie? Well, then, perhaps you can explain to me why you think you are finished your assignment?"

I started to say, "Because all of the work is done," but then I finally understood what she was saying. "You're telling me that we need more feedback on the assignment?" Martha nodded. "And that getting that feedback is the final stage in the assignment?" Martha nodded again. "But what else is there to know? We finished on time, only slightly over budget, and the production facilities work."

"Your problem, Willie, like everyone else's, is that you can't look beyond the short-term, the immediate! Look, let's review our picture again." She picked up the pad of paper from beside her rocker and wrote some familiar words:

**Genesis**
**Design**
**Execution Plan (Project)**
**Execution**
**Reviews:**
- **1) Acceptance of the deliverables**
- **2) Assessment of project management**
- **3) Evaluation of the original concept**

"We haven't talked about the review process yet, but it is just as important as all of the others, although it is usually done in as perfunctory a manner as you have done it, so a lot of the benefit is lost." She turned to me. "Now, Willie, just like we've done for the other phases, I want you to answer a simple question: What should be the result of the review phase?"

After all of the talk about feedback, I could hardly get this one wrong. "Information or feedback about how to improve the way assignments get done."

Martha blew a congratulatory smoke ring in my direction. "Precisely, Willie. The difficulty occurs because no one wants to spend time looking back at an assignment at this point. For better or worse, it's done now! Let's get on to the next one! What do you suppose happens when that attitude prevails?"

I only had to look at my own past to answer that. "The same mistakes, except for maybe the biggest ones, are repeated on the next assignment."

Martha nodded. "They are indeed. And often, a combination of many little mistakes makes big things go wrong. Without a review, the little things get forgotten or missed. What about the good things?"

I looked at her. "What good things?"

Martha smiled and looked at me over the top of her spectacles. "Don't be so cynical, Willie. Good things happen on every assignment too, you know."

"I suppose that, like the bad things, only the major successes are remembered. All the little stuff gets forgotten." Personally I had always found that good things were always forgotten, but mistakes haunted you forever.

"Yes indeed, Willie, things do get done right, but if no one gets any recognition for them, they may not do the right things next time. So would you agree that a review is important?"

I had a Martha-esque answer for that one. "Only if you want to improve how you do assignments."

Martha smiled. "There is hope for you yet, Will. Now, do you want to improve the way you and Hyler manage assignments?"

"I suppose I do, Martha." I don't know why I agreed; it certainly was not in my current job description.

Martha nodded with satisfaction. "Well, then, let's talk about the review process in a little more detail." She turned the pad of paper around so that she could draw on it, and added three lines to what she already had. When she was done it looked like this:

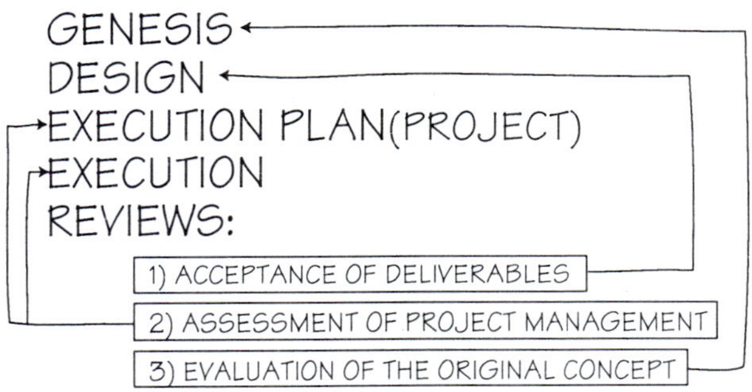


"There are actually three stages to the review process, and each stage is simply a series of questions that need to be answered. The answers provide the feedback, and the basis for improving the next assignment." She traced the line she had drawn from the first review up to the Design stage. "This first review is all about accepting the deliverable. This is the simplest one, because there is only one question to be asked: To what extent does the deliverable match the design?"

I stared at it for a second and then said, "I don't quite get that, Martha. Shouldn't the question be more along the lines of: Is the deliverable acceptable?"

Martha smiled as she took another puff on her pipe. "No Willie, that comes later. You see, the design was already approved by the sponsor, and, if done properly, by the users. Now is not the time to be questioning that decision. All we want to know is: Did we deliver what we said we would?"

I thought about this for a moment. "So if we were looking at my assignment, we would pass this review if the production facilities were all working, the staff were hired and trained, and all of the new computer systems were up and running. Because if so, we passed this one with flying colors."

"That's right Willie, although it's usually not a completely black and white answer. Was everything perfect when you handed over the production facilities?"

I had to admit that it was not. There were still some bugs in the inventory software, and some of our new hires had already washed out. And some of the interior finishing work on the factory additions was still incomplete. "There was a bunch of little stuff that wasn't quite finished, but we got all of the important stuff done," I said, a little defensively.

Martha smiled her knowing smile. "That's how it is at the finish of all executions. Small things here and there need to be tidied up or redone. The extent to which those things are minor or unimportant is what this review is all about. In your assignment it sounds like those little things aren't a problem."

I nodded in agreement. I suppose if we had installed the machinery upside down or something like that, we would have failed this review.

Martha was talking again. "The second review, which I think of as the review of 'project management', looks at the planning and execution. The questions that need to be asked are pretty straightforward. For example...", Martha paused and leaned forward in her rocking chair.

We sat in silence for about 30 seconds. I started to think that maybe she had had a stroke and been frozen in position. Finally I realized that she was waiting for me to provide some questions. "Oh, sorry. Let's see, what might be asked here...How about questions about the plan, how accurate was it? Was the logic correct? Were the contingency plans good? That kind of stuff." Martha nodded and motioned for me to go on.

"Well, this is probably where you would have the standard questions like: Was it completed on time? On budget? Were all items in the scope done? Um..." I decided to let loose and free-associate. "Was the plan kept up-to-date? Was the sponsor kept informed? Was the plan revised when major changes occurred? Was the objective statement revised? Were the team members kept informed? How was morale? Who shot JFK? That kind of thing."

Martha nodded her head and idly tapped her pencil on the pad of paper. "Very simple questions, aren't they? Taking the time to ask them and record the answers is a very simple way of improving assignments. All together, they ask: How well did we create and manage the project?

"Now we go on to the third review. The review of the original idea." She paused, then leaned forward and continued in a subdued voice, producing what I thought was a good dramatic effect. I leaned forward too.

"The third review almost never gets done. Do you know why that is, Willie?" I shook my head. "Because," she said, her voice suddenly so loud it made me jump back, "once you've spent $2 million building a new factory, you'd like to think it was a good idea!" Martha smiled and sat back in her chair.

"By the time you've reached the senior management level in corporate America, you've gotten damn good at covering your mistakes. This third review goes back to the sponsor level to ask if the whole thing was a good idea in the first place, and a lot of sponsors don't like that. It should be, but seldom is, part of the strategic planning process."

I was mightily impressed by all of this, but I could see a problem with this kind of review. "Martha, determining if an idea is good isn't always straightforward. With the WindSailor it'll be two or three seasons before we know if it's a hit."

"That's exactly right, Will! The third review is at a much more strategic level, and often takes some time to complete. However, if we want to continue to pursue good objectives, or avoid bad ones, we have to try to understand the process. And to do that, we need to ask: Was the objective of the assignment appropriate?"

"Seeing as how Ralph is the President of the company, as well as my sponsor, who is going to review the WindSailor idea? Don't you think Ralph might be a little biased?"

"How about your Board of Directors? I expect they would be in a position to do that."

Actually, I thought to myself, that is exactly who will do the review. Ralph's promotional hopes were riding with the Hyler board, and the success or failure of the WindSailor would probably be a big part of their decision.

Martha ran a pipe cleaner through her pipe. "It isn't supposed to be the Spanish Inquisition, though. In fact, in my experience, using the review process to point fingers has a net negative result. It must be treated as an opportunity for the project team and sponsor to learn. And once the review questions are known, all concerned should adopt the behaviors that lead to happy answers all the way through the assignment. It's no good waiting until the very end to tell someone about a little thing they did two months ago. At the same time, the formal process is important to close out an assignment and highlight the lessons learned, for future assignments."

"I'll talk to Ralph about it," Stu promised me. "I think he'll be interested. He loves everything you do these days, Will." I could see that Stu was pleased with me as well.

I was sitting in Stu's office, telling him about my recommendations for a formal assignment review to be conducted by Ralph. I had gotten to thinking about my talk with Martha and decided that maybe my job description did include a little project management improvement.

Stu continued. "The Hyler board met again last night in New York. Ralph flew in to give them an update on the WindSailor, and I guess they were pretty happy with how things are going, despite the fact that we aren't going to meet our projected return on investment." The advent of competition and the extra expense for the new marketing campaign were expected to reduce the assignment's ROI. But it was still healthy enough that, combined with the benefit of continuing to position Hyler on the cutting edge of the small-craft sailing world, everyone was pleased about the decision to pursue it.

"Ralph did mention something that he wanted me to discuss with you, Will. We both agree that you managed to do this assignment, both assignments really, in a different way. I know that you've been telling the people on your project team that you've been using an outside consultant, but I also know that you haven't spent any money on consulting fees."

"Well, um..." I started to explain, but Stu held up his hand.

"I understand the trick. Sometimes if you want to introduce a new idea it's easier to say it was someone else's. I've used it myself. Honestly, Will, I think you're onto something here, and we want to start managing all of our assignments like you did.

"So what Ralph and I would like you to do is write up some kind of procedure manual that details the process you worked out for this assignment. Nothing too long and complicated, but something that captures the essence of what you did."

I could not believe it. The more success I had, the more work I got loaded with! Here I was, looking forward to anonymous retirement from project management, and now I was being asked to write a company procedure manual. "I don't know, Stu, I'm way behind in my other work. And besides, you know what I think of procedure manuals. People just look at them sitting on the shelf, and they fall asleep. No one ever uses them."

Stu looked amused. "I'm afraid you're stuck with it, Will. I'll tell you what. Don't make a standard procedures manual. Use your imagination. But give us something. We don't want to lose this process."

I called my project team together later that day to wrap things up, and to let them know about the upcoming review. As had become our tradition, we met over donut holes and coffee at the Dunkin Donuts across the street from the plant.

"Review?" Sheila said. "Inquisition is more like it, don't you think?"

"Yeah," agreed Amanda. "I hate report cards. They're so impersonal."

"Something must have gone wrong." Mark Goldman did his part to cheer everyone up. "Maybe California Water Sports is already taking market share."

"Actually, I've got some news about them," Leslie Frame told us. We all turned toward her expectantly. "Apparently they were a little optimistic about their implementation. It looks like their WindSailor knock-off won't be making it to the market for this season."

I forgot all about the review. "You're kidding me. You mean we went to all that trouble and extra expense, and now they're not even going to introduce their product this year?" I was not sure whether to be happy or upset.

Leslie smiled. "Relax! We didn't spend that much more money. And anyway, our introduction was probably more effective the way we did it. We just found that out today, so there was nothing we could have done."

"What happened?" Amanda asked.

"Apparently their project got off schedule, and they couldn't get it back on track in time for this season. Something about design problems they didn't discover until after they had installed their new production equipment. Anyway, it's nothing but good for us. We're starting to get orders from CWS's unhappy customers!" Leslie took a donut hole and toasted us all.

"I wonder if Al Burton is going to be looking for another job," Sheila wondered out loud. She was still 'temporarily' assigned to his position.

I tried to get things back in focus. "Anyway folks, back to the review process. I think you're all being just a little negative. We can't improve how we do things if we don't have an objective look at our performance, and the review process does just that." Everyone looked at me skeptically. "Hey, everything has gone well so far, hasn't it?" They all nodded grudgingly. "Well, trust me, this won't be any different. And anyway, I've got something to help us prepare." I handed everyone a sheet of paper.

"These are the questions I've submitted to Ralph to be used during the review session. Over the next few days I want each of you to think about them in terms of the project we just completed."

"You mean, assignment," Amanda corrected.

"Thank you," I said. "We'll meet before the session with Ralph, to talk about our answers."

"Isn't that cheating a little?" Alice Sorensen asked.

I smiled. "Not really. I want to make sure that we all get something out of this process, so we won't depend entirely on Ralph to give it to us."

Everyone started shuffling papers and putting away pens in preparation for leaving. All of the donut holes and coffee had been consumed, leaving nothing but the check, so I thought it would be a good time for my 'good-bye' speech.

"Before you go, I just wanted to say something to all of you. This assignment has been different for me, and I guess for you too.

We tried out some new ideas in a do-or-die situation, and they worked. And in the process, I think we all, and me especially, learned a lot about doing assignments that require projects.

"I want to thank all of you for the effort you put into this. I've often been grateful that all of you are so competent and professional. We didn't have personal problems working together, and you are all well enough organized that we could focus on the bigger picture of doing this assignment without having to get bogged down in the little stuff." I paused and dabbed my eye with a napkin. "Thanks for everything, guys."

There was a moment of silence, then Sheila spoke for everyone when she said, "Are you paying for this?"

# The Project Manager's Survival Manual

# CHAPTER 23

"Daddy, why don't you come outside and play with Jake and me?" Sarah asked me as I slumped in front of our home computer.

" 'Jake and I', honey," I corrected.

"What?" she looked at me questioningly.

"You should say 'Jake and I', not 'Jake and me'."

"She was right the first time," Jenny called from the kitchen.

I looked at Sarah and she laughed. "Why don't you go outside and play, and I'll come out and join you in a minute."

I got up and walked into the kitchen with what I hoped was a sufficiently ferocious look on my face. "Dear," I said to Jenny, "how many times have I asked you not to embarrass me in front of the children?"

Jenny laughed, just like Sarah. I scowled at her, and said, "Let me tell you about one of my favorite quotes. It goes like this: 'Any man can support me when I'm right. What I want is a man who will support me when I'm wrong'. You can just substitute 'woman' for 'man'."

"Who said it?"

I looked back at her. "I think you're missing the point."

Jenny laughed again. "But Sarah was right. I didn't want her to learn the wrong way from her dad. In 12 years she might be valedictorian of her graduating class, and she would make that mistake in her speech, thanks to you, and be embarrassed about it forever. It would ruin her self-esteem. And she'd probably resent you for the rest of your days. You should be thanking me for saving you from a terrible fate."

As I groped in vain for a sufficiently snappy comeback, Jenny turned back to the dishes. I gave up and grabbed a dishtowel to help her dry.

"You don't have to do that, honey," she told me. "I know you have to get those project management procedures written. I'll finish up here."

"You don't understand, Jen. I don't want to do that. Drying dishes, however dull it may seem, has suddenly become the most fascinating thing in the world, given the alternative." I held a glass up to the light to check for errant moisture.

"Getting a little writer's block?" Jenny asked.

"Not really. I would have to have written something to be able to call myself a writer. Then when I got blocked it would be writer's block. Since I haven't written a thing since I was asked to do this more than two weeks ago, I would say I have mental paralysis."

"You're getting silly, Will."

I sighed and put my now-dry glass on the shelf and picked up another wet one. "I think I am getting a little foolish about this whole thing. I mean, how hard can it be? I'm just supposed to write some procedures that will govern how we do projects at Hyler, based on what I did on the WindSailor. Piece of cake."

"So what's the problem?"

"For one thing, there just seems to be so much to tell! It would take me at least a couple of hundred pages to explain it all. And if I did that, it would be boring as hell! Who in their right mind is going to read through 200 boring pages of project management policies and procedures?" I paused and put my now-well-dried second glass up on the shelf next to the first one.

"The thing that is really bothering me is the idea of detailed procedures in the first place. Every situation is different from every other one, which means that just about every detailed procedure you specify is going to be a little bit wrong in every new situation. And policies are worse. Their only purpose is to make sure that people don't think for themselves."

Jenny frowned at me. "I don't think I understand what you mean, Will."

"Let me give you an example, one that is near and dear to my own heart because it almost had a big impact on me during the WindSailor assignment. At the start, Ralph wanted me to do earned value costing. That is a specific way of reporting costs on projects. The only problem, when I looked into it, was that there were a whole lot of cost indexes and reporting formats that made absolutely no sense for keeping track of costs on the WindSailor. So my team and I figured out what we needed to know, and kept track of that."

"And what about Ralph?" Jenny asked.

I smiled. "That's the funny part. We just reported to him by summarizing our information in what we thought was a simple, useful format. Apparently Ralph thought the same thing, because he never complained or mentioned earned value costing again. In fact, when we did the project review last week, he commented that the costing reporting was especially well done from his perspective."

"I don't see the problem then, Will. Obviously you figured out a better way of doing costing. What's wrong with specifying your procedure in the manual?"

I sighed. "That's just it, Jen. I did find a better way: for this project. Maybe on a different project it wouldn't make sense to chuck out all the earned value stuff. Maybe some of it would be useful.

"I guess what I'm getting at is that the requirements of the particular assignment should determine a lot of the detailed procedures. If you try to specify them and make them law, you would have to make them as generic as possible so they would fit all situations. And of course, in the process, you would make it so they would fit no situations."

"Will, are you saying that there should be no standards, no specific procedures? That everyone should start from scratch every time? I don't know if I can agree with that. Think of all the effort required to re-invent the wheel over and over again."

One of the many things I like about my wife is her ability to make me think, and to clarify my thoughts. "No Jen, I don't intend to re-invent the wheel for every assignment. But I think that I have to move upstream of the detailed procedures, and not even try to specify them if I want to produce something useful."

Jenny nodded. "So why not write something that covers only the fundamentals, and leaves the details to the individual project manager?"

"Yeah, but is the world ready for that? Is it ready to work from first principles, and let the situation determine the specific details? I guess that's what I'm really wrestling with. I could probably write down the fundamental steps on a page or two, but I get the feeling that Ralph is expecting a whole lot more."

Jenny passed me another glass. "All you can do is try, Will."

I finished drying the dishes and went outside to play with the kids. It was a relatively simple game (for me) of Monkey in the Middle, so I devoted the 2 percent of my brain that wasn't working on catching the ball, to thinking about my conversation with Jenny.

I still had the same problems I did a few minutes ago, but she had helped me articulate them for myself. They were:

1) While all assignments were governed by some fundamental principles, they were all different beyond a certain level of detail. A detailed procedure manual would be boring, unread, and worst of all, wrong for most situations.
2) Ralph was expecting a boring, detailed procedure manual on how to do projects at Hyler.
3) People might not be ready to work from fundamental or 'first' principles, and might instead prefer to have a 'recipe' book that didn't require them to figure out a lot of things on their own.

Just for fun I also threw in:

4) How did I know that I was working from the most fundamental level of principles for an assignment? Maybe what I thought of as first principles were still too specific.

Just then something hit me. It was the ball. "Daddy," Jake yelled, "You have to watch. Now you're the monkey."

"Sorry son. I'll try harder." I decided to focus a little on playtime and worry about procedure manuals later.

Later found me back in front of the computer, wishing I had figured out something sooner, so I could go to bed. I took a moment to jot down my difficulties on a piece of paper so I could stare at them all at once, instead of having to think about them one at a time inside my head.

The fourth one turned out to be the one I disposed of first. Maybe I hadn't learned the most essential principles of assignments from Martha, but they were the most fundamental ones I knew, and they had worked for me. While I would try to keep my eyes open for more fundamental things, I decided to go with what I had. Scratch one problem.

Next I tackled number two, Ralph's expectations. I decided that my success on this assignment had earned me some respect for my ideas. If what I came up with did not exactly fit with his expectations, I hoped he would at least be willing to listen to why that was the case.

I looked at number one. If I believed this, and I did, it meant that all of the effort I would have to put into writing detailed procedures would be mostly wasted; unappreciated by most people, and resented by those who actually read my manual, did projects by it, and found it to be wrong. I could not do that, in all conscience.

That left only problem number three: Were people ready to work from first principles instead of detailed procedures? Considering the outcome of the other problems, this one seemed almost moot. If people were not up to doing the right thing, was it right to let them do the wrong thing because they wanted to? Clearly, it was not. I had to try to help them do the right thing.

So what was the best way to get people to think out their own detailed procedures? As I chewed on my pencil, it occurred to me. Why not offer myself as a coach to other people at Hyler who were working on assignments? Why not try to help them in much the same way that Martha helped me? (They, of course, would not have to put up with pipe smoking and sarcastic comments). The drag on my time certainly wouldn't be a problem. The time Martha had spent with me over the past year, long as it had seemed, could be counted in hours, not days. I could certainly afford that kind of time.

I could provide a simple framework of general steps in an assignment, and then coach people to help them with specific details as they created and managed their own projects. The more I thought about it, the more sense it seemed to make. I turned on the computer and started to write.

"Gee Will, a whole two pages? I can certainly see why it took you three weeks to produce that!" I think Stu must have been reading books about leadership in the '90s, because he seemed to be trying to change his leadership style from very directed, dictatorial military, to positive consensus building via sarcasm. On the whole, I had liked him better the way he was.

"Stu, give me a chance to explain it a little. I realize it's not exactly what you and Ralph were expecting."

Stu shook his head. "To be honest Will, this is what I was expecting from you. After the tricks you pulled off with the WindSailor, I'm really not surprised that your procedure manual is only two pages long. However, I should warn you, Ralph may not be too pleased with this."

"That's why I'm showing it to you first, Stu. I wanted to do a little pretesting on the whole idea before going to Ralph."

I went into my little song and dance to explain how I had arrived at the two-page procedure manual for projects at Hyler. As I talked, Stu interrupted me occasionally with questions. Finally I asked him, "Well, what do you think? Will Ralph buy it?"

Stu took his time answering. He leaned back in his chair and stared up at the ceiling as if he were in deep thought. He sat forward and studied the palms of his hands. Finally he said, "Well, I don't think so." My face fell, and Stu looked like he was suppressing a smile. "Sorry Will, but I really don't think he will. You should have seen the struggles I had with him behind the scenes during the WindSailor assignment. Whenever things weren't like Al Burton would have done them, Ralph wanted to get on your case. I managed to keep him from doing anything rash, and you came through every time."

"So why won't he buy this?" I interrupted. "He trusted you before and it worked."

Stu sighed and stared up and the ceiling again. "The thing is, Will, he's trusted you about as far as he's going to. A guy like Ralph can only stray so far from the organizationally accepted norm, and he's done that with the WindSailor. I know," he said, holding up his hand to stop me from interrupting again. "I know it made him look successful this time. But the fact is, it's almost always safer to do what everyone else is doing, whatever the flavor of the day may be. And for a guy like Ralph, who wants to get ahead in the corporation, that's the path he will follow. It's always worked for him in the past.

"Believe me, Ralph will not be thrilled about a two-page procedure manual for project management. He wants thick books that will collect dust on every shelf in the plant. He wants something substantial to point to when Henry Stanton, President of Mantec, tours the place." Stu had been speaking louder and louder as he went along, and now he came to a furious crescendo. "Ralph wants the Bible on project management. And in case you haven't looked lately Will, the Bible has a lot more than two pages!"

I had been slouching lower and lower in my chair. After Stu finished, there was a moment of silence while he caught his breath. Finally I said, "Well, I guess I better get writing." I stood up to leave.

"You know," said Stu, still staring at the ceiling, "I've always been a great fan of Socrates."

I looked at him. "Really?"

"Yes, indeed," he cracked his knuckles. "And I have to say that while Ralph wouldn't like your ideas about working from first principles, and coaching others by asking them questions and letting them discover things for themselves, I do."

"I suppose it reminds you of the good old days when Socrates taught you in high school." I was a little sarcastic because of my disappointment. "Did you have him in the 9th grade or 10th?"

Stu just smiled at me, and didn't say anything.

I looked back. "I give up Stu, why are you telling me about Socrates?"

"Oh, no particular reason, Will. It's just that as the new President of Hyler, you might find me a little more open to your ideas than Ralph was."

I stared at him. "You're kidding me."

Stu shook his head. I gave a little war cry and jumped over his desk to shake his hand. Unfortunately I caught my toe on his desk blotter and ended up in his lap, his desk papers all over the floor. He didn't seem to mind. "Congratulations Stu! That is the best news I've had since I finished the WindSailor! This is fantastic!"

Stu was all smiles. "It seems that Harry Carpenter, one of the vice-presidents over at AlphaChem, is retiring. The WindSailor really was Ralph's ticket out of here to bigger and better things. Of course that left his job open, and yours truly, also riding the success of the WindSailor, will be stepping into it. As of September 1st, you can call me 'Mr. President'."

# The Survival Manual for Project Managers

**Structure of an assignment:**

**Genesis**
**Design**
**Execution Plan (Project)**
**Execution**
**Reviews: 1) Acceptance of the deliverables**
**2) Assessment of project management**
**3) Evaluation of the original concept**

**When asked to do an assignment:**

1) **Identify the sponsor.** You'll recognize him or her because he or she is the one who can spend the money.

2) **Make sure that the sponsor knows who the sponsor is.** The sponsor must understand his/her responsibilities. This should be part of the culture, but never assume.

3) **Write the first objective statement.** Make sure that you answer all of the questions in the standard objective statement:
   What is wrong with the existing situation?
   How will things be better when we are done?
   What are the performance criteria for the deliverables?
   What is the scope of the assignment (i. e., what is in the assignment, and what is not in the assignment)?
   What are the specific constraints regarding cost, time, quality, and so on?
   Who is the sponsor?
   Who is the project manager?
   What authority is being given?

4) **Have the sponsor sign the objective statement.** Always get an actual signature on the document.

5) **Collect the best project team that you can.** Remember, the same responsibilities must be fulfilled on every assignment, but team members may double up on some roles, depending on the assignment. After sponsor and project manager, roles include: designer, users' rep, project administrator, implementor.

6) **Create the conceptual design.**

7) **Get the sponsor's signed approval of the conceptual design and funding to complete the detailed design.**

8) **Detail the design.** You'll know it's complete if you can do a useful Execution Plan.

9) **Get the sponsor's signature on the detailed design.**

10) **Create the Execution Plan with the project team.** Use the logic of interrelation of the activities (dependency chart). Then determine things like costs, schedule and resource requirements.

11) **Get the sponsor's signature on the Execution Plan.**

12) **Execute the plan.**

13) **Review the assignment.** Make sure that you complete all three review steps.

# New Frameworks

# CHAPTER 24

The elm-lined trees of Darfield worked their usual magic as I drove slowly through the town toward my in-laws' house. Most of my trips along that street during the past year had found me in such a distracted state of mind that I had failed to notice the regal splendor of the old trees and the beautiful old houses. Today was different. I purposefully took my time, drinking in the exquisite visual…

"Hey, mister, watch where you're going!" I jerked the steering wheel to the left, barely avoiding a 12-year-old on a skateboard. "You been drinking, buddy? Or just learning to drive?" I found myself thinking that I had been a little more polite when I was 12. Or maybe this guy was a 30-year-old midget with an attitude.

"Daddy, you should be more careful," Sarah told me solemnly. She had asked to come along with me to visit her grandmother.

My reverie spoiled, I quickly drove the remainder of Elm Street to Fred and Natalie's place and pulled into the driveway. I had intended this trip as kind of a 'thank you' pilgrimage so I could pay homage to Martha's wisdom. It was now August 28th, almost a year to the day since I had been tapped for the WindSailor assignment. Demand for our product had continued unabated. By adding extra shifts, we had managed to exceed even the most optimistic production estimates, and everyone at Hyler was feeling very good about the prospects for next year and beyond. More important to me, there had been no problems with the production facilities, all of the information systems were operating without glitches, and our new workforce was fitting in well at the plant. From everything I could see – and Stu had agreed – our assignment went just about perfectly. Realist that I am, I had to give credit where it was really due. That was why I was back at Elm Street without a problem.

As I stepped out of my car, I saw Martha in her regular place on the porch, rocking in her chair and smoking her pipe. The number of smoke rings hanging in the still air over the flower bed were silent testimony to her ongoing vigil. For a moment I stopped and admired the tableau. The defiant, crotchety-but-wise old woman with her rocking chair and pipe, undoubtedly thinking deep thoughts about important management issues.

"Well, it's about time you came to visit, Willie! No problems for a while, eh? No need for old Martha to kick around. Just like the youth of today." She saw Sarah getting out of the car, and her tone changed. "Hi honey! How are you today?"

It was the second time within a few moments that my illusion had been shattered and it was getting a bit annoying. I choked back my unpleasant reply, and said, "In fact, Martha, I made a special trip out here to thank you for all of the help you gave me on the WindSailor assignment. Everything has been a big success, and it is all thanks to you." I reached into the car and brought out a gift-wrapped box. "And as a token of my appreciation, I got you a little gift." I climbed the porch steps and walked over to her. I held out the box. "Here."

Sarah was on Martha's lap by this time. "You go off and see your grandmother, Sarah. Your dad and I have to talk." Sarah jumped down and banged through the screen door into the house.

As she eyed the gift in my outstretched hand, I could tell she was pleased, but in true Martha fashion, she tried not to show it. "I didn't do it for any gift, you know," she said crustily. "And besides, there isn't much I need at my age. I'll be dead soon anyway." So saying, she tore off the wrapping paper eagerly.

Inside was a tin of high-grade Turkish pipe tobacco. After a lot of research – and over the objections of Jenny, who didn't think Martha needed any more help killing herself – I had hunted down this tin of what was supposed to be a pipe smoker's delight. "Good brand," was all Martha said, and I didn't expect more. I could tell that she was pleased.

I sat down in the chair beside her. "To be honest Martha, I came out here to thank you, but to also ask you a few questions about some things that are still puzzling me."

"Just a few questions?" Martha gave me a sidelong glance which seemed to say that someone as dumb as me should ask more than just a few questions.

I ignored the implication, and continued. "There were some things that Ralph talked about at the beginning of the project that I thought might cause us a lot of problems during the implementation. The Total Quality Management stuff, and the self-directed work teams. Not to mention things like earned value costing and work breakdown structures. I did everything I could to avoid having anything to do with them, because I've always had bad experiences with them before.

"But inside I worried that I was missing the boat. I mean, quality is important. The thing is, we never had a problem with quality. We worked well as a team. We didn't need earned value costing or work breakdown structures; we just did what worked." I paused.

"So?" prompted Martha, "What is your problem?"

"I guess the problem is, why is Hyler trying to do all of those other things? Why don't we just manage our work like projects or assignments? It works so well. Everybody at the company is talking about the job we did. Why not try to implement 'management by projects' at Hyler and get rid of all of that other crap?"

Martha didn't say anything for a few minutes, she just sat there puffing her pipe and thinking. Finally she said, "People are funny, Will. You ask them to drive nails with their bare hands, and they'll get frustrated real quickly. The human hand isn't a very good tool for driving nails.

"Funny thing is, if you give them a hammer, they are happy as a pig in– well, you know what I mean. They'll drive nails like there's no tomorrow. The only problem is that pretty soon everything starts looking like a nail. Everything you ask them to do, they try to do with a hammer, because it works so well for driving nails. Of course, not everything is a nail."

She paused again and smoked some more. I could see the point she was trying to make. "The same thing holds true in business. Something that works well for a person in one situation gets applied to every other problem that the person can find. Often the results are disastrous. Do you understand what I am saying?"

I nodded sheepishly. "Not everything is an assignment or a project. Trying to force everything into that framework means trouble."

Martha smiled. "Exactly."

"What about Total Quality Management then? It seems to be all-pervasive."

"Have you ever heard of the Bentskin Award?" she asked me with that sly look on her face.

"Of course I have," I replied, knowing she was getting at something, but not sure quite what.

"What is it?"

"It's an award that is given out every year to a company or companies that demonstrate significant improvement in and devotion to the quality of their product. " I thought it sounded pretty good, considering I really didn't know all that much about it.

"Close enough," she told me. "And if a company were to win this award, what would you imagine some of its" – here she added an aside in her usual droll way – "the company's, not the award's, characteristics might be?" She paused expectantly.

I knew there was a trap in here somewhere, but I couldn't be sure where it was. As always in these types of situations, I figured it was best to just soldier on. If I ever figured out in advance what the old gal was getting at, it would deprive her of her fun.

"Well," I began, "I suppose that a company that won this award would likely be a leader in its particular niche, would be highly profitable, have happy employees, and maybe have been pulled from the brink of disaster by the introduction of all this total quality stuff. Maybe it would be a real turnaround story."

She smiled in her shark-like manner, which told me I had guessed wrong – as usual. "What would you say," she asked me, "if I told you that more than 60 percent of the companies that have won that award filed for Chapter 11 bankruptcy protection within 18 months of the ceremony?" She waited patiently.

I didn't say anything. Part of me could well believe it, considering the experience at Hyler. "Look," I said finally, "you know something here. Why don't you just save us some time and tell me?" I knew from recent experience that this was futile.

"Because," she explained patiently, "the best way for you to really know it is to figure it out. So what would you think?"

I gave in and thought.

It seemed to me that if a bunch of these award winners in the field of quality were going under shortly after reaching the pinnacle of success, there were three pretty simple possibilities.

First, the guidelines for choosing the winners must be pretty fuzzy, and their lack of clarity was allowing a lot of unqualified companies to slip through – companies that weren't really achieving the quality they claimed.

Second, it could be that companies who were into quality in a big way were frequently in very high-risk sectors, susceptible to downturns in the economy. When things got bad, poof, they went under. But this seemed even less probable than the first possibility.

Third, using the same tool to fix everything means that you are using the wrong tool most of the time.

This last one seemed to be the most likely, and that's what I told Martha.

"You are starting to think," she said. "But we really haven't gotten to the heart of the problem. For starters, what is 'quality'?"

"Excellence," I said without hesitation.

"What is 'excellence'?" she rejoined, with no hesitation herself.

"Well," I said, stalling for a second because I didn't have a ready answer, "good; better than the rest."

"What is 'good'?" she asked in the same tone.

Damn, I thought, this was how all of the project stuff started. "What," I said, "is the point of all of these definitions?"

Martha just admonished me with a stare that said I was getting out of line. I thought for a moment. "I don't know. 'Good' is not 'bad'. How's that?" When Martha didn't say anything I admitted that she had made her point. "I guess I don't really know what quality or even excellence means."

This seemed to perk the old girl right up. "No!" she exclaimed, "You've made the point. All I did was help you to do it. You're right, you don't really understand what the words 'quality' and 'excellence' mean. Or, more correctly, you understand the definitions, but you haven't thought very carefully about what they mean." She settled back in her rocker and tried to puff on her pipe. It had gone out, so she began the relighting procedure.

"You did define 'quality' correctly. In fact, 'excellence' is usually the fourth or fifth definition of the word. The first definition has to do with the features or characteristics that make something what it is – its attributes. The degree of excellence that a thing possesses implies some judgment about the thing we're discussing. In other words, someone has decided that the combination of qualities this thing possesses makes it excellent or superior.

"All of that is fine and dandy, but you know how I like to harp on words. There is a characteristic of this definition that you need to understand in order to use the word effectively. I've given you all the clues. What is that characteristic?"

Martha finished up her pipe-lighting procedure while she waited for an answer.

I didn't have a pipe to light, so I just sat there feeling (and if you were to ask Martha, probably looking) stupid. Again I resigned myself to thinking. What was it about the word "quality," or even, apparently, the word "excellence"? What was the key characteristic? Nothing came to mind, so I tried a different approach.

Who or what could be described as "quality" or "excellent"? I've often found that working at a problem from a different angle yields different results, and even answers.

In high school I had been a pretty fair basketball player, at least until my height – or lack thereof – started to get in the way. People had described me as a "quality player," and some had even gone so far as to say a "college prospect." What did they mean? That I was good? But that didn't help me. All I could say about "good" was that it wasn't bad – nothing very helpful.

Martha was still engrossed in her pipe. If she was feeling impatient with my slowness, she wasn't showing it. She started to blow smoke rings in my direction. I sighed and leaned back in my chair and tried to think some more.

If quality is excellence (or the characteristic of excellence), and excellence is goodness, and goodness is not badness, what is badness? Madness, undoubtedly, or not goodness.

I got up. "I need to take a little stroll to the bathroom. I'll be back in five minutes."

"You take your time Willie. I'll be right here. And don't worry, the answer won't go anywhere either. That's the beauty of first principles, they're always around." She snuffled to herself and went back to blowing smoke rings.

I headed inside, and couldn't help noticing all of the reference books that Natalie and Fred kept on the bookshelf in their living room. This included several dictionaries. I decided to take a moment and look up some words.

Sure enough, "quality" was just as Martha defined it. The first definition was "the attributes or characteristics of a thing." It wasn't until third definition that the word "excellence" came into it. Dead end. I looked up "excellence." Again, as expected. "Superior, surpassing goodness." It sounded like little boys in Sunday school, and it didn't shed any light.

"Good" was little help either. The definition actually included the word "excellence"! "Good" was one of largest entries in the dictionary.

I decided to be different and look up the word "bad." That was the ticket, take the radical, underworld track.

"Bad" was defined as "a lack of goodness," and I felt like tearing out my hair (although to be honest, I couldn't afford to tear much before I would start blinding people with the glare). Interestingly, "bad" was also defined as "lacking in quality" and "defective." The two were obviously connected. It was also clear that I could define the words, but that I was, at least according to Martha, missing the point.

I kept reading, only to discover that (as I already knew but had not considered) "bad" in slang means "good." I tried not to think about the implications, and hoped that Martha was unaware of this development.

The dictionary listed some synonyms for "bad", and one of the sentences describing the synonyms started out "In this comparison..." A little farther along, the light went on.

Unfortunately, the light was not in my head, it was in the room.

"Are we ready to go yet, Daddy?" Sarah asked me. "I'm getting hungry."

"Not quite yet, honey," I told her. "If you ask your grandma, she'll probably give you a cookie."

I turned back to the dictionary. My subconscious was tickling me about that phrase "In this comparison..." What was I trying to tell myself?

Finally it dawned on me: the word was "comparison." For something to be bad, it had to be bad in comparison to something else that was good (or at least less bad than the item in question). Something could only be excellent in relation to something else, even if it was only a person's expectation. And therefore, for something to be "quality" – the way it is used in respect of Total Quality Management – there had to be some kind of comparison. "Quality" is a relative term.

I started to rush back out to the porch, but paused at the door to catch my breath and put on a nonchalant exterior. I strolled back out, looking, I thought, like a man who had worked it out for himself. I would simply state what I had learned, and leave out any reference to the dictionary that had actually done the illuminating for me. Let Martha think I was brighter than I looked.

"Any luck with the dictionary?" she asked. Smart-ass.

"In fact," I said, attempting to maintain my worldly exterior, "I think I did have some luck. The key quality of quality," I smiled at my clever use of the word, "is that when it is defined as 'excellence' or 'superiority', it is a relative term, not a stand-alone, not an absolute."

"Well, well," said Martha, "You surprise me every time you do that." She continued: "You're absolutely right. The word 'quality' is frequently used today to mean the characteristic of excellence. And when it is used in that fashion, it is a relative term. So what do you suppose the words 'Total Quality Management' mean?"

That was easy. " 'Total Quality Management', means relative to everyone else, or to how the company was in the past."

"Right again, Willie. Pretty vague isn't it? Now, what do you suppose that the managers of companies were doing before TQM came along?" She smoked her pipe and watched me to see if I could continue my success.

"I would think," I ventured, "that before TQM, most companies were still trying to do a good job."

"So what would something like TQM do for them?" She asked.

I shook my head. "As it was introduced at Hyler, nothing. It actually made things worse."

Martha sighed. "A technique called Statistical Quality Control, which essentially involved using statistics to help improve manufacturing operations, gained a great deal of popularity in Japan in the '50s. Many management gurus attributed Japan's comeback from the ruin of World War II to the use of SQC. By the time the Japanese were out-performing North America, the 'hammer' had been found: its name was Quality Control.

"A simple technique, and one that worked well in certain situations and sold like hotcakes as the answer to all problems. Sadly, it was not. Ironically, most of the people who attempt to apply TQM today weren't even with us in Japan."

"Wait a minute," I interrupted. "You were in Japan?"

"That's another story, Will, for another day. The point is, a great deal of harm has come from the misapplication of that particular hammer to every situational nail."

"And the fact that it didn't cover all situations meant that it has mutated over the years into many different, fuzzy forms," I added.

"That's what has happened, Will, and it hasn't been a pretty sight." I had this sudden, weird image of Martha surveying the American business scene from the vantage point of her porch, shaking her head and rolling her eyes at the various blunders made by people like me.

We sat in silence for a few moments while we contemplated the implications of the misapplication of hammers. Finally Martha said, "What do you think now about managing your company entirely by projects?"

I thought a lot differently. "I guess the techniques that you taught me should only be applied to those assignments that need to include projects. Project management shouldn't be the universal tool, just like TQM shouldn't be. But to be honest, Martha, I'm having trouble thinking of what those other processes might be. I mean, what doesn't fit into the framework of an assignment?"

"Many things, Will, many things," she said. "The strategic planning process, production control, performance management – just to name a few. The techniques that we have talked about over the last year are merely one small but important set of management tools available for improving the overall situation. Don't think that you know it all yet!" She smiled and sent a smoke ring my way.

We sat for a few moments more in silence, and then Martha grunted and got slowly up off her rocker. "I'm glad the WindSailor worked out, Will. Believe it or not, old as I am, I still get quite a thrill out of helping somebody. Now all of this talking has made me tired. Why don't you get off home and feed my great-granddaughter. Pretty selfish of you to keep her here past dinnertime! Come see me next time you have a problem." That was Martha, crusty to the end.

I left that night with a lot on my mind, but very little of it had to do with projects.

# Epilogue

*In a novel, it is permissable to introduce elements of luck and coincidence that would be out of place in other forms of communication. So it is in this book. Although Martha exists, in a somewhat different form, and the other characters are drawn from real life, happy endings are often elusive.*

*That is largely because the necessary support sometimes does not come together in the right time and place. The rarity of real life characters like Stu Barnes is remarkable. Organizations often lack the will, rather than the tools and techniques, to succeed. We are all poorer because of this.*

*Rather than trust chance, Manageering Associates has developed the following:*

- *A rational and effective framework for dealing with assignments involving projects.*
- *A course which has enabled thousands to test run - in a low risk setting - the powerful ideas mentioned in the preceding pages.*
- *A Project Planning Kit™ containing all the physical tools required for the Execution Planning method described in chapter 17.*
- *Coaching skills to ease the transition of entire organizations to higher levels of project management.*
- *A strategic planning process that avoids the now painfully obvious difficulties of those popular since the 1960's. It's little comfort to do the wrong assignments well.*

*We welcome enquiries.*

*For additional copies of this book, try the business section of leading bookstores, or order direct from:*

*Manageering Associates*
*325 Hector Road*
*Victoria, B.C., Canada*
*V8X 3X1*

*Phone (250) 479-5553*
*Fax (250) 479-8936*
*Toll Free (North America)*
*1-888-322-5553*
*Web Site: http://www.islandnet.com/manageering.*

*Single copies $24.50 (Canadian) plus shipping and all taxes.*
*Volume discounted prices upon request.*

*Manageering also provides*
*Consultation to Management Teams, Project Training, Coaching and Project Planning Kits™ to clients in many parts of the world.*